VOCABULARY GAMES

FOR THE CLASSROOM

LINDSAY CARLETON

ROBERT J. MARZANO

Marzano Research Laboratory
Powered by Solution Tree

555 North Morton Street
Bloomington, IN 47404

888.849.0851
FAX: 866.801.1447

email: info@marzanoresearch.com
marzanoresearch.com

Visit **marzanoresearch.com/reproducibles** to download the reproducibles in this book.

Printed in the United States of America

14   13   12   11   10   3   4   5

Library of Congress Control Number: 2009942821

ISBN: 978-0-9822592-6-9 (paperback)

         978-0-9822592-7-6 (library binding)

FSC
Mixed Sources
Product group from well-managed
forests and other controlled sources
Cert no. SW-COC-002283
www.fsc.org
© 1996 Forest Stewardship Council

Vice President of Production: Gretchen Knapp

Managing Production Editor: Caroline Wise

Senior Production Editor: Risë Koben

Copy Editor: Rachel Rosolina

Proofreader: Sarah Payne-Mills

Text and Cover Designer: Orlando Angel

ACKNOWLEDGMENTS

Marzano Research Laboratory would like to thank the following reviewers:

Brian Albert
Special Education Teacher
East High School
Buffalo, New York

Doug Golden
Math Department Chair
South Cobb High School
Austell, Georgia

Dean Kalahar
Social Studies Teacher
Sarasota High School
Sarasota, Florida

Joseph E. O'Brien
Associate Professor, Department of
    Curriculum and Teaching
University of Kansas
Lawrence, Kansas

Jill Roach
Science Teacher
East High School
Buffalo, New York

Maria N. Trejo
Project Director and Consultant
Margarita Calderón and Associates
Washington, D.C.

TABLE OF CONTENTS

VOCABULARY LISTS

ABOUT THE AUTHORS

Lindsay Carleton is a staff writer at Marzano Research Laboratory. She received a Master of Fine Arts degree from the University of Iowa Writers' Workshop, where she was a fiction editor for the *Iowa Review* and a creative writing instructor.

Robert J. Marzano, PhD, is CEO of Marzano Research Laboratory. Robert Marzano focuses on translating research and theory into practical programs and tools K–12 teachers and administrators can put to use in their classrooms for immediate gains. During his forty years in education, Dr. Marzano has worked with educators in every U.S. state and a host of countries in Europe and Asia. He has authored more than 30 books, 150 articles and chapters, and 100 sets of curriculum materials. His work focuses on reading and writing, instruction, thinking skills, school effectiveness, restructuring, assessment, cognition, and standards implementation.

INTRODUCTION

Direct vocabulary instruction is fundamental to effective teaching. Our knowledge about and understanding of any topic is rooted in our mastery of the terms relevant to that topic. To some degree, this is common sense. Consider social studies students learning about the U.S. government. Certainly they must have a firm grasp on terms such as *executive*, *legislative*, *judicial*, *presidency*, *bill*, *amendment*, and *vote* (among others) in order to demonstrate proficiency for learning goals on this topic. In other words, there is a direct link between an understanding of academic vocabulary and an understanding of academic content.

What is also clear is that there is a vast difference in the vocabularies of low- versus high-achieving students. Data collected as far back as 1941 indicate there is roughly a 6,000-word gap between students at the 25th and 50th percentiles on standardized tests in grades 4–12. Since the 1980s, researchers have estimated the difference to be anywhere between 4,500 and 5,400 words for low- versus high-achieving students (for a discussion, see Marzano, 2009). This means we can take the commonsense connection between vocabulary and content one step further and conclude that the size of a student's vocabulary is directly related to his or her academic achievement.

The purpose of *Vocabulary Games for the Classroom* is to provide all K–12 teachers with a wide variety of games to build both academic and general vocabulary in their classrooms. While games have been sometimes misused or underestimated by classroom teachers, roughly sixty studies done by Marzano Research Laboratory showed that, on average, the use of academic games in the classroom is associated with a 20 percentile point gain (Haystead & Marzano, 2009).

To a great extent, this book is a complement to three other books on vocabulary instruction: *Building Background Knowledge for Academic Achievement: Research on What Works in Schools* (Marzano, 2004), *Building Academic Vocabulary: Teacher's Manual* (Marzano & Pickering, 2005), and *Teaching Basic and Advanced Vocabulary: A Framework for Direct Instruction* (Marzano, 2009). Together, those books lay out the rationale for a comprehensive schoolwide or districtwide approach to direct instruction in academic terms as well as terms necessary for general literacy. Those books recommend a process for teaching new terms, which includes the following six steps:

1 Provide a description, explanation, or example of the new term.

2 Ask students to restate the description, explanation, or example in their own words.

3 Ask students to construct a picture, symbol, or graphic representing the term.

4 Engage students periodically in activities that help them add to their knowledge of terms in their notebooks.

5 Periodically ask students to discuss the terms with one another.
6 Involve students periodically in games that allow them to play with terms. (Marzano & Pickering, 2005, pp. 14–15)

The focus of this book is obviously on the sixth step of the overall process—playing with new terms through games.

Although this book does not address the first five steps, it is important to keep them in mind when using the games described in this book. That is, vocabulary games should not be played just for fun (although they are fun, and teachers should capitalize on the energy and excitement that they generate). Rather, vocabulary games should be seen as one part of a systematic approach to direct vocabulary instruction. As the steps in the preceding list indicate, the teacher should introduce new terms to students in an informal manner via descriptions, explanations, or examples (step 1). Next, students should restate the description, explanation, or example in their own words (step 2) and construct a picture, symbol, or graphic representation of the term (step 3). Ideally, the results of steps 2 and 3 are recorded in a vocabulary notebook. A sample page from a vocabulary notebook is provided in figure I.1.

Term: Circulatory System My Understanding: 1 (2) 3 4

Describe: The circulatory system pumps blood through the heart. Old blood comes in one side and new blood is pumped into the body from the other side.

Draw:

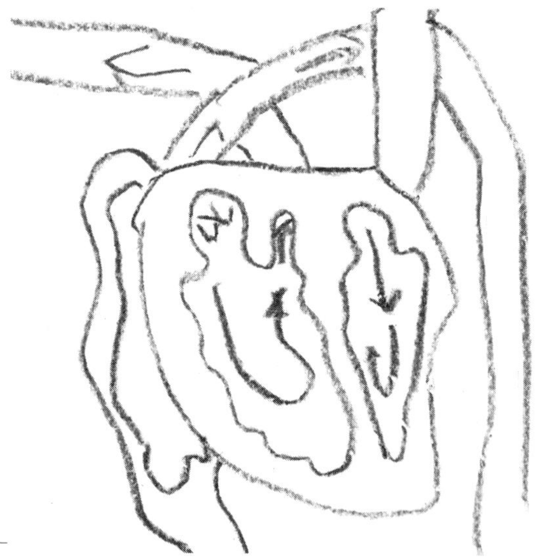

Subject: Science

Figure I.1: Sample page from a student's vocabulary notebook.

The sample page in figure I.1 depicts a lower elementary student's understanding of the circulatory system. Notice that the page has room for only one vocabulary term. This is because students need room to record their descriptions and their nonlinguistic representations of terms. At the higher elementary grade levels and in middle school and high school, each page of the notebook can contain more terms, since more mature students can write legibly in smaller places.

As shown in figure I.1, the top part of each box contains a space for a student's description, explanation, or example. The bottom of each box contains a space for a student's picture, symbol, or graphic representation. In figure I.1, both of these sections are filled in. This would be the case after a teacher has gone through the first three steps of the six-step process. Steps 4, 5, and 6 are then employed—in any order—to reinforce the new term. One week, a teacher might set aside ten or fifteen minutes to have students discuss the entries in their notebooks in pairs or trios (step 5). The next week, that same teacher might set aside ten or fifteen minutes to have students engage in a comparison activity to help them add to their knowledge of the terms in their notebooks (step 4). Throughout both weeks, the teacher might have students play games using the terms in their notebooks (step 6). After each step, the teacher would have students go back to their vocabulary notebooks and add new information they had gleaned from the activities. To illustrate, consider figure I.2.

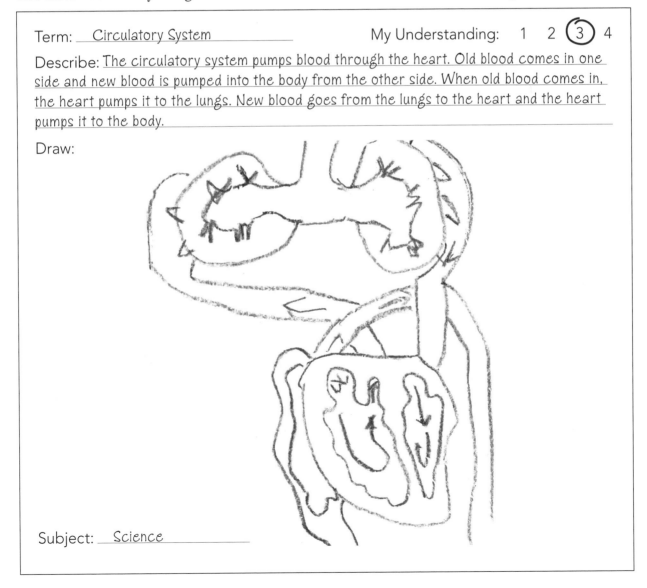

Figure I.2: Student vocabulary notebook after steps 4, 5, and 6.

Notice that the student has made some corrections in his or her initial entry regarding the circulatory system. By asking students to record terms in a vocabulary notebook and asking them to reexamine their knowledge of terms after steps 4, 5, and 6, the teacher ensures that students systematically deepen their understanding of terms that were directly taught.

As described in *Building Background Knowledge for Academic Achievement* (2004) and *Building Academic Vocabulary: Teacher's Manual* (2005), it is recommended that schools or entire districts create lists of academic terms for core content areas at each grade level. If the school or district has done this, then teachers will want to incorporate those terms into the games described in this book. Teachers might also use the terms in the appendix to supplement the list generated by the district or school. However, if the school or district has not developed such a list, we have put together some terms that are commonly the focus of direct vocabulary instruction in the areas of language arts, mathematics, science, and social studies. This list was compiled from our work with schools, districts, and even entire states that have developed such lists. In effect, the appendix is a fairly good representation of the terms considered important in these subject areas. In the appendix, the terms in each subject area are organized into four broad categories: (1) lower elementary, (2) upper elementary, (3) middle school/junior high, and (4) high school. Table I.1 lists the number of terms at each of these four levels for each of the four content areas.

Table I.1: Number of Terms by Content Area and Grade-Level Band

	Language arts	Math	Science	Social studies
Lower elementary	96	96	96	330
Upper elementary	251	190	179	1268
Middle school	253	204	218	1166
High school	217	218	299	1291

As table 1.1 shows, social studies has more terms than the other three content areas. Because social studies encompasses a number of subject areas, we have split the terms at each grade-level band into the following categories: general history (applicable only to lower elementary), U.S. history, world history, civics, economics, and geography (see table 1.2).

Table I.2: Number of Social Studies Terms by Category and Grade-Level Band

	General history	U.S. history	World history	Civics	Economics	Geography
Lower elementary	137	n/a	n/a	42	33	118
Upper elementary	n/a	265	358	182	100	363
Middle school	n/a	133	409	235	122	267
High school	n/a	156	392	233	224	286

Other than the appendix, this book includes thirteen games that can be played in class:

1 *Word Harvest*
2 *Name It!*
3 *Puzzle Stories*
4 *Two of a Kind*
5 *Opposites Attract*
6 *Magic Letter, Magic Word*
7 *Definition Shmefinition*
8 *Which One Doesn't Belong?*
9 *Who Am I?*
10 *Where Am I?*
11 *Create a Category*
12 *What Is the Question?*
13 *Classroom Feud*

Each game is described briefly but in enough depth to provide adequate guidance for classroom use. Additionally, the depth of understanding of terms required to play each game is addressed. Some games can be used even if students are relatively new to the terms; other games require more in-depth knowledge to be played effectively. Suggestions on how and when to award points are offered as well, though you may opt out of awarding points and choosing a winner. The focus of these games is on vocabulary enhancement through *friendly* competition, so students should not feel undue pressure to "win" points or games. Only teachers know their class well enough to decide how much competition is appropriate. Should teachers decide to award points and select winners, we do not recommend that points from games be used when grading students. This does not mean that a game cannot be used for formative evaluation, quite the contrary. During play, teachers can glean valuable information as feedback to guide instructional discussions.

It is important to remember that each game and the feedback garnered from it should be used to enhance students' knowledge of the incorporated terms. To ensure that this goal is met, teachers must do three things: (1) note terms students have trouble with, (2) identify what students know and do not know about a term, and (3) have students make changes in their vocabulary notebooks.

First, teachers should make note of the terms students have trouble with. This is usually evident if a large proportion of students miss a particular term during the game. For example, assume a science teacher is playing a game such as *Classroom Feud* (modeled after *Family Feud*) in which the class is split into two teams. He asks one team the following question: "The system of the body that includes both the heart and the lungs is the _____ system." The correct answer is *circulatory*. After their time to confer is up, however, the team agrees on the answer *respiratory*. According to the rules of the game, the other team gets an opportunity to steal the point, but in this case, the other team doesn't provide the correct response either. The teacher stops the game momentarily to ask who has the right answer and discovers that only one student can answer correctly. Accordingly, he makes a mental note that the students are having trouble with the term *circulatory* and returns to it in class the next day.

Second, teachers should identify what students know and do not know about the difficult terms. When it is clear that students are having difficulty with a term, the teacher should determine whether their difficulty arises because they do not understand critical characteristics of the term or because they are inaccurate about some of the critical characteristics of a term. For example, suppose the science teacher in the previous example revisits the circulatory system in class the day after the game. Through a class discussion, he realizes the students believed the lungs were only part of the respiratory system. Most of them had not understood that a single organ can be involved with more than one body system. He reviews important organs that are part of more than one body system to clear up the confusion.

Third, teachers should have students make changes in their vocabulary notebooks. Ideally, after each game is played, students should review the terms in their vocabulary notebooks that were addressed in the games. While students are reviewing the terms in their vocabulary notebooks, they should be asked to add anything new they learned about the terms as a result of the games and change anything about a term they realized was inaccurate. For example, in the preceding classroom scenario, the students might go back to the vocabulary notebook entry they had about the circulatory system and make a second drawing, one which depicts the lungs as part of that system. These changes should be recorded in their academic notebooks as depicted in figure I.2 (page 3).

Teachers using this book should feel free to make adaptations and additions. Just as it is important for students to have fun with the vocabulary games, so should teachers. Therefore, feel free to adapt, augment, and change the games in any way that enhances students' knowledge of new terminology. Some of the games require, or can be enhanced by, visual images used in conjunction with the vocabulary terms. For example, the term *airplane* may need to be accompanied by a simple illustration or photograph of an airplane. Teachers should feel free to include students in the process of obtaining these images. For example, you might ask students to draw simple pictures, create collages, or find images on the Internet to be used during play.

1

WORD HARVEST

For lower elementary language arts, math, science, and social studies

Design

This game is modeled after the game *Apple Picking* in Susan L. Kasser's (1995) book *Inclusive Games: Movement Fun for Everyone!* However, where that game focuses only on movement, *Word Harvest* focuses on vocabulary as well. It is best for lower elementary students, and uses terms from language arts, math, science, and social studies. Teachers in a self-contained classroom can use a variety of terms from different content areas as well as general literacy terms. Because students will need a working understanding of the terms and phrases used in the game, select only those with which they will be familiar.

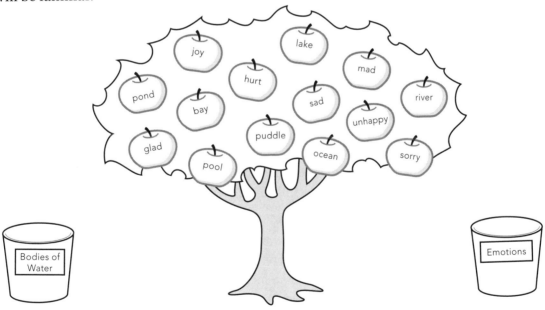

Materials

You will need construction paper and/or poster board (brown, green, and red), scissors, tape, two buckets or baskets, and note cards.

Set Up

To set up the game, begin by writing one "word category" on each note card. For example, you might write "colors" for a category that includes different words for colors (such as *red* or *purple*) or "time" for a category that includes words depicting increments of time (such as *second* and *minute*). You can use the word categories we have crafted in the vocabulary list on pages 9–11, or create your own. If you choose to create your own, be sure to consider the size of the categories you choose. Each category should include approximately the same number of terms or phrases. For example, if you choose ten terms that belong in a category called "clothing" (words like *skirt* or *shoe*), then the other categories you choose should also have roughly ten words each. We recommend each category have between five and ten words.

Prepare in advance by creating a big paper tree. The tree should be roughly the height of your students and large enough to display all of your vocabulary words (more than one tree can be used for bigger classrooms). Each vocabulary word is written on a separate paper apple (see page 12 or visit **marzanoresearch.com/reproducibles** for a reproducible illustration of an apple). Be sure that each word you write on an apple corresponds to a word category you created. For example, if you have a category called "money," then you might write words like *coin, dollar,* or *nickel* on the paper apples. Make sure every apple is placed low enough for students to reach.

On game day, tape the tree(s) to a wall at one end of the classroom, tape all of the apples to the tree(s), and place two buckets at the opposite end of the classroom. Tape one word-category note card to each bucket. For example, one team might have a bucket labeled "foods," while the other team might have a bucket labeled "days of the week."

Play

Begin play by splitting the class into two teams. Be sure that each team has students at various stages of vocabulary development (each team should have students who are advanced, students who are on target, and students who are at more remedial vocabulary levels). The members of each team line up near the bucket you designate as their home base (each team has one bucket). Point out the word-category note card taped to their bucket so that every student knows what kinds of words he or she will be looking for on the vocabulary tree. For example, you might tell one team they will be looking for "clothing." Ask them to repeat the phrase and give you examples of clothing words. Once the students understand what kinds of words they are looking for, the game begins.

On your signal, the first student in line from each team hurries to the tree and reads the words written on the apples. When she finds the kind of word she is looking for, she plucks it and hurries back to place it in her team's home-base bucket. For example, a student who is looking for "numbers" finds the word *three* written on an apple and plucks it. He hurries back and drops it in his team's bucket so that the next student can have a turn.

There are two ways to define a round. One involves stopping play when one team has plucked all of the words in their designated category. That team receives a point, and two new word categories (one for each team) are designated for the remaining apples before play resumes. The second way to play is that once one team has plucked all of the relevant words, you quickly designate a new word category for that team only by taping another note card on the bucket and making an announcement. In this version of the game, play does not end until each student has had a turn or until the allotted time is up. At that point, the apples are counted, and the team with the most correct words wins.

If you choose, you can create special word categories and word apples for a bonus round. These categories, terms, and phrases might be more difficult or less familiar. The idea of a bonus round is to challenge students rather than frustrate them, so take care in choosing terms and phrases.

Vocabulary Words

Make sure you choose words that are at least relatively familiar to the students. All of them should clearly fit into the categories you designate. Nouns work the best, but proper nouns such as names of important people, states, countries, and continents might be used as well. If you use verbs, be sure they fit into a clear category, such as the "eating/drinking" category used in the provided vocabulary list (page 10). The game can be modified as necessary. For instance, if a social studies teacher is covering basic geography, he or she might designate categories such as "cities," "states," or "countries" and even a category such as "words you find on a map."

Following are sample lists of categories and terms aimed at a lower elementary level. Because many of the terms appropriate for lower elementary students are general enough to be used in more than one subject area, we have listed twenty-seven categories with ten or more corresponding terms alphabetically instead of by subject. Feel free to modify terms and/or categories as necessary and mix them as appropriate for your class. For a more detailed list of categories and terms, see *Teaching Basic and Advanced Vocabulary: A Framework for Direct Instruction* (Marzano, 2009). A reproducible outline of an apple is also included (page 12).

Baby Animals
baby
bunny
calf
chick
fawn
foal
kitten
pup
puppy
tadpole

Birds
chicken
crow
duck
eagle
fowl
goose
hen
jay
owl
parrot
robin
rooster
seagull
turkey

Bodies of Water
bay
creek
lake
ocean
pond
pool
puddle
river
sea
stream

Colors
black
blue
brown
gold
gray
green
orange
pink
purple
red
silver
white
yellow

Days and Months
April
August
December
February
Friday
January

continued →

July
June
March
May
Monday
November
October
Saturday
September
Sunday
Thursday
Tuesday
Wednesday

Directions and Locations

above
across
ahead
behind
below
beside
between
close
east
far
left
middle
north
right
south
under
west

Eating and Drinking

bite
chew
dine
drink
eat
feed
gnaw
nibble
swallow
sip

Family Members

aunt
brother
cousin
dad
daughter
father
grandparent
mom
mother
sister
son
uncle

Five Senses

blind
deaf
hear
listen
look
see
smell
stare
taste
touch

Foods

biscuit
bread
candy
cheese
fruit
hamburger
hotdog
macaroni
milk
muffin
noodle
oatmeal
omelet
pizza
pretzel
salad
sandwich
taco
toast
vegetable
waffle
water

Emotions

cry
mad
glad
hurt
joy
play
sad
silly
sorry
unhappy

Parts of the Body

arm
belly
chest
ears
elbow
eyes
face
finger
foot
hand
head
hip
knee
leg
mouth
neck
nose
toe
waist

Jobs

actor
baker
clown
coach
doctor
fireman
judge
maid
mailman
pilot
police officer
president
soldier
teacher

Land Animals

bear
camel
cat
cow
deer
dog
donkey
elephant
fox
giraffe
horse
kangaroo
lion
monkey
moose
mouse
pig
rabbit
raccoon
sheep
skunk
wolf
zebra

Measurements

centimeter
cup
foot
gallon
inch
meter
mile
pound
quart
tablespoon
yard

Forms of Money

cash

cent

coin

cost

dime

dollar

nickel

penny

price

quarter

Numbers

eight

eighty

fifty

five

forty

four

hundred

nine

ninety

one

seven

seventy

six

sixty

ten

thirty

thousand

three

twenty

two

Places in the Community

bakery

bookstore

church

hospital

library

neighborhood

office

park

restaurant

school

temple

zoo

Places to Live

apartment

cabin

castle

home

hotel

hut

igloo

palace

teepee

tent

Plants

berry

blossom

branch

bush

flower

grass

leaf

root

tree

vine

Rooms in a House

attic

basement

bathroom

bedroom

closet

garage

hall

kitchen

playroom

porch

Sports

baseball

basketball

boxing

football

golf

hockey

skiing

soccer

swimming

tennis

Time

calendar

clock

date

day

decade

hour

minute

past

present

second

today

tomorrow

watch

week

year

yesterday

Things to Read

book

cartoon

chapter

diary

dictionary

magazine

map

menu

newspaper

textbook

webpage

Tools

drill

fork

hammer

rake

saw

scissors

screwdriver

shovel

spoon

tweezers

Water Animals

dolphin

fish

salmon

seal

shark

shrimp

starfish

tuna

walrus

whale

Weather and Seasons

air

fall

flood

lightening

rain

snow

spring

storm

summer

thunder

wind

winter

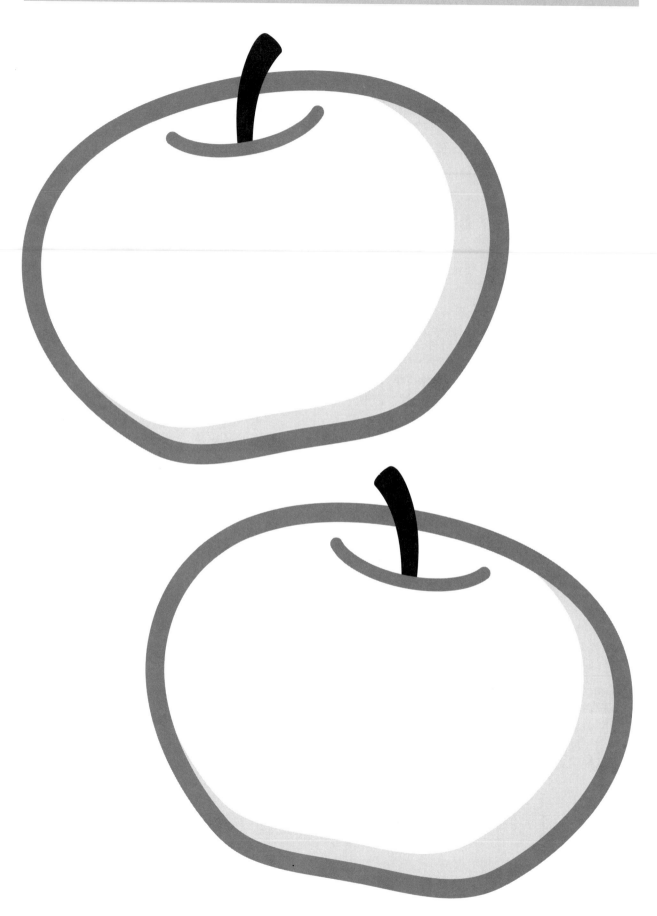

2

NAME IT!

For lower elementary language arts, math, science, and social studies

Design

This game is modeled after the game *Peanut Butter and Jelly* in Susan L. Kasser's (1995) book *Inclusive Games: Movement Fun for Everyone!* However, the game in that book focuses only on movement while this game focuses on vocabulary as well. It is best played with lower elementary students, and can include general vocabulary terms as well as relevant terms from any of the four main content areas (language arts, math, science, and social studies). Students will need to have been introduced to the relevant terms and phrases and have a working understanding of them.

Materials

You will need a chalkboard or whiteboard, a large bucket or basket, and pictures or illustrations of the terms you will be using. For example, if you want to use the term *bear*, you will need a picture or illustration of a bear. Because this game involves the use of many images, you should feel free to include your students in the process of obtaining them. Students might create illustrations themselves, or they might find them in books at home or in the classroom or on the Internet. Once students find images, they should give them to you for approval and safe keeping until game day.

Set Up

In advance, choose your terms and phrases along with a separate illustration or picture to accompany each one. Before beginning, place the images in the bucket. Be sure they are folded or turned facedown so that students must choose one at random.

Play

Begin by setting the bucket of pictures in the middle of the room. After explaining the rules and giving a few examples of how the game is played, split the class into two teams, with each team forming a separate line at the back of the room. On your cue, the first member of each team hurries to the bucket and selects a picture. After looking at the picture, each student hands it to you and then writes on the board, in one word, what he or she sees. For example, if a student selects a picture of a bird, she writes the word *bird* on the board. When she is finished, you give her a "thumbs up" for a correct word or a "thumbs down" for an incorrect word.

You can decide whether or not you want to give second chances or clues. For example, if a student selects a picture of a butterfly and writes the word *bug* on the board, you can choose to give him the "thumbs down" and move on to the next student, or you can tell him that his word was not specific enough (for example, you might ask, "What kind of bug?"). You can give students between one and three chances to get the word right and earn a point for the team. After he earns the point or uses up his chances, he erases what he has written and hurries back to tag the next member of his team in a relay fashion.

After each student has taken a turn, a round of play is over and points are tallied. You can play as many rounds as you wish, but make sure you have new images for each round.

Vocabulary Words

It is best to use common nouns with this game because verbs and prepositions can be difficult to communicate with a picture. Be sure that the image you select has enough clues to enable the student to figure out the correct term. For example, it would be difficult for a student to translate an illustration of a woman into the term "mom." This game can be tailored in highly specific ways for every classroom. For instance, if your students are learning to tell time, you might use illustrations of clocks showing different times and ask the students to write the time they see on the board. In the following list, the sample terms and illustrations appear in categories listed alphabetically because many of the terms and phrases used at the lower elementary level are general and can be applied in more than one content area. Visit **marzanoresearch.com/reproducibles** to download sample illustrations associated with this list.

Animals

alligator
bear
dog
elephant
giraffe
horse
lion
monkey
pig
sheep

Clothing

coat
dress
mittens
pants
robe
scarf
shirt
shoes
shorts
skirt
socks
tie

Cooking and Eating Utensils

bowl
fork
glass
knife
mug
pot
spoon

Fruits and Vegetables

apple
banana
broccoli
carrot
corn
grapes
orange
pear
potato
pumpkin

Insects

ant
bee
butterfly
caterpillar
fly

grasshopper
ladybug
moth
slug
spider
worm

Furniture

bed
bookcase
chair
couch/sofa
crib

desk
table

Musical Instruments

drum
flute
guitar
piano
saxophone
tuba
violin

Shapes

circle
cube
cylinder
diamond
oval
pyramid
rectangle
sphere
square
triangle

Sports Equipment

ball
bat
glove
goal/net
ice skates
skis
surfboard

Vehicles

airplane
balloon
bicycle
boat
bus
car
helicopter
motorcycle
rocket
train

3

PUZZLE STORIES

For upper elementary and middle school language arts, math, science, and social studies

Design

Puzzle Stories gets its name from the overall object of the game: to create a story based on the image on a puzzle. It is best played with upper elementary or middle school students, but can be modified for lower elementary or high school students as well. In addition to increasing vocabulary, this game can be used to practice writing skills and enhance creativity. It can be played using terms from any of the four main content areas (language arts, math, science, and social studies), but is probably the most easily adapted to language arts, social studies, and science classes. Students will need to have a working understanding of the terms and phrases used.

Materials

You will be splitting the class into small groups for this game and will need as many puzzles as you have groups. For example, if your class splits evenly into five groups, you will need five puzzles. The puzzles you select should be easy to put together. They should also depict a simple scene, such as a hummingbird sucking nectar or a sailboat on the sea. The idea is simply to give students a starting place and then let them apply vocabulary terms and phrases and make use of their creativity. You also need a chalkboard or whiteboard.

Set Up

Create one or more lists of vocabulary words in advance. The list should be between five and ten words long. If you are teaching all four subjects in one classroom, you can choose words from more than one content area. For example, your list might include two social studies vocabulary terms, three language arts terms, one math term, and two science terms.

Play

Begin by splitting the class into small groups of three to five students. It is best if each group contains students who are advanced and students who are struggling with vocabulary. Once the students understand the game, provide each group with a puzzle and handout with a list of vocabulary words. You can also write the list on the board.

On your cue, the students in each group race to put the puzzle together. Once they have done that, their next task is to write a story about the scene or object depicted in the puzzle using their vocabulary list. For example, an elementary school science teacher might provide the groups with a puzzle that depicts a hummingbird sucking nectar from a flower. He or she might provide the following list of terms:

home	observe	sound
grow	parent	machine
light	summer	creek

After the students put together the puzzle, one group might come up with a story like the following, based on the theme of the puzzle:

> Harry is a blind hummingbird. He can't tell when it is light and when it is dark, so he finds his nectar using sound. Flowers make noises people can't hear. Sometimes, on summer nights, he hears the flowers open up. Most people have never seen a hummingbird out at night, so it takes them by surprise. They will leave their homes and follow Harry through the park or along the creek, wherever he goes. They are like machines. Harry knows they are there, but he doesn't mind. He follows the sound of the flowers until he finds the best ones, the ones that grew the most during the day and smell the strongest. Sometimes, a whole crowd gathers to observe Harry sucking his nectar. Kids don't get in trouble with their parents for being out at night because usually their parents are there too. Everyone likes him so much that they are going to rename their town after him.

After students finish, one representative from each group can read the story aloud. The game can be for enjoyment only, or students can vote on their favorite story to designate a winning group. You can adapt the game for younger students in a few ways: (1) provide students with a shorter list of terms, maybe two or three words long; (2) provide a photograph instead of a puzzle that students must put together; or (3) ask students to construct only a sentence about what they see rather than a whole story.

Adapting the game for older students is possible as well. Instead of puzzles, each group might be given a magazine and asked to select a photo or advertisement to use as the basis of their story. The key to adapting the game to older students is to provide more difficult or focused terms that require more creativity. Teachers can use vocabulary words from the current unit and ask students to find photos in the magazines that relate to each term. For example, a physics teacher asks students to describe what is happening in any photo they find in a given magazine in terms of exothermic or endothermic reactions. One group finds a photo of women sunbathing and equates this to an endothermic reaction in that the women must absorb the heat and energy of the sun to change the color of their skin.

Vocabulary Words

No sample terms are provided for this game, as each list will be unique. The best lists include both nouns (common or proper) and verbs. Relevant adjectives or prepositions can be used as well. The key is to include a variety of parts of speech so that students can more easily combine them into a story. The vocabulary lists for older students might be shorter because the terms are more complex conceptually.

4

TWO OF A KIND

For lower and upper elementary
general vocabulary

Design

Two of a Kind is modeled after the game *Memory* and focuses on homonyms. It is best suited for building the general vocabulary of elementary students. Students must have familiarity with the words being used.

Materials

You will need blank note cards.

Set Up

In advance, write one word (a homonym) on each note card, leaving the other side of the card blank. For example, if you write *steel* on one card, write *steal* on another. Create a master set of cards constituted by pairs of homonyms (between five and fifteen pairs works best), then make enough copies of the set to distribute among your students. The class will be broken up into small groups or pairs, and each group will need an identical set of cards.

Before playing, set up a separate station for each group by laying the cards facedown in rows. The idea is that when they begin, none of the students know what or where any of the words in their set of cards are.

Play

Just like *Memory*, a student takes a turn by flipping over two of the note cards. If the two words he finds are homonyms, he keeps both cards; if they are not, he turns them back over, and another student gets a turn. The object is to collect as many cards as possible. The game is over when all of the cards have been collected. Rounds can be set up so that the winner of one game plays the winner of another until one student has prevailed (keep in mind that you will need new sets of cards for each round), or it can be played just for fun—no points awarded or winners declared.

If you wish, you can require that each student explain the homonym before getting to keep the pair or trio of cards. For example, if a student picks up the pair of homophones *whole* and *hole*, you can require that she raise her hand to get your attention as you circulate throughout the room and define both words or use them in a sentence before she is able to keep the cards. This requirement is especially useful with homonyms of the same spelling. If students must give both definitions of the word, you know they are not collecting the pair of cards by sight recognition only.

Vocabulary Words

Following are sample homonyms. They are not split into content areas. Rather, they appear in three groups: one for homonyms with the same spelling, one for homonyms with different spellings, and one for trio homonyms such as *they're*, *their*, and *there*.

Same-Spelling Homonyms

bit/bit
cell/cell
document/document
left/left
object/object
official/official
pass/pass
pound/pound
race/race
right/right
second/second
sound/sound

Different-Spelling Homonyms

acts/axe
aid/aide
ant/aunt
bail/bale
bare/bear
base/bass
beat/beet
bow/beau
bow/bough
break/brake
butt/but
ceiling/sealing
cellar/seller
cents/sense
chance/chants

choose/chews
chute/shoot
clause/claws
course/coarse
cymbal/symbol
days/daze
die/dye
doe/dough
dual/duel
due/do
ewes/use
eye/I
fair/fare
feat/feet
find/fined
flee/flea
flier/flyer
flour/flower
grate/great

guys/guise
hair/hare
heal/heel
heard/herd
hole/whole
idle/idol
its/it's
knead/need
knight/night
knows/nose
leak/leek
loan/lone
made/maid
mail/male
main/mane
meet/meat
minor/miner
mite/might
moose/mousse

nun/none
or/oar
owed/ode
packed/pact
paste/paced
pause/paws
peace/piece
peek/peak
peer/pier
plane/plain
pore/pour
pray/prey
prints/prince
profit/prophet
rain/reign
raise/rays

read/red
right/write
road/rowed
root/route
sail/sale
scene/seen
see/sea
seem/seam
sew/so
sighs/size
sink/sync
soar/sore
some/sum
son/sun
stair/stare
stake/steak

steel/steal
suite/sweet
Sunday/sundae
tacks/tax
tale/tail
tents/tense
threw/through
tide/tied
tow/toe
vane/vain
vice/vise
wait/weight
waive/wave
way/weigh
we/wee
weak/week

weather/whether
which/witch
whose/who's
wood/would

Trio Homonyms

present/present/
  present
role/roll/roll
they're/their/there
to/too/two
wail/whale/wale
yore/your/you're

OPPOSITES ATTRACT

For lower and upper elementary
general vocabulary

Design

Opposites Attract gets its name from its focus on antonyms. It can be used for building the general vocabulary of lower and upper elementary students. Students should have a working understanding of the terms and phrases used.

Materials

You will need blank note cards and tape.

Set Up

In advance, write one word in big letters on one note card and its antonym on another card. For example, if you write *inside* on one card, write *outside* on the other. Each set of card should have complete pairs of antonyms, and there should be as many cards as there are students in the class.

Play

Each student is given a card with a word written on it. Once the student has read and understands the word, he tapes it to his shirt so that other students will be able to easily see and read it. On your cue, everyone walks around the room and reads the words on other students' cards. Each student is looking for his or her antonym. For example, if a student's word is *giant*, she would be looking for someone with a word like *tiny*.

This game can be played nonverbally if you choose, and you can set time limits as well. If you want to play more than one round, simply gather up the cards and reshuffle them so that each student gets a new word. Another option is to create different sets of cards in advance, each with more difficult antonyms than the last. Points are not necessarily awarded in this game, and there does not need to be any clear winner. Any student who finds his or her antonym is a winner.

Vocabulary Words

Following are sample antonyms. They are categorized as easy, intermediate, or advanced. Choose the pairs that would be familiar to students in your class but would challenge them as well.

Easy Antonyms

add/subtract
best/worst
big/small
clean/dirty
easy/difficult
empty/full
fast/slow
fat/skinny
happy/sad
hot/cold
hungry/full
inside/outside
less/more
light/dark
loud/quiet
mean/kind
polite/rude
pretty/ugly
rich/poor
sharp/dull
short/long
sick/well
smooth/rough
soft/hard
stand/sit
stop/go
strong/weak

top/bottom
war/peace
wet/dry
young/old

Intermediate Antonyms

always/never
awake/asleep
begin/finish
bitter/sweet
blessing/curse
brave/cowardly
bright/dim
build/destroy
buy/sell
expensive/cheap
frequent/rare
friend/enemy
hurt/heal
many/few
multiply/divide
open/closed
remember/forget
safe/dangerous
serious/silly
shout/whisper
succeed/fail

together/alone
tough/fragile
truth/lie
work/play

Advanced Antonyms

adore/shun
create/erase
fierce/meek
introvert/extrovert
modern/old-fashioned
plant/harvest
popular/outcast
sow/reap
tropical/polar
waste/conserve

MAGIC LETTER, MAGIC WORD

For lower and upper elementary or middle
school language arts, math, science,
and social studies

Design

Magic Letter, Magic Word asks students to use clues they are given (including a "magic letter") to
find the "magic" vocabulary term or phrase. Students need to have a good understanding of the
terms and phrases to play this game. It is best played with lower and upper elementary students
but can be modified for middle school students as well.

Materials

The only material necessary is a chalkboard or white board.

Set Up

In advance, create a list of vocabulary terms and phrases and corresponding "clues." The object of
the game is for the students to use these clues to find the correct term or phrase. For example, assume you want students to understand the term *astronomy*. You might provide the following clue:
"The study of objects in space is called _____." Or, if you are looking for a term such
as *Wednesday* that comes in a sequence (the sequence of the days of the week), you might provide
the following clue: "Sunday, Monday, Tuesday, _____." You can also provide a brief
definition as a clue. For example, if you are looking for the phrase *president of the United States*, you
might provide this clue: "He lives in the White House." Finally, synonyms make good clues. For example, if the term you are looking for is *proofread*, you might provide the following clue: "Another
word for *edit*."

Clues can be more or less specific, depending on the level of difficulty you want to achieve. For example, if you are looking for the term *inherit*, you may choose to go with a descriptive clue such as

"traits like eye color and height you _____ from your parents," or you may choose a more open-ended clue such as "genetic hand-me-down." Obviously, this second clue is more abstract and requires more from students. Tailor the clues to the level of difficulty appropriate to your class.

Along with the clue, provide students with the "magic letter." The letter is another clue to the term or phrase you are looking for. To make the game simple, each magic letter might be designated as the initial letter in the term. For example, if your magic letter is *P*, students know that the correct term or phrase begins with a *P*. You can also designate the magic letter as the last letter in the correct term. The most advanced level of the game is to designate only that the magic letter appears somewhere in the term you are looking for.

Be aware that more general clues may lead to students providing more than one correct answer. For example, a social studies teacher covering a unit on U.S. history might provide *M* as the magic letter and the following clue: "early U.S. presidents." Given such a broad clue, one group might say "James Monroe," while another might say "Martin Van Buren." Or, if you write the magic letter *T* on the board and a clue such as "a journey," you may get answers such as "trip," "trek," or "travel." It is perfectly acceptable to allow more than one correct response, but you may prefer to narrow it down by providing a more specific clue. For example, if the answer you are looking for is *Martin Van Buren*, you might provide a specific clue such as, "This early U.S. president was also Andrew Jackson's vice president." Likewise, if the term you are looking for is *travel*, you might provide a specific clue such as, "I think the best way to get to grandma's house is to _____ by train." Given these more specific parameters, students will come up with one correct response.

Play

Break the students into small groups, and write a magic letter and a clue on the board. Students must find a word that fits the clue and utilizes the magic letter in the way you have designated. When they have found an answer, they signal by raising their hands or a flag you provide at the start of the game. You can set up point systems and designate winners if you choose, or you can leave the game open-ended with the fun of it being simply finding the right term.

Vocabulary Words

Virtually any part of speech can be used with this game, as the key is creating an appropriate clue for the term. You can also open up the game so that it encompasses more than vocabulary. For example, a language arts teacher might provide open-ended clues such as "coming-of-age theme" and have students use the clue and magic letter to write the title of a book with that theme. Only limited examples of terms and corresponding clues have been provided in each of the four main subject areas, as this game will be highly specialized in each classroom. Some of the math examples use illustrations; if you decide to make use of these examples, you should reproduce them on the board or via overhead. All of the examples that follow assume the magic letter to be the initial letter of the relevant term or phrase.

Language Arts

Magic Letter: **A**

CLUE: A list of all of the letters is called an _____.
ANSWER: **alphabet**

CLUE: A person who writes a book is called an _____.
ANSWER: **author**

CLUE: People in plays or movies are called _____.
ANSWER: **actors**

Magic Letter: **P**

CLUE: *For*, *an*, and *by* are all examples of _____.
ANSWER: **prepositions**

CLUE: Commas, periods, and question marks are all examples of _____ marks.
ANSWER: **punctuation**

CLUE: When you read over your work to correct spelling errors, you are _____.
ANSWER: **proofreading**

Magic Letter: **F**

CLUE: Metaphors and similes are examples of _____.
ANSWER: **figurative language**

CLUE: An author can describe events that took place before the time of the story by using a _____.
ANSWER: **flashback**

CLUE: If you speak Spanish well enough to live in Mexico, you are said to be _____ in the language.
ANSWER: **fluent**

Magic Letter: **S**

CLUE: A genre that intends to make political statements by using parody is called a _____.
ANSWER: **satire**

CLUE: A speech given by only one character is called a _____.
ANSWER: **soliloquy**

CLUE: A style of writing that primarily focuses on following an author or narrator's train of thought is called _____.
ANSWER: **stream of consciousness**

Math

Magic Letter: *S*

CLUE: 7 − 3 = 4 is an example of a _____ problem.
ANSWER: **subtraction**

CLUE: When you add two numbers together you get a _____.
ANSWER: **sum**

CLUE: A shape that has four sides of equal length is called a _____.
ANSWER: **square**

Magic Letter: *I*

CLUE: The _____ tells you that 7 + 0 = 7 and that 7 × 1 = 7.
ANSWER: **identity property**

CLUE: A triangle with at least two sides of equal length is called an _____.
ANSWER: **isosceles triangle**

CLUE: 3 < 5 and 7 > 2 are examples of _____.
ANSWER: **inequalities**

Magic Letter: *C*

CLUE: Two angles that add up to be 90° are called _____.
ANSWER: **complementary angles**

CLUE: Any number that is greater than one and is not a prime number is called a _____.
ANSWER: **composite number**

CLUE: Two triangles that have the same shape and size but are in different positions are called

_____.

ANSWER: **congruent**

Magic Letter: *T*

CLUE: A straight line that just touches a curve at a single point is called a _____ line.
ANSWER: **tangent**

CLUE: A statement that can be proven true based on statements previously proven true is
called a _____.
ANSWER: **theorem**

CLUE: A line that passes through two parallel lines is called a _____.
ANSWER: **transversal**

Science

Magic Letter: **L**

CLUE: The sun gives us heat and _____.
ANSWER: **light**

CLUE: Soda, milk, and orange juice are all in _____ form.
ANSWER: **liquid**

CLUE: Another word for *find* is _____.
ANSWER: **locate**

Magic Letter: **A**

CLUE: A car that speeds up on the highway to pass another car is _____.
ANSWER: **accelerating**

CLUE: The study of space and all of the objects in space is called _____.
ANSWER: **astronomy**

CLUE: The Earth is separated from space by the _____.
ANSWER: **atmosphere**

Magic Letter: **I**

CLUE: Your body can fight off sickness and infection because of its _____.
ANSWER: **immune system**

CLUE: Antibacterial and antifungal medicines are used to prevent _____.
ANSWER: **infection**

CLUE: An animal with no backbone is called an _____.
ANSWER: **invertebrate**

Magic Letter: **D**

CLUE: Inherited characteristics such as height and eye color are determined by your _____.
ANSWER: **DNA**

CLUE: The siren of an ambulance sounding louder as the ambulance gets closer and then getting quieter as it passes you is an example of the _____.
ANSWER: **Doppler effect**

CLUE: A force that can slow an object in motion is called _____.
ANSWER: **drag**

Social Studies

Magic Letter: **F**

CLUE: George Washington is often called the _____.
ANSWER: **father of our country**

CLUE: Each country participating in the Olympics is represented by a unique _____.
ANSWER: **flag**

CLUE: Products such as cars and toys are assembled in _____.
ANSWER: **factories**

Magic Letter: **A**

CLUE: The immigration station that processed thousands of immigrants, the majority of whom were Chinese, in the early 1900s is known as _____.
ANSWER: **Angel Island**

CLUE: _____ was the American female pilot who disappeared on an around-the-world flight.
ANSWER: **Amelia Earhart**

CLUE: A person living in the United States who is not a citizen is called an _____.
ANSWER: **alien**

Magic Letter: **J**

CLUE: _____ was the U.S. senator known for making unsubstantiated claims of communist subversion within the government.
ANSWER: **Joseph McCarthy**

CLUE: The Supreme Court is part of the _____ branch of the government.
ANSWER: **judicial**

CLUE: _____ is another word for a person under the age of eighteen.
ANSWER: **juvenile**

Magic Letter: **C**

CLUE: The passing of the _____ made discrimination in public places illegal and required equal opportunity employment practices nationwide.
ANSWER: **Civil Rights Act of 1964**

CLUE: _____ was the founder of the League of Women Voters.
ANSWER: **Carrie Chapman Catt**

CLUE: The doctrine regarding the government's right to regulate free speech is called the _____.
ANSWER: **clear and present danger rule**

7

DEFINITION SHMEFINITION

For upper elementary through high school
language arts, math, science, and social studies

Design

This game, modeled after *Balderdash*, requires little or no knowledge of the relevant terms and phrases. In fact, the fun of the game is *not* knowing the definitions. It can be played in any content area (language arts, math, science, and social studies), and is best suited to upper elementary through high school students.

Materials

You will need a basket or bowl and a dictionary.

Set Up

Prepare a list of at least ten to twenty terms ahead of time (only you will see the list). Be sure the definitions for your terms are in a dictionary or similar reference book.

Play

First, break the class into teams of three, four, or five. Give one team the dictionary. You begin by writing the first term on the board and saying it aloud. On your signal, the team with the dictionary looks up the real definition of the term and writes it down while the other teams work together to come up with their best guess as to what the word means. They can use knowledge of prefixes, roots, and suffixes as well as any background knowledge. For example, if a fifth-grade class is analyzing the word *autobiography*, one student might pick up on the root *auto-* and suggest the word had something to do with performing an action without thought, like *automatic*. Another student might know that a biography is the story of someone's life because she sees her dad reading biographies at home. The group might put together these and other suggestions to write the definition, "Autobiography: the things in life we all know are boring but still have to do." You might even ask students to write the word in a sentence. Their definition will probably not be correct, but the important thing is that students have seen and started thinking about the word.

The team with the dictionary should mark their definition in some way, such as putting a *D* on the top right-hand corner of the page before turning it over to you. The other teams do not need to mark their definitions in any way. After you have collected all of the definitions, including the real definition, read them aloud. After everyone has heard and thought about every definition you read, have the teams discuss which one they think is correct. The team who used the dictionary to write down the correct definition will sit out this round of play. When the other teams have agreed on an answer, one member of each team announces which definition they believe is correct.

Points are awarded in two ways: First, if a team guesses the correct definition, a point is awarded to them. Second, a point is awarded to any team who wrote the definition another team voted for. For example, if Team A wrote the definition that Team B voted for, Team A is awarded a point. The object of the game, then, is not only to guess the correct definition, but also to write a realistic definition for the given word, one that will fool other teams into voting for it.

Finally, if any team writes down the real definition, an automatic three points are awarded. For example, assume each team has written their own definition for the word *corruption*. You find that you have two slips of paper with the correct definition when you collect all of the definitions. One slip was written by the team with the dictionary, but another was written by a team that did not have the dictionary. This is why the team with the dictionary must mark their definition before giving it to you. If you have two slips of paper with the correct definition, simply discard the one written by the team with the dictionary. This way, you can inform the class that one of the teams has written the correct definition and, because the team with the dictionary sits out that round of play, the answer will not be given away by being read twice. You award the team with the correct definition three automatic points only after everyone has voted. As the game continues, each team gets a turn to write down the real definition using the dictionary.

You can modify this game if you wish (which is helpful for younger students in particular) by writing out the definitions for each term in student-friendly language beforehand. If you do this, the dictionary team is not necessary. Make sure you write your definitions on slips of paper similar to the paper students will be using so as to avoid giving the answer away when you read the definitions aloud.

After the correct definition is revealed and points have been awarded, you might ask each student to write down the word and its true definition in his or her vocabulary notebook. Through playing this game then, students will have been introduced to new vocabulary terms because they will have looked at each term, thought about its meaning, and then written down the correct definition.

Vocabulary Words

At any level, common nouns and verbs that would be fun to invent definitions for should be used. It is best to choose terms that students may recognize but not necessarily know the formal definitions for. At the lower levels, simple compound words are good choices, and at the higher levels, words with clear roots work well. Proper nouns, such as the names of important people, do not work as well with this game, because there is nothing in a person's name that would suggest his or her accomplishments.

Again, it does not necessarily matter how close students get to the exact definition, only that they are introduced to the terms in a fun way. You will need to adapt the game for your specific vocabulary needs, but following are some sample terms with age-appropriate definitions. Keep in mind that if you are going to have students write down the real definitions in vocabulary notebooks, you may need an example to accompany the definition. For instance, after defining the term *prime factor*, you may want to give an example: "The two prime factors of 100 are 2 and 5."

Language Arts

Upper Elementary

action word: a word that tells you what someone or something is doing

audience: the people who read a book or watch a movie

brainstorm: to come up with writing ideas

checklist: a list of things to do

chronology: events listed or told in order from first to last

decode: to use clues to figure out what a word means

edit: to correct a mistake in writing or change writing to make it better

express: to let someone know how you feel

heading: the title of a page, section, or chapter of a book

imagery: a written description of exactly how something looks

index: an alphabetical list of names, places, and terms that are used in a book that also includes page numbers on which they appear

newspaper: the publication that reports on current events

nonfiction: writing about a real person's life or an event that really took place

novel: a long story the author made up

outline: a sketch that shows the main ideas or features of an essay or a project

paragraph: a small section of writing that begins with an indentation and contains an idea or thought

plot: the storyline; the main events of a story

prefix: an affix placed before a root word that changes the meaning of the word

preview: an advance showing or view of things to come

text: the writing that appears in books

thesaurus: a resource that helps you find synonyms, or words that are similar in meaning

timeline: a representation of events in the order they happened or will happen

tone: the feeling or mood that comes across in speech or writing

software: programs used with a computer system

summary: a short retelling of the main ideas in a speech or text

Middle School

autobiography: a book someone writes about his or her own life

bibliography: the alphabetical list of sources used in a research paper

body language: the gestures or movements a person makes that tells you how he or she feels

caption: the title for or short explanation of a drawing or picture

criticism: the evaluation of a text or performance

dialogue: the written record of the exact words of a conversation between two or more people or characters

elaborate: to add details to a text or performance; to expand

exposition: writing intended to inform or explain

feedback: information given to someone about his or her performance or product that is intended to help him or her improve

figurative language: language with meaning other than literal

footnote: a note at the bottom of a page that explains or documents something in the text

foreshadowing: the technique an author uses to hint at what will happen next in a story

interjection: words or phrases that convey emotion

interpretation: an explanation of the meaning of a text or performance

jargon: words or language specific to a profession or group

juxtaposition: the act of positioning two different things side by side for emphasis or comparison

mass media: any medium of communication that reaches large numbers of people

meter: the regular pattern or rhythm in which words, lines, and verses in poems appear

modifier: a word or phrase that limits or qualifies another word in the same sentence

monologue: text that conveys the inner thoughts of a character or narrator

paraphrase: to restate the main ideas of a text in one's own words

stereotype: a simplified and generalized statement about a group of people that is often untrue and/or offensive

subplot: a secondary or minor storyline

tension: the suspense the audience feels when watching a performance or reading a text

word origin: the time and place in which a word was created

High School

acronym: a word formed from the first letter or letters in a phrase or set of words, such as NAFTA representing North American Free Trade Agreement

analogy: a comparison based on similarity

allusion: an implicit or indirect reference often found in literature

ambiguity: uncertainty in meaning or multiple possible meanings

archetype: an original model or type

articulation: the act and quality of speaking

censorship: the prevention of communication by some authoritative body

circumlocution: the use of more words than necessary to express a thought or convey meaning

cognate: words that originate from the same language

couplet: a pair of rhyming lines in a poem

denotation: the direct or literal meaning of a word

diction: word choice

epic poem: a long poem about the journey of a hero

idiom: phrases unique to a specific culture or time period

logical fallacy: a flaw in the logic of an argument

narrator: the teller of a story

nuance: a very slight difference in expression or variation

overview: a general outline or summary

parody: a funny imitation, usually of a piece of literature

poise: a person's composure or self-confident manner

résumé: a formally written document that outlines a person's education and work history

rhetorical question: a general question that does not require an answer

thesis statement: a statement found in the introduction of an expository essay that sums up the argument the author intends to make

understatement: a statement that underplays actual seriousness or intensity

universal theme: a theme that appears in many different cultures across time

Math

Upper Elementary

acute angle: an angle with less than 90°

addend: one number that is being added to another number

bar graph: a way to display data

capacity: how much liquid a container, like a glass, can hold

circumference: the measure of the outside edge of a circle

data: a collection of facts that can be used to draw a conclusion

decimal: parts less than one

diagram: a drawing that illustrates how an object, like the engine of a car, is put together

division: the process by which large groups or numbers are separated into smaller groups or numbers

estimate: a guess about the weight, size, or amount of something

fraction: a ratio showing parts of a whole

improper fraction: a fraction with a numerator that is larger than the denominator

investigation: the process of finding out about something

mean: the number you get when you add up all of the numbers in a set and then divide the sum by how many numbers appear in the set

obtuse angle: an angle with a measurement more than 90°

odd number: a number that does not divide evenly in half

perimeter: the measure of all of the sides of a polygon

pie chart: a diagram that shows proportions of a whole or a set as a percentage of a circle

prism: a three-dimensional shape made of triangles, rectangles, or parallelograms

ruler: a tool used to take measurements up to a foot in length

rotation: a complete turn

sphere: a three-dimensional circle

three-dimensional shape: a shape that has length, width, and depth

two-dimensional shape: a shape that has length and width but no depth

Venn diagram: a diagram intended to show the similarities and differences between two things

Middle School

addition of fractions: the process by which two fractions with common denominators are added by adding the numerators to get one sum ($1/4 + 3/4 = 4/4$)

algebraic expression: a mathematical expression that contains variables and exponents

array: an arrangement of a series of terms according to some specific pattern

circumference formula: an equation used to measure the outside edge of a circle (πr^2)

constant ratio: the relationship expressed when one quantity is an unchanging multiple of another

coordinate plane: a plane made up of an x axis and a y axis that is meant to create a pattern of data points measured by their respective distances from each axis

dilation: the act of taking a shape and making it bigger without changing the shape in any other way

measures of dispersion: any form of measuring the variability of data in a particular set

exponent: the superscript number that determines to what power its connected number will be raised (4^2)

line of symmetry: the line through the exact middle of a symmetrical shape

maximum: the largest value in a set or function

minimum: the smallest value in a set or function

conjecture: a theory that does not have enough evidence to support it

ordered pairs: two numbers that represent the exact location of a point on a coordinate plane

intercept: the point at which a line or shape intersects with another line or shape

polygon: a shape that has three or more sides

prime factor: all of the prime numbers that are factors of a given quantity

range: the set of all values in a function throughout its domain

scale drawing: a rendering of an object based on specific ratio dimensions to the original object

scientific notation: a number multiplied by the number ten raised to a particular power (6×10^4)

slope: a quantity that reports the inclination of a line graphed on a coordinate plane

sample error: the inaccuracies that result from drawing conclusions by looking at only a small segment of an entire population

rate: a particular ratio in which both numbers bear some relationship to one another

variable: a symbol in an equation that stands for an unknown quantity

vertex: the common endpoint of two lines

High School

acceleration: the rate of change in velocity with respect to time

angle of depression: the angle at which you look down to see something that is below you

bivariate data: data with two variables

circle without center: the impossible or incomprehensible

density: mass per unit of volume

decibel: a unit used to express the intensity of a sound wave

absolute value: the value placed on a number based only on its distance from zero (−3 and 3 are |3|)

Richter scale: a scale used to measure the amount of energy released in an earthquake

factorial notation: a number multiplied by every descending number to zero ($4! = 4 \times 3 \times 2 \times 1$)

Fibonacci sequence: a sequence in which each number is the sum of the preceding two numbers (1, 1, 2, 3, 5, 8, 13 . . .)

force: the push or pull on an object that is the result of contact with another object

categorical data: data that can be easily separated into groups

natural number: any whole number in the set {0, 1, 2, 3, 4 . . .}

negative exponent: an exponent with a base that belongs on the bottom of the fraction line ($x^{-2} = 1/x^2$)

reciprocal: a multiplicative inverse; for instance, 4/5 is the reciprocal of 5/4

regression line: a line that passes straight through two or more variables on a graph

theorem: a rule based on evidence we know to be true

standard deviation: the average difference of the scores from the mean of distribution

statistic: the informative result of applying some function to a set of data

synthetic geometry: the branch of geometry that does not use algebra to solve problems

tangent: the point at which a straight line (line of tangency) touches a curve

transversal: a line that passes through two parallel lines

univariate data: data with only one variable

vector: a quantity that has both magnitude and direction

velocity: a vector quantity that has speed and direction

Science

Upper Elementary

bedrock: the solid layer of rock underneath soil on the Earth's surface

birth: the process of an animal being born

boiling point: the point at which water boils

carnivore: an animal that only eats other animals

condensation: the process by which water in a vaporous state becomes liquid

constellation: a group of stars that have been given a name

core: the very center; as in the center of the Earth

disease: any sickness that causes a part or system of the body to breakdown or fail

drought: a prolonged period of time without water

earthquake: a natural disaster characterized by the shaking of the ground that is caused by the shifting of the Earth's crustal plates

electricity: electrical charges and currents

food chain: the feeding chain between animals in an ecosystem

fossil: the remnants of a plant or animal from the distant past

glacier: the huge pieces of ice in the Arctic and Antarctic climates on which many animals live during winter months

herbivore: an animal that only eats plants

landslide: a natural disaster caused by a massive amount of earth coming loose from the top of a steep slope and sliding down

life cycle: the cycle of birth, growth, reproduction, and death that all living things go through

light reflection: the act of light rays hitting a surface and bouncing off in the opposite direction

light refraction: the act of light rays bending as they pass through a clear or cloudy surface

melting point: the temperature at which ice melts, becoming water

migration: the seasonal or systematic movement of a group of animals of a particular species for reasons related to survival

omnivore: an animal that eats both animals and plants

organism: any living thing

planet: any of the eight large bodies that revolve around the sun and shine because of the light reflected by the sun

rock cycle: the cycle in which rocks are formed, changed, destroyed, and formed again

Middle School

acquired trait: a trait a person comes to exhibit over time as opposed to a trait a person is born with

asexual reproduction: reproduction involving one parent without sexual intercourse

atmosphere: the layer or layers of gas surrounding a celestial body

atom: the smallest part you can break an element into without changing the element

cell: the basic unit of structure of all living things

decomposer: an organism that breaks down the bodies of dead plants and animals

Earth's age: the length of time the Earth has existed

eclipse: the appearance of either the moon blocking the sun or the Earth's shadow blocking the moon

ecosystem: the way organisms within a particular environment interact with each other

experimental control: an attempt to predict events that will occur in a scientific experiment by neutralizing the effects of other factors

fungus: an organism that survives by decomposing and digesting the material on which it grows

galaxy: a large system of stars and space debris held together by gravity

gene: the most basic unit of heredity

homeostasis: the tendency of the internal system of more complex animals to maintain internal stability and consistency

hypothesis: a prediction about the outcome of a scientific experiment based on observation

light-year: the distance light travels in one mean solar year

meteor: a rock or large object in space that enters the Earth's atmosphere

molecule: the smallest physical unit of an element or a compound

organ: a group of specialized tissues that perform a distinct task, such as the stomach or heart

parasite: an organism that lives on or inside another organism on which it depends for survival

species: a class of individuals that resemble each other and breed with only one another

sperm: a male reproductive cell

taxonomy: any system that classifies, names, and describes organisms

vertebrate: an animal with a spine

wavelength: the distance between two successive points in a wave at the same oscillation

High School

big bang theory: a theory of the conception of the universe

buoyancy: the upward force fluid exerts on a submerged body

catalyst: a substance that causes or quickens a chemical reaction without being affected itself

chlorophyll: the green pigment in plants necessary for the process of photosynthesis

chromosome: string-like bodies that carry genes

chemical bond: a force that binds atoms or ions in a molecule

elasticity: the property of a substance that allows it to be stretched or shaped and then return to its original shape

electromagnetic spectrum: the entire range of radiation, beginning with radiation exhibiting very high frequencies (short wavelengths) to radiation exhibiting very low frequencies (long wavelengths)

electron: the part of an atom with a negative charge

entropy: the measure of energy that cannot be accessed for work

Fahrenheit: a system of temperature measurement

fossil fuels: organic substances derived from the remains of long dead organisms and extracted by humans for energy use

genetic diversity: the total number of genetic characteristics in a particular species

genetic mutation: any alteration in a gene or genetic sequence that results in a new or altered inherited trait

geochemical cycle: the chemical interactions that exist between the lithosphere (earth), hydrosphere (water), and atmosphere (air)

neutron: the part of an atom with a neutral charge

ozone: a form of oxygen that is present in the upper atmosphere and absorbs harmful ultraviolet light rays

plate tectonics: the theory of the Earth's crust being broken into plates that move independently and can collide or move under or past other plates

proton: the part of an atom with a positive charge

recessive trait: a trait that can be inherited by a child only if both parents carry the right gene

speed of light: the constant speed at which light travels

thermal equilibrium: the transfer of heat and energy between two regions connected by a diathermic wall

vacuole: a cavity created by a membrane on the inside of a cell

viscosity: the measure of resistance to flow present in a fluid

X-ray: a form of electromagnetic radiation that is capable of penetrating solid matter

Social Studies

Upper Elementary

Africa: a continent south of Europe

armed forces: a country's military, naval, and air force

Asia: a continent between Europe and the Pacific Ocean

archeology: the study of ancient peoples and their cultures

Bill of Rights: Amendments I to X of the U.S. Constitution

campaign: the process competitors for the same government job go through in order to convince people to vote for them in an election

Canada: the country that borders the United States on the north

caste system: a social structure in which a person's class is permanently determined by the class of his or her family

Christianity: one of the world's five major religions; followers believe in only one god and believe that Jesus Christ was the son of God

citizenship: the legal awarding of the duties, rights, and privileges afforded a citizen

cold war: a war between two nations fought without armed conflict

communism: a system of government in which the state is run by a single party that controls the economy and its means of production; an economic system in which production and goods are commonly owned, but private property does not exist

developing country: a country mostly poor and dependent on agriculture but moving in the direction of industrialization

emancipate: to free from slavery

Europe: a continent north of Africa and east of the Atlantic Ocean

geology: the study of the physical history of the Earth

Great Depression: the period starting in October 1929, and including most of the 1930s in which the United States was in grave economic crisis

hemisphere: one of the halves in which a sphere or globe can be divided, such as into top, bottom, left, right

industrial revolution: changes in the social and economic systems of a country that come about because people begin to build and use machinery

immigrant: a person who is living in a country other than the one he or she was born

Islam: one of the world's five major religions; followers believe in one god and believe that Muhammad is the primary and last prophet of God

labor: another word for work

majority rule: a way of making decisions by vote or opinion in which the party with the most votes wins

Mexico: the country that borders the United States on the south

Statue of Liberty: the statue given to the United States by France that stands on Ellis Island

Middle School

adaptation: to change customs or habits in order to fit in to a new surrounding

atomic bomb: an explosive weapon that uses nuclear fission and can cause great destruction

blue-collar sector: the section of the working population that typically performs manual labor and earns an hourly wage

capitalism: an economic system in which individuals or corporations can hold private ownership of goods and resources

civil disobedience: the nonviolent refusal to obey laws considered to be unjust

clergy: the people formally approved to perform religious services

colonization: the process of settling on land and establishing a town or city

discrimination: the practice of making a biased judgment of a person based on assumptions about his or her race, gender, class, or other characteristics

emigration: the process of leaving one country to reside in another

ethnicity: the belonging to a group or groups based on common customs, language, or beliefs

exchange rate: the ratio used to determine how much currency in one country is equal to the currency of another country

feminism: the doctrine that advocates women having rights equal to men

Holocaust: the mass slaughter of Jews and other peoples by the Nazis during World War II

imperialism: the process by which the rule of one nation is extended by force into another nation

Korean War: the war fought between 1950 and 1953 in which the United States aided South Korea in their fight against North Korea

labor union: an organization of employees formed to deal collectively with employers

monarchy: a system of government in which one person, often from a noble family line, has total control

mortality rate: also known as the death rate; the ratio of deaths in a year to the total population

pandemic disease: a widespread disease affecting many people in one or more areas

political alliance: an agreement between two or more politicians or political groups based on common interests

segregation: the voluntary or involuntary separation of groups of people

urbanization: the process by which a city expands

welfare: the assistance given by the government to a person or family in need

white-collar sector: the section of the working population that typically performs office work and earns a salary

High School

affluence: abundance or wealth, usually financial

amnesty: a pardon or forgiveness for past offenses

anti-Semitism: discrimination against Jewish people

arms embargo: the refusal of one nation to export weaponry to another nation because of a political dispute

assimilation: the process of blending into a new culture

black market: the buying and selling of illegal goods; the market created by such buying and selling

cartography: the process of creating maps

creditor: a person or corporation who lends money and credit and to whom debt is repaid

cultural identity: the influence a particular culture and the practices of that culture have over an individual

democracy: a system of government in which the power rests with the people or officials elected by the people

demographics: the data gathered about a population, such as the life expectancy rate, infant mortality rate

due process: formal judicial proceedings designed to ensure individuals are treated in a fair and just manner

entrepreneur: a person who assumes risk to start and/or run a business or enterprise

free enterprise: the idea that citizens acting as entrepreneurs in a capitalist economy are not restricted by government intervention

genocide: the intentional and systematic mass murder of a particular race, nation, or cultural group

hearsay: invalid information; gossip

ideology: the manner of thinking characteristic of an individual, group, or culture

jihad: a holy war waged on behalf of Islam as a religious duty

mercenary: a person who takes action solely for money rather than out of pride or necessity, and often serves in another country's army

monotheism: belief in only one god

postindustrial society: the stage of economic development following industrialization in which the emphasis is on production of services and intellectual property rather than material goods

profiteering: a corporation or individual who makes excessive gain on any good or service in short supply, and who benefits from manipulating the sale of their good or service

realism: an artistic movement emphasizing the experience of everyday life as opposed to the bizarre or abstract

socialism: an economic theory advocating that ownership and control of economic goods and services rest with the entire community instead of with individuals; often described as a middle ground between capitalism and communism

sovereignty: the independence and authority of rule

utopian community: a group of people who have isolated themselves from society as a whole and established a unique colony based on principles they believe to be ideal

8

WHICH ONE DOESN'T BELONG?

For lower elementary through high school
language arts, math, science, and social studies

Design

This game is modeled after the one played on the children's television show *Sesame Street*, though it is more versatile as described here. It can be played in elementary through high school classes in any of the four major subject areas (language arts, math, science, and social studies), and can be tailored to students who have very little knowledge of the content terms and phrases, students who are practicing and deepening their knowledge, or students who have a firm grasp of the vocabulary. The idea, as the name implies, is that students look at a group of terms or phrases and pick out the one that does not belong.

Materials

You will be splitting the class into pairs or teams, and each team will need a flag (or something to signify when they are ready to provide an answer). You will also need a chalkboard or whiteboard.

Set Up

Prepare the sets of terms or phrases beforehand, with each set consisting of three terms that share some common theme or link, and one term that "does not belong." For example, if you choose the terms *yellow*, *green*, and *blue*, you would choose a fourth term that is not a color word, such as *one* or *coin*. You need between ten and thirty sets, depending on how familiar the students are with the terms and phrases you have chosen and how challenging you want the game to be.

Play

Begin by splitting the class into pairs or small groups. Ideally, each group will consist of students at all levels of vocabulary proficiency. Next, write the first set of four terms or phrases on the board; in some cases you might need to draw simple illustrations or reproduce images. The teams are given a specific amount of time to figure out which of the terms does not belong with the other three and why. Each team has a flag that they raise when they have an answer, and at end of the allotted time, everyone shares their answers and a point goes to any team who got the right answer. A point can also be awarded to the team that comes up with the best explanation as to why their choice does not fit (the best explanation likely includes correct use of relevant vocabulary terms). If you so choose, you can add time as a factor as well, awarding more points to the first team to come up with the correct answer.

You can use this game with students who have limited familiarity with the terms and phrases if you tailor the items to the students' level of knowledge. For example, in a game for a second-grade class designed to introduce a social studies unit on natural disasters, the following set might appear:

> landslide
> earthquake
> hurricane
> hunger

Students just being introduced to natural disasters might not know what these words mean, but they can use previous knowledge and knowledge of compound words to take a guess and articulate why they chose their answer. For example, a student might be familiar with the word *hurricane* after hearing personal stories from family members or friends about Katrina. He might not be familiar with the words *earthquake* or *landslide*, but he can break down the compound words and make a pretty reasonable guess about their general meanings. He might offer an explanation such as, "An earthquake sounds like it might be bad, so I thought it would go with a hurricane." Finally, he is most likely familiar with the concept of hunger and has probably heard the word before. Given this peripheral prior knowledge, the student would be able to identify *hunger* as the term that does not belong.

At this point, the game is being used as an introduction to the terms and phrases, so in addition to properly tailoring the items, you can give hints if necessary and accept vague answers in the interest of opening up a discussion. In this way, the game can be used as an informal pretest to help you get a feel for what kind of background knowledge students have.

You can also use this game to help students deepen their knowledge of terms and phrases that have been previously introduced. To do so, select items that require a bit more analysis—that is, the term that does not belong should be more difficult to pick out. For example, if the teacher of the second-grade social studies unit on natural disasters chose to play this game after the students had been introduced to the relevant vocabulary, she might use the following set:

> tsunami
> cyclone
> tundra
> avalanche

Second-grade students with no introduction to these terms would most likely not be able to pick out the item that does not belong. In fact, they might feel frustrated by such an item. Students who have seen these terms before, though, and heard them used or perhaps written down their definitions would be able to look closely, think about each item, and determine that *tundra* is the only term that does not refer to a natural disaster.

If you use the game with students who have a firm grasp on the terms, you can tailor the items to be even more challenging. The individual terms don't need to be harder or more advanced, but there should be finer distinction between the items that belong and the item that does not. For example, if the teacher of the same class and unit discussed in the preceding text wanted to play the game at the end of the unit, she might create a set such as the following:

> avalanche
> landslide
> tsunami
> drought

The students would need to think a bit harder to pick out the term that does not belong here. After all, a drought, if severe enough and long enough, could be considered a natural disaster; however, it is the only one among the terms that would not *necessarily* be categorized as such. Students would have to have a deep and working understanding of the vocabulary presented in the unit to be able to determine the right answer.

Vocabulary Words

Because the focus of the game is categorization, it is usually best to use terms that can easily be categorized and are the same part of speech. For example, if you select three nouns that belong together, the item that does not belong should also be a noun.

Following are five to ten sets of terms and answers each for the lower and upper elementary, middle, and high school levels in all four major content areas. We have also included a hint you can give your class if they clearly cannot recall the correct answer independently. The majority of these hints involve revealing the category to which three of the terms belong. Even if students have been given the category, they still have to use what they know to pick out the term that does not belong.

For the sake of simplicity, these items assume at least a working knowledge of the relevant terms and phrases. The exact vocabulary terms students need to know to answer each item correctly are in bold; the boldface terms also appear in the appendix (page 203). Keep in mind that these are general examples only, and make any necessary adaptations for your classroom and units.

Language Arts

Lower Elementary

A. *Hop on Pop*
B. *Goodnight Moon*
C. *The Stinky Cheese Man*
D. *Aladdin*

ANSWER: The first three options are all **books**, but *Aladdin* is a **movie**.

HINT: Which ones did you read? Which ones did you watch on television or at a theater?

A. "Cinderella"

B. *Green Eggs and Ham*

C. "Beauty and the Beast"

D. "Hansel and Gretel"

ANSWER: *Green Eggs and Ham* is the only option that is not a **fairy tale**.

HINT: We talked about different kinds of stories; what kinds of stories are these?

A. *A*

B. *B*

C. *d*

D. *G*

ANSWER: While *A*, *B*, and *G* are all **uppercase letters**, *d* is a **lowercase letter**.

HINT: We have written all of the letters in the alphabet in two ways, big letters and little letters. Which ones are big, and which are little?

A. AD 35

B. 05/05/07

C. July 7, 2010

D. 6:15

ANSWER: 6:15 is a time while all of the other options are **dates**.

HINT: If you wanted to remember an event by writing down the day or year it happened, how would you do it?

A. *A*

B. *N*

C. *E*

D. *O*

ANSWER: *N* would be the letter that does not belong because it is not a **vowel**.

HINT: If a letter is not a consonant then it must be a . . .

ANSWER: The last image is a **photograph**, but the other three images are drawings.

HINT: Which one of these lets you see something in the real world? How does it do that?

A. Michael
B. Toby
C. Richardson
D. Lisa

ANSWER: Michael, Toby, and Lisa are traditionally **first names**, but Richardson is traditionally a **last name**. (Note: You can tailor this item to fit the first names and last names of students in your class.)

HINT: We talked about kinds of names. For example, first names, last names, and nicknames. Which kind of names are these?

A. *time* and *mime*
B. *cat* and *hat*
C. *fold* and *bed*
D. *tent* and *rent*

ANSWER: Only *fold* and *bed* are not rhyming words.

HINT: Let's say them out loud and see which words don't sound like they go together.

A. I ate breakfast with Teddy.
B. Do you know Maria?
C. Can we go outside and play?
D. When is your birthday?

ANSWER: Only the first sentence is not a **question**.

HINT: Which one of these can you answer? What is a sentence that needs an answer?

A. Mom and I went to the store.
B. Dad and Toby.
C. I don't like candy canes.
D. I wish we could get a puppy.

ANSWER: The second option is not a **complete sentence**.

HINT: Which one of these doesn't have an action word? If there is no action word, what does that mean for the sentence?

Upper Elementary

A. *big* house
B. *blue* napkin
C. *sad* clown
D. *quickly* walking

ANSWER: The first three options are **adjectives**, but the last option is an **adverb**.

HINT: Which one of the italicized words tells you more about an object, and which ones tell you more about an action?

A. We need milk, juice, and eggs at the store.
B. The aliens landed in New York; they had a huge ship.
C. Dad went to work this morning, and he accidentally took my backpack.
D. Melroy yelled, "Hey Fran, can you come outside?"

ANSWER: The second sentence uses a semicolon, but the other sentences use **commas**.

HINT: Look carefully at the punctuation. What marks do each of the sentences use?

A. I'm
B. Mrs.
C. Jan.
D. Ave.

ANSWER: While *I'm* is a **contraction**, the others are **abbreviations**.

HINT: Three of these words are short for longer words, and one is short for two words.

A. snowflake
B. chapter
C. barnyard
D. everyday

ANSWER: Every word except *chapter* is a **compound word**.

HINT: Which one of these can't be split into two separate words?

A. cow
B. goats
C. bear
D. dolphin

ANSWER: *Goats* is the only **plural** word in the group. (Note: Students may also be familiar with the term **singular**.)

HINT: How many cows are there? How many goats are there? How many bears and dolphins are there?

A. mom
B. playground
C. cowboy
D. draw

ANSWER: While *draw* is a **verb**, the other three terms are all **nouns**.

HINT: Which words are things or people, and which words are action words?

A. Phil told Sylvia he would come to the party after he walked his dog.
B. "Bring your dog to the party!" Sylvia said.
C. Phil told her, "My dog is very nervous, and he pees when he meets new people."
D. Sylvia laughed. "We'll only introduce your dog to people we don't like," she said.

ANSWER: The first sentence is the only one that does not contain a **direct quote**.

HINT: Look closely at the punctuation. In which sentences do you hear the exact words of Phil or Sylvia? How do you know?

A. small, tiny
B. rough, smooth
C. happy, excited
D. run, jog

ANSWER: The words *rough* and *smooth* are **antonyms**, while the other pairs of words are all **synonyms**.

HINT: Which pairs of words are similar in meaning and which are opposite in meaning?

A. sound effect
B. science fiction
C. mystery
D. fable

ANSWER: A **sound effect** does not belong in the group because **science fiction**, **mystery**, and **fable** are all terms that refer to different **genres**.

HINT: Can you name a specific book that would match each of these literature types? If you can't, why not?

A. email
B. personal letter
C. diary
D. Internet

ANSWER: The **Internet** is an electronic **medium**, while **email**, **personal letter**, and **diary** all refer to things people write.

HINT: One of these you can't write.

Middle School

A. Martin looks like a fox.
B. The house felt like a cave.
C. The car was a pigpen.
D. The taffy was as smooth as butter.

ANSWER: The other three options are **similes**, while "The car was a pigpen" is a **metaphor**.

HINT: Look at the comparisons in each of the sentences. What technique is being used to make those comparisons?

A. flashback
B. foreshadow
C. enunciation
D. dialogue

ANSWER: The terms **flashback**, **foreshadow**, and **dialogue** all refer to literary techniques, but the term **enunciation** has to do with verbal speaking.

HINT: Which one of these are techniques you can use in writing?

A. Her voice was deep and gravelly.
B. The sunset was full of reds and oranges, and even blues.
C. The railing was smooth from so many people running their hands over it.
D. The dance was the most fun I've had.

ANSWER: The last item in the list is the only one that does not include **descriptive language**.

HINT: Which sentence puts a picture in your head? How can you write a sentence that does this?

A. a news broadcast
B. an editorial
C. a research paper
D. a biography

ANSWER: A **news broadcast**, a **research paper**, and a **biography** are all based in **fact**, but an **editorial** is based in **opinion**.

HINT: Which one of these sources would be most likely used in a research paper? Why?

A. I went to bed early last night.
B. We are going out for dinner.
C. I didn't want a little brother at first.
D. Sam took Nona out on a date.

ANSWER: The second item is in **present tense**, but the others are in **past tense**.

HINT: When you read each sentence, think about *when* it happened. How do you know?

A. information from a biography for a research report on a particular person
B. an article from the *New York Times* for a research report about a current event
C. an interview with an author for support in a report on an interpretation of that author's book
D. *US Weekly* for a research report on the life of a famous film director

ANSWER: The first three options are the only ones that demonstrate responsible and appropriate use of **resource material**.

HINT: If you were writing a research paper, which of these would you use? Why?

A. bear, bare
B. torn, ripped
C. steal, steel
D. rain, reign

ANSWER: The second option contains two words that are **synonyms**, but the rest of the words are **homonyms**.

HINT: Which of these pairs of words sound alike, and which sound different? Why? Which of these pairs of words are alike in meaning?

A. using a statistic in a report without citing where it came from
B. paraphrasing a quote from another source and listing a citation
C. using the same ideas and arguments found in another paper without citation
D. buying a paper off of the Internet and passing it off as your own

ANSWER: All but the second option are examples of **plagiarism**.

HINT: Which of these things would you get in trouble for? Why?

A. italic
B. ballad
C. sonnet
D. haiku

ANSWER: **Italic** is a type of font, but a **ballad**, a **sonnet**, and a **haiku** are all types of poems.

HINT: Which of these can be classified as types of poems?

High School

A. kick the bucket
B. dunk tank
C. apple of my eye
D. the cat's pajamas

ANSWER: All but the second option are examples of **idioms**.

HINT: Which of these are sayings? Which ones mean exactly what they say?

A. a story about a man battling Alzheimer's disease

B. a story about a man who committed a crime and is torn between turning himself in and keeping the secret to avoid punishment

C. a story about a woman's abusive relationship with her husband

D. a story about a woman's path to recovery from alcoholism

ANSWER: The third option is an example of an **external conflict**, while the other three options are examples of **internal conflicts**.

HINT: Who is battling outside forces, and who is battling him or herself?

A. By the time Wanda finished the race, she was panting like a dog.

B. The leaves rested lazily on the roof.

C. The warm room hugged Priscilla when she came in from the cold.

D. The lighthouse welcomed the sailors home from a long journey.

ANSWER: The first option is the only one that does not contain **personification**.

HINT: Which of these sentences can be true on a literal level? Why or why not?

A. She didn't want to talk to James by herself.

B. They went to the courthouse by themselves?

C. I planted everything in the garden myself.

D. We hardly recognized each other in costume.

ANSWER: All but the last option contain **reflexive pronouns**.

HINT: Are there pronouns in each sentence? What makes them unique?

A. a commercial for toothpaste that uses an endorsement by the National Dental Association

B. an advertisement for a nicotine patch endorsed by the surgeon general as the best product to help a person to quit smoking

C. a commercial for a nonprofit organization that uses pictures of underprivileged children in third-world countries to elicit donations

D. a commercial for a car that emphasizes safety ratings from J. D. Power and Associates

ANSWER: All but the third option contain an **appeal to authority**. The third option contains an **appeal to emotion**.

HINT: How are each of these advertisements trying to persuade you? Do any of the advertisements want you to feel something?

A. the play date
B. the child
C. the trickster
D. the artist

ANSWER: The first option is the only one that cannot be characterized as an **archetype**.

HINT: Three of these things refer to archetypes, assonance, reticence, or alliteration.

A. assonance
B. consonance
C. alliteration
D. allegory

ANSWER: **Assonance**, **consonance**, and **alliteration** are all poetic elements involving sound. (Note: the teacher may or may not require the correct definition for **allegory**.)

HINT: Using two words, try to give an example of each term's technique.

A. whistle
B. boom
C. meow
D. woof

ANSWER: *Whistle* is not an **onomatopoeia**.

HINT: Which of these words are things people do naturally, and which are noises?

A. Your house is the size of Wyoming.
B. I am a million times smarter than you are.
C. The summer in Iowa is an inferno.
D. The Willis Tower, formerly the Sears Tower, is the tallest building in Chicago.

ANSWER: The first three options contain **hyperbole**, while the fourth does not.

HINT: Which of these sentences use exaggeration?

A. *Richard III*
B. *Beowulf*
C. *The Odyssey*
D. *The Divine Comedy*

ANSWER: *Richard III* is the only option not characterized as an **epic**. (Note: Texts can be altered according to the reading lists/discussions of a class.)

HINT: Which of these are poems? Which are mainly about the journey of a hero?

Math

Lower Elementary

A. 3 < 5
B. 5 < 13
C. 4 < 10
D. 9 > 1

ANSWER: The last option uses the **greater than** symbol, but the first three options use the **less than** symbol.

HINT: Which of these are expressing "greater than," and which are expressing "less than"? Are any of these number pairs equal? Which ones are bigger, and which ones are smaller?

A. 1st place
B. 2 flowers
C. 3rd time
D. Eighth try

ANSWER: The second option uses a **cardinal number**, but the others use **ordinal numbers**.

HINT: Are any of these cardinal numbers? Ordinal numbers? Whole numbers? Number lines?

A. 2
B. 1/2
C. 3
D. 6

ANSWER: Only 1/2 is not a whole number.

HINT: Are any of these numbers whole numbers? Cardinal numbers? Ordinal numbers? Coins?

A. 3 + 2 = 5
B. 4 + 3 = 7
C. 7 − 2 = 5
D. 1 + 6 = 7

ANSWER: The third option (7 − 2 = 5) is a **subtraction** problem, while the others are **addition** problems.

HINT: Look at the symbols. What act is being performed, and would you say "plus" or "minus" if you read it out loud?

ANSWER: The last shape is a **triangle**, but the other three shapes are **rectangles**.

HINT: Count the corners of each shape. Which shapes have three corners, and which have four?

A. 0, 1, 0, 1, 0, 1
B. 1, 2, 3, 1, 2, 3
C. 0, 4, 2, 7, 1, 5
D. 3, 3, 2, 3, 3, 2

ANSWER: The third list of numbers does not contain a **pattern**.

HINT: Let's go through these one by one and see if you can tell me what number would come next in that sequence. If you can predict what will come next, how are you able to do that?

A. inches
B. pounds
C. ounces
D. grams

ANSWER: Inches are not a **measure of weight**.

HINT: If you were going to weigh something, which of these terms could you use?

ANSWER: 17 is not where it belongs on the **number line**.

HINT: Which of these numbers is out of order? How do you know?

A. The library is down the hall and to the left.
B. My house is two streets east of the school.
C. We always watch TV in the afternoon.
D. Brandon's mom takes the bus north to get downtown.

ANSWER: Only the third sentence is not referring to **direction**.

HINT: Which of these sentences uses words like *left* or *north*? When do you use those kinds of words?

A. 40

B. 03

C. 10

D. 55

ANSWER: 55 is the only number listed that does not contain a **zero**.

HINT: Look carefully at both digits in these numbers. One digit appears in three options, while the others don't.

Upper Elementary

A. inch

B. centimeter

C. foot

D. mile

ANSWER: A centimeter is the only option that is a **metric unit** of measurement as opposed to **U.S. unit** of measurement.

HINT: Which of these units belong to the same system of measurement? What is that system called?

A. $1.4 + 1.2 = 2.6$

B. $2.3 + 5.2 = 7.5$

C. $2.1 - 1.0 = 1.1$

D. $11.1 + 2.6 = 13.7$

ANSWER: The third option shows **decimal subtraction**, but the other three options show **decimal addition**.

HINT: What kinds of numbers are being used? How are they being used? What kind of process is taking place in each one?

A. midpoint

B. mean

C. median

D. mode

ANSWER: **Mean**, **median**, and **mode** are all **measures of central tendency**, while midpoint is not.

HINT: Which of these are measures of central tendency?

A. 10%

B. 12.1

C. 50%

D. Ten percent

ANSWER: The second option is a decimal, but the other three refer to **percents/percentages**.

HINT: Let's say these out loud. Which one doesn't sound the same? Why?

A. 1/2
B. 2/3
C. 2 1/2
D. 3/4

ANSWER: 2 1/2 is a **mixed number**, and 1/2, 2/3, and 3/4 are all **fractions**.

HINT: Let's say these numbers out loud. Which one sounds different? Why?

A. 3
B. 5
C. 7
D. 15

ANSWER: Only 15 is not a **prime number**.

HINT: Are these even numbers? Odd numbers? Prime numbers? Fractions?

A. −2 < 3
B. 3 < 70
C. 70 = 70
D. 50 > 3

ANSWER: All but the third option are **inequality statements**.

HINT: Look carefully at the symbols. Which of these pairs of numbers are equal to one another and which aren't?

A. 2/5 + 2/5 = 4/5
B. 3/8 + 2/8 = 5/8
C. 3/4 + 2/4 = 5/4
D. 5/6 − 4/6 = 1/6

ANSWER: The first three options involve the **addition of fractions**, but the last option involves the **subtraction of fractions**.

HINT: What kinds of numbers are being used? What processes are being used?

A. sum
B. difference
C. quotient
D. divisor

ANSWER: **Sum**, **difference**, and **quotient** all refer to the product of an operation, but a **divisor** refers to a number within an operation.

HINT: What do you get when you add two numbers? What do you get when you subtract two numbers? What do you get when you multiply or divide two numbers?

A. centimeter

B. inch

C. meter

D. gram

ANSWER: A gram is a **measure of weight**, but centimeters, inches, and meters are all **measures of length** or **measures of height**.

HINT: If you were going to measure the dimensions of a box, which of these could you use? Why?

Middle School

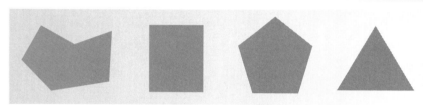

ANSWER: Only the first shape is an **irregular polygon**.

HINT: If you folded all of these shapes in half, would the two halves match? What do you call a shape with two sides that match? A shape with two sides that don't match?

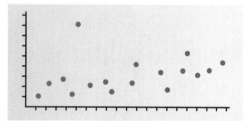

ANSWER: The dot that is furthest removed does not belong because it is an **outlier**.

HINT: Is that dot that is furthest away a quotient? A mean? An outlier? A denominator?

A. 2

B. 16

C. 72

D. 112

ANSWER: 2 is not a **composite number**.

HINT: Which of these are whole numbers, square numbers, decimals, or composite numbers?

A. 13 = 1.3

B. 4/6 = 2/3

C. 8/16 = 4/8 = 1/2

D. 20/5 = 4/1 = 4

ANSWER: Only the first option is not a **simplification**.

HINT: Look at the processes in each option; can you name each one?

A. iiii
B. IV
C. ix
D. VIII

ANSWER: Only the first option is not a **Roman numeral**.

HINT: Which of these are Roman numerals, standard units of measure, and variables?

A. $2x^2 + 5x + 3 = 0$
B. $x^2 + x(4y + 6) = 0$
C. $3x^2 + x + -2 = 0$
D. $x(2x - 3) + -1 = 0$

ANSWER: The second option is not a **quadratic equation**.

HINT: Let's look at the variables. Which one has one variable, which has more than one? What does that mean?

A. angle 2
B. angle 4
C. angle 6
D. angle 5

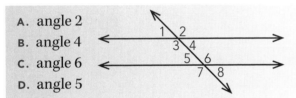

ANSWER: Angle 2 is not an **interior angle**.

HINT: Which of these are acute angles, interior angles, exterior angles, and complementary angles?

A. $\sqrt{64} = 8$
B. $8^2 = 64$
C. $8 + 8 + 8 + 8 + 8 + 8 + 8 + 8 = 64$
D. $-8^2 = 64$

ANSWER: The third option does not refer to **squares** and **square roots**.

HINT: Let's say these out loud. Which one sounds different? Why?

A. $\sqrt{2}$
B. $2/1$
C. 4
D. -2

ANSWER: The square root of 2 is an **irrational number**, but the other three options are all **rational numbers**.

HINT: How could you express these numbers as fractions? Which kind of numbers can be expressed as fractions using integers and which can't?

A. square

B. parallelogram

C. rhombus

D. octagon

ANSWER: Only an octagon is not a **quadrilateral**.

HINT: How many corners does each shape have? What is a shape with four corners called?

High School

A. The square of the hypotenuse of a right triangle is equal to the sum of the squares on the other two sides.

B. $a^2 + b^2 = c^2$

C. $c = \sqrt{a^2 + b^2}$

D. $a^2 + b^2 + c^2 = 0$

ANSWER: Only the last option is not the **Pythagorean theorem**.

HINT: Three of these examples are expressing the same thing. They are expressing a theorem.

A. $-|3 + 3| = -|6| = 6$

B. $|2 - 4| = |-2| = 2$

C. $|6 + -5| = |1| = 1$

D. $-|3 + -6| = -|-3| = -3$

ANSWER: The first option is not a correct use of **absolute value**.

HINT: All of these equations use absolute value; which one uses it incorrectly?

A. $3(x^2 + 1)$

B. $2x^2 + 3x$

C. $2xy$

D. $(x^3 + 7x) \times (x^5 - 3xy)$

ANSWER: The second option is a **polynomial**, but the other options are all **monomials**.

HINT: Which of these are monomials? Polynomials? Quadratic equations?

A. The constant ratio between a circle's circumference and its diameter.

B. A/r^2

C. 3.14

D. $D = r/t$

ANSWER: All but the last option refer to **pi**.

HINT: All but one of these options refer to pi, distance, surface area, or the Pythagorean theorem.

A. The rate in change in distance with respect to time
B. $\Delta d/\Delta t$
C. A quantity that has both magnitude and direction
D. A quantity that is measured in respect to displacement as opposed to direction

ANSWER: All but the last option refer to **speed**. The last refers to **velocity**.

HINT: Which of these refer to speed, velocity, direction, and force?

Science

Lower Elementary

A. computer
B. automobile
C. microwave
D. snake

ANSWER: A snake is not a **machine**.

HINT: Which one of these can you turn off and on? Can you turn an animal on and off? Can you turn a plant on and off? Can you turn a machine on and off?

ANSWER: The last animal pictured is not a **dinosaur**.

HINT: Which of these do you think you could see in a zoo?

A. toys
B. food
C. shelter
D. water

ANSWER: Only toys cannot be considered **requirements for life**.

HINT: Which of these things could you live without?

A. mountain
B. boulder
C. gravel
D. cloud

ANSWER: A cloud is not a **kind of rock**.

HINT: If you could hold each one of these, what would it feel like?

A. trees losing their leaves
B. days getting shorter
C. dogs having puppies
D. air getting colder

ANSWER: Dogs having puppies is not a **seasonal change**.
HINT: Which of these changes happen when the seasons change?

A. campfire
B. oven
C. furnace
D. closet

ANSWER: Only a closet does not produce **heat**.
HINT: If you were cold, which of these would not help warm you up?

A. water
B. rock
C. plants
D. clothing

ANSWER: Clothing is not one of the **Earth's natural materials**.
HINT: Which of these things is made by the earth, and which are made by man?

A. microscope
B. binoculars
C. telescope
D. observation

ANSWER: Microscopes, binoculars, and telescopes all **magnify** things.
HINT: Which of these make objects look closer?

A. ice melting
B. doorbell ringing
C. child crying
D. car horn honking

ANSWER: Melting ice is the only option not obviously associated with **sound**.
HINT: What noises do these things make?

A. planet
B. star
C. galaxy
D. lightening

ANSWER: Lightening is not an object that can be found out in the **universe**.

HINT: Which of these exist inside the Earth, and which exist outside of the Earth?

Upper Elementary

A. cricket
B. crocodile
C. iguana
D. Komodo dragon

ANSWER: Of the four animals listed, crickets are the only ones without **bones**.

HINT: One of these animals doesn't have bones.

A. elephant
B. giraffe
C. deer
D. lion

ANSWER: Elephants, giraffes, and deer are all **herbivores**, but a lion is a **carnivore**.

HINT: What do each of these animals eat?

A. newspapers
B. typing paper
C. aluminum cans
D. gasoline

ANSWER: Only gasoline cannot be **recycled**.

HINT: Which one of these things can only be used once? What process do we use into order to use the other three things again?

A. condensation
B. evaporation
C. precipitation
D. reproduction

ANSWER: **Condensation**, **evaporation**, and **precipitation** are all parts of the **water cycle**, but **reproduction** is part of the **life cycle**.

HINT: Which of these involves water in some form? What is the name for how those three terms interact?

A. the cloud of smog caused by the many cars in a city

B. the waste and chemicals a company dumps into a river instead of properly disposing them

C. the washable water bottle that can be used many times

D. the trash left behind by a group of campers

ANSWER: Only the third option is not an example of **pollution**.

HINT: Which of these refer to pollution, recycling, a fossil fuel, or reproduction?

A. wooly mammoth

B. velociraptor

C. fern

D. human

ANSWER: Only humans are not considered **prehistoric organisms**.

HINT: Three of these things are dinosaurs, prehistoric organisms, machines, or fossils.

A. table salt

B. vegetable oil

C. sugar

D. baking powder

ANSWER: Vegetable oil is the only item on the list that is not **soluble** in water.

HINT: How do each of these things mix with water?

A. absorption

B. refraction

C. reflection

D. conduction

ANSWER: **Absorption**, **refraction**, and **reflection** are all ways light behaves when it hits a surface. **Conduction** is the transfer of energy through matter.

HINT: Three of these things refer to the way light behaves when it hits a surface.

A. helium

B. nitrogen

C. oxygen

D. carbon dioxide

ANSWER: Helium is the only gas that cannot be found in the makeup of the **atmosphere**.

HINT: Which of these are found in our atmosphere?

A. B vitamins
B. calcium
C. fluoride
D. carbohydrate

ANSWER: Fluoride is the only item on the list that is not a **nutrient**.

HINT: Three of these things are minerals, vegetables, reptiles, or nutrients.

Middle School

A. clay
B. glass
C. Teflon
D. copper

ANSWER: Clay, glass, and Teflon are all **insulators**, but copper is a **conductor**.

HINT: Three of these are insulators, conductors, filters, or radiators.

A. polar
B. temperate
C. tropical
D. volcanic

ANSWER: Only the first three options are examples of **climate**.

HINT: Three of these things refer to rocks, climates, energies, or ecosystems.

A. snakes
B. bald eagles
C. humans
D. krill

ANSWER: Snakes, bald eagles, and humans are all **predators**, but krill is **prey**.

HINT: Think about what each of these organisms eat. Does any other organism commonly eat them?

A. lungs
B. stomach
C. large intestine
D. esophagus

ANSWER: The stomach, large intestine, and esophagus are all part of the **digestive system**, but the lungs are part of the **respiratory system**.

HINT: What systems of the body do these organs belong to?

A. permanent tissue

B. nervous tissue

C. connective tissue

D. muscle tissue

ANSWER: Permanent tissue is a **plant tissue**, while connective, nervous, and muscle are all **animal tissues**.

HINT: Which of these tissues are found in animals, and which are found in plants?

A. chemical energy

B. thermal energy

C. electrical energy

D. sound

ANSWER: Only chemical energy is **potential energy**. Thermal energy, electrical energy, and sound are all **kinetic energies**.

HINT: Which of these can be classified as a potential energy? Which as a kinetic energy?

A. marble

B. slate

C. soapstone

D. coal

ANSWER: Marble, slate, and soapstone are all **metamorphic rocks**, but coal is a **sedimentary rock**.

HINT: Which of these are metamorphic rocks? Which are sedimentary? Which are igneous?

A. humans and oxygen

B. bees and flowers

C. anemones and anemone fish

D. ants and aphids

ANSWER: The first option is the only one that is not an example of **mutualism**.

HINT: The organisms in three pairs participate in one kind of relationship: parasite/host, prey/predator, mutualism, or photosynthesis.

A. titanium

B. platinum

C. iridium

D. gold

ANSWER: Titanium is a **reactive metal**, but iridium, silver, and gold are all **nonreactive metals**.

HINT: Which of these metals can be classified as reactive? Which as nonreactive?

A. spinal chord
B. heart
C. blood
D. lungs

ANSWER: The spinal chord is associated with the **nervous system**, but the heart, blood, and lungs are all associated with the **circulatory system**.

HINT: What body system do each of these belong to?

High School

A. the amount of sunlight present in an ecosystem
B. the availability of water in an ecosystem
C. the number of trees that produce fruit all year long in an ecosystem
D. the temperature at different seasons in an ecosystem

ANSWER: The third option is a **biotic** factor, but the others are all **abiotic** factors in an ecosystem.

HINT: Which of these represent biotic factors? Which represent abiotic factors?

A. the decrease in temperature when citric acid is mixed with baking soda
B. the increase in temperature when vinegar is poured on steel wool
C. the increase in temperature during the combustion reaction of fuels
D. setting of concrete and cement

ANSWER: Only the first option is an **endothermic reaction**. The other three options are all **exothermic reactions**.

HINT: Which of these are endothermic reactions, and which are exothermic?

A. X-rays
B. ultraviolet light
C. radio waves
D. gamma rays

ANSWER: **Radio waves** are the only option with low frequency on the **electromagnetic spectrum**. **Gamma rays, X-rays**, and **ultraviolet light** all have high frequencies.

HINT: Think about the frequency of the waves in each option.

A. red giant
B. blue giant
C. white dwarf
D. Polaris

ANSWER: **Red giants**, **blue giants**, and **white dwarfs** are all types of stars. Polaris is the name of a specific star.

HINT: Which can be categorized as star types?

A. KOH
B. HCl
C. HI
D. HBr

ANSWER: KOH is a **base**, but the other three options are all **acids**.

HINT: Which of these are bases, and which are acids?

A. the force that holds protons and electrons together in atoms
B. the force that holds atoms together to make molecules
C. the force that operates via photons
D. the force that creates gravity

ANSWER: The first three options refer to **electromagnetic force**. The last option refers to **gravitational force**.

HINT: Think about the kinds of force demonstrated in each option.

A. amplitude
B. volume
C. frequency
D. period

ANSWER: Only volume is not one of the **properties of waves**.

HINT: Which of these can be categorized as a property of a wave?

A. hydrogen bonding
B. hydrophobic forces
C. ion bonding
D. electrostatic forces

ANSWER: Ion bonding is the only option that is not a controlling factor in **protein structures**.

HINT: Which of these bonds is involved in protein structures?

A. nitrification
B. denitrification
C. decay
D. drag

ANSWER: Drag is the only option that is not part of the **nitrogen cycle**.

HINT: Three of these are involved in one of the following: nitrogen cycle, oxygen cycle, carbon cycle, or sedimentation.

A. allopatric
B. peripatric
C. sympatric
D. parasympathetic

ANSWER: Parasympathetic is not an evolutionary process of **speciation**.

HINT: Which of these are involved in speciation?

Social Studies

Lower Elementary

A. policeman
B. doctor
C. hero
D. teacher

ANSWER: Policeman, doctor, and teacher are all **job** titles.

HINT: Which of these things are jobs?

A. Christmas
B. Friday
C. Martin Luther King Jr. Day
D. Fourth of July

ANSWER: Only Friday is not a **holiday**.

HINT: Which of these is a holiday?

ANSWER: Only the last image is not of an **automobile**.

HINT: Which of these fly, and which travel on the road?

A. boats
B. trains
C. laws
D. airplanes

ANSWER: Boats, trains, and airplanes are all modes of **transportation**, but laws are not.

HINT: Three of these things are related to one of the following: time, transportation, beliefs, or England.

A. Sunday
B. Tuesday
C. Friday
D. August

ANSWER: **August** is a month of the year, but **Sunday**, **Tuesday**, and **Friday** are all days of the week.

HINT: Which of these are months of the year? Which are days of the week?

A. graduation
B. monument
C. wedding
D. bar mitzvah

ANSWER: A monument is the only option that is not a **ceremony**.

HINT: Three of these things are days, laws, ceremonies, or crops.

A. dollar bills
B. quarters
C. years
D. pennies

ANSWER: Years are not a form of **money**.

HINT: Can you buy a candy bar with these things?

A. crop
B. printing press
C. telephone
D. computer

ANSWER: A crop is not a form of **technology**.

HINT: Three of these things are associated with farming, yesterday, religion, or technology.

A. dogs
B. horses
C. sheep
D. lions

ANSWER: A lion is not a **domestic animal**.
HINT: Which of these would you find in a house or on a farm?

A. teepee
B. igloo
C. apartment
D. bridge

ANSWER: A bridge is not a form of **housing**.
HINT: Which of these things can you live in?

Upper Elementary

A. Africa
B. Asia
C. United States
D. Europe

ANSWER: **Africa**, **Asia**, and **Europe** are all **continents**, but the **United States** is a **country**.
HINT: Which of these are continents? Which are countries?

A. a man buying groceries
B. a family paying for a meal at a restaurant
C. a factory that makes cars
D. a kid buying baseball cards

ANSWER: The third option represents a **producer**, but the other three options represent **consumers**.
HINT: Three of these are producers, consumers, artifacts, or workers.

A. Cesar Chavez
B. Frederick Douglass
C. Harriet Tubman
D. Jackie Robinson

ANSWER: Cesar Chavez is a **Hispanic American**, but Frederick Douglass, Harriet Tubman, and Jackie Robinson are all **African Americans**. (Note: You can change the names to be more recognizable to your students.)
HINT: Which of these are African Americans? Which are Hispanic Americans?

A. Statue of Liberty
B. Olympic rings
C. American flag
D. bald eagle

ANSWER: Only the second option is not an **American symbol**.
HINT: Which one of these reminds you of the United States?

A. teacher
B. president
C. mayor
D. governor

ANSWER: **President**, **governor**, and **mayor** are all elected government positions, but teacher is not.
HINT: Which of these jobs do you have to be elected to get?

A. Declaration of Independence
B. Trail of Tears
C. Bill of Rights
D. Constitution of the United States

ANSWER: The **Declaration of Independence**, the **Bill of Rights**, and the **Constitution of the United States** are all written documents designed to establish a new country, but the **Trail of Tears** was an event in which Native Americans were forced to walk hundreds of miles to reservations.
HINT: Which of these are documents?

A. Henry Ford
B. Barack Obama
C. Franklin D. Roosevelt
D. Andrew Jackson

ANSWER: **Barack Obama**, **Franklin D. Roosevelt**, and **Andrew Jackson** were all presidents of the United States, but **Henry Ford** was not.
HINT: Which of these people served as the president of the United States?

A. Revolutionary War
B. Civil War
C. the Texas War for Independence
D. World War I

ANSWER: The **Revolutionary War**, the **Civil War**, and the **Texas War for Independence** were all fought on U.S. soil, but **World War I** was not.
HINT: Think about where these wars were fought.

A. Cherokee
B. Sioux
C. Hopi
D. Maori

ANSWER: The **Cherokee**, **Sioux**, and **Hopi** were all **Native American** tribes, but the Maori are native to New Zealand.

HINT: Think about where these tribes live/lived.

A. salary
B. income
C. debt
D. investment

ANSWER: **Salary**, **investment**, and **income** are all words associated with earning or making money, but **debt** is associated with losing or owing money.

HINT: Which of these is associated with losing money? Which are associated with gaining money?

Middle School

A. Islam
B. Judaism
C. federalism
D. Hinduism

ANSWER: **Islam**, **Judaism**, and **Hinduism** are three of the world's major religions, but **federalism** is a system of government in which both national powers and state powers govern.

HINT: Which of these are religions?

A. Mao Zedong
B. the Great Leap Forward
C. People's Republic of China
D. Shang Dynasty

ANSWER: The **Shang Dynasty** was not in power at all during the time of **Mao Zedong**, the **Great Leap Forward**, and the **People's Republic of China**.

HINT: Think about the time in which these terms are associated.

A. legislative power
B. executive power
C. autocratic power
D. judicial power

ANSWER: The only branches of power in the U.S. government are **legislative power, executive power**, and **judicial power.**

HINT: Three of these are branches of the U.S. government.

A. *Marbury v. Madison*
B. Scopes trial
C. Dred Scott decision
D. Declaration of Sentiments

ANSWER: **Marbury v. Madison**, the **Scopes trial**, and the **Dred Scott decision** were all influential court cases in U.S. history that set precedent for future practices, but the **Declaration of Sentiments** was a document demanding the equal treatment of women that was signed at the first women's rights convention in 1848.

HINT: Three of these were important judicial decisions.

A. energy that comes from hydroelectricity
B. energy that comes from fossil fuels
C. energy that comes from solar power
D. energy that comes from wind power

ANSWER: **Hydroelectric energy**, **solar power**, and **wind power** are all **renewable energy sources**, but **fossil fuel** is a **nonrenewable energy source.**

HINT: Which of these energy sources are renewable? Which are nonrenewable?

A. Little Rock in 1957
B. "Letter From a Birmingham Jail"
C. equal rights amendment
D. "I have a dream" speech

ANSWER: **Little Rock in 1957, "Letter From a Birmingham Jail,"** and the **"I have a dream" speech** are all associated with the **civil rights movement**, but the **equal rights amendment** concerns **women's suffrage.**

HINT: Think about the movements these terms are associated with.

A. freedom of assembly
B. freedom of speech
C. freedom of press
D. freedom of taxation

ANSWER: **Freedom of assembly**, **freedom of speech**, and **freedom of press** are all real and afforded in the United States. There is not freedom of taxation.

HINT: Which of these are real freedoms in the United States?

A. literacy rate
B. death rate
C. HIV
D. gross domestic product

ANSWER: **Gross domestic product**, **death rate**, and **literacy rate** are all used to find statistical data about the state of a nation. HIV is a disease.

HINT: Which of these are data recorded in order to find out about the state of a nation?

A. guns and ammunition
B. slaves
C. sugar
D. rum

ANSWER: Guns and ammunition were not the major objects of trade in the **triangular trade route**.

HINT: Three of these things were associated with the triangular trade route.

A. socialism
B. fascism
C. feminism
D. communism

ANSWER: **Fascism**, **socialism**, and **communism** are all political theories, but **feminism** is a social movement that advocates equal rights for women.

HINT: Which of these are movements?

A. Storming of the Bastille
B. Reign of Terror
C. Jacobins
D. Opium Wars

ANSWER: The Storming of the Bastille, the Reign of Terror, and the Jacobins are all associated with the **French Revolution**, but the **Opium Wars** were between Great Britain and China.

HINT: Think about the nations in which these things took place.

High School

A. publisher of the *Wall Street Journal*
B. second-oldest U.S. market index
C. index that includes Bank of America, Exxon, and Citigroup
D. major provider or credit ratings

ANSWER: The first three options are all associated with the **Dow Jones**, but the last is associated with the **S&P**.

HINT: Which of these are related to the Dow, and which to the S&P?

A. the power Congress has to impeach and convict the president of the United States
B. the power the president of the United States has to veto a bill passed by Congress
C. the implied power of the Supreme Court to overturn laws it deems unconstitutional
D. the power of the electoral college members to vote in any way they see fit

ANSWER: The first three options refer to the constitutional powers associated with **checks and balances**.

HINT: Which of these is part of a system put in place by our forefathers to ensure no one person has too much power?

A. economic depression of 1819
B. economic depression of 1857
C. economic depression of 1893
D. economic depression of 1919

ANSWER: Only the **economic depressions of 1819**, **1857**, and **1893** actually happened.

HINT: Only three of these depressions actually happened.

A. the philosopher known for his attempts at finding a set of true and undeniable principles
B. the philosopher known for *cogito ergo sum*
C. the philosopher known as the father of modern philosophy
D. the philosopher known for his conclusion that man does not act purely in accordance with reason

ANSWER: Only the first three options refer to **René Descartes**.

HINT: Three of these refer to one person: John Locke, Andrew Jackson, Socrates, or René Descartes.

A. John Roberts Jr.
B. Ted Kennedy
C. Clarence Thomas
D. Ruth Bader Ginsburg

ANSWER: Only Ted Kennedy has not been a **Supreme Court justice**.

HINT: Which of these people have been Supreme Court justices?

A. secretary of housing and urban development

B. secretary of defense

C. secretary of agriculture

D. secretary of airport security

ANSWER: The secretary of airport security is not a member of the **president's cabinet**.

HINT: Who is part of the president's cabinet?

A. a person who believes the system of government in another country to be inferior to the system of government in his own country

B. a person from an affluent background who believes people from poverty to be less intelligent

C. a person who believes a religion different from his own to be silly or wrong

D. a person who believes cats to be better pets than dogs

ANSWER: The first three options all refer to someone exhibiting **ethnocentrism**. The last option exhibits only a personal preference.

HINT: Which of these illustrate a belief of personal superiority?

A. a treaty that required Germany to completely disarm

B. a treaty that required Russia to take complete responsibility for starting a war

C. a treaty signed during the presidency of Woodrow Wilson

D. a treaty drafted by France, Great Britain, and Italy

ANSWER: The second option listed is incorrect. The **Treaty of Versailles** required Germany to take full responsibility for World War I.

HINT: Which of these has to do with Versailles?

A. a school attended by many different races, but each race tends to spend personal time with people of their own race

B. a restaurant that has one bathroom for people of one race and another for people of a second race

C. a country that allows citizens of one race but not of another race to vote in elections

D. a store owned by a person who only hires people of one race

ANSWER: The third option is an example of **de jure segregation**, and the other three options are all examples of **de facto segregation**.

HINT: Which of these are types of segregation?

9

WHO AM I?

For upper elementary through high school
language arts, math, science, and social studies

Design

Who Am I? requires that the students have a relatively deep understanding of the terms and phrases being used. Usually, the game is played using the names of important people being studied, and the students must have an understanding of those people and the time in which they lived. This game is rooted in vocabulary, but it is unique in that it requires students to apply what they already know about the terms, therefore reinforcing their knowledge. It can be played in any of the main subjects (language arts, math, science, and social studies) with upper elementary through high school students.

Materials

You will need large note cards and a baseball or top hat.

Set Up

Prepare in advance by writing the name of someone your class has been studying on each card. For example, if you have been teaching a unit on the civil rights movement, you might write "Martin Luther King Jr." on one card, "Medgar Evers" on another, and so on. You need at least as many terms as there are students in the class.

Play

This game is best played with the entire class, though you can modify it to be played with small groups if you wish. To begin, one student takes a turn by sitting on a chair or stool in front of the class. He selects a note card from a pile you present; all cards are face down to ensure the student cannot see the term you have written. After taping the card on the hat, place the hat on the student's head so that the class can see the name but he cannot. Tell him this is his secret identity. If the other students in the class cannot read the card, you can also write it on the blackboard or use an overhead projector, but be sure the term is being displayed behind the student who selected the card. The point is simply that everyone but the student with the secret identity knows what that identity is.

The student in the chair's job is to figure out who he is. To do this, he is allowed to ask yes or no questions. For example, he can begin by asking general questions such as, "Am I a man or a woman?" or "Am I alive or dead?" He then asks more specific questions such as, "Am I an author?" and then, "Did I write *Slaughterhouse 5*?" Finally, he gets down to specific terms or phrases by asking questions like, "Am I Kurt Vonnegut?" Once he guesses his identity, his turn is over.

Note that because this game asks students to independently consider the people or characters they have learned about in class and apply that knowledge, the questions each student asks will be unique. For example, if the identity the student is trying to guess is Kurt Vonnegut, the student might use a different line of questioning. He might begin by asking "Am I alive or dead?" and continue with questions such as "Did I serve in World War II?" and "Did I die in the war?" He could then narrow the field of possible identities by asking "Did I write about my experiences during the war?" Students should be familiar with the people whose identities they are assuming, but they will apply that knowledge in different ways. At any point in time he can make a guess about who he thinks he is.

The game can be relatively lax in its allowances, or it can be more difficult. For example, you can choose to set time limits and/or limit the number of questions and guesses each student is allowed. If the student follows the rules and correctly guesses his identity, he gets a point. If he does not make a guess or guesses incorrectly, no point is awarded. Alternatively, each student can be timed. The goal in this case is to use as little time as possible to determine a correct answer.

Vocabulary Words

Who Am I? works best if you use the names of people or characters your class has been studying. The strength of this game is that it allows teachers to see what students know about the people or characters they have studied and the contexts in which they lived. Other proper nouns can be used as well, but we recommend that if you elect to do this, you give the student a hint, telling her whether she is a person, place, or thing. The following list of sample terms is limited to the subject of social studies, because in other subjects, the game will be highly specialized.

Social Studies

Upper Elementary

Abraham Lincoln

Adolf Hitler

Augustus

Andrew Jackson

Alexander Graham Bell

Alexander Hamilton

Alfred the Great

Amelia Earhart

Aztec Indians

Barack Obama

Bartholomew de las Casas

Benito Mussolini

Benjamin Franklin

Betty Zane

Billy the Kid

Booker T. Washington

Buddha

Cesar Chavez

Charlemagne

Charles Finney

Christopher Columbus

Clara Barton

Commodore Matthew Perry

Confucius

Constantine

Nicolaus Copernicus

Czar Nicholas II

Daniel Boone

Davy Crockett

Edmund Cartwright

Eleanor Roosevelt

Elizabeth Blackwell

Eric the Red

Francisco Franco
Francisco Vasquez de Coronado
Ferdinand Magellan
Franklin D. Roosevelt
Frederick Douglass
Galileo Galilei
Garibaldi
George H. W. Bush
George W. Bush
George Washington
George Washington Carver
Genghis Khan
Gerald Ford
Geronimo
Harriet Tubman
Harry S. Truman
Henri Matisse
Henry Ford
Jackie Robinson
Jacqueline Kennedy Onassis
Jacques Cartier
James Armistead
James Hargreaves
James Monroe
James Watt
Jedediah Smith
Jesus of Nazareth
Jim Bowie
Jim Crow
Jimmy Carter
Joe Magarac
Jonas Salk
John Adams
John F. Kennedy
John Glenn
John Hancock
John Henry
John Kay
Joseph Stalin
Julius Caesar

Louis Pasteur
Lydia Darragh
Lyndon B. Johnson
Marcus Aurelius
Martin Luther King Jr.
Marco Polo
Marie Curie
Mary McLeod Bethune
Mother Mary Jones
Muhammad
Napoleon Bonaparte
Nathan Beman
Pablo Picasso
Paul Bunyan
Pecos Bill
Peter Cartwright
P. T. Barnum
Rasputin
Richard Arkwright
Richard Henry Lee
Richard Nixon
Robert E. Lee
Ronald Reagan
Rosa Parks
Sam Houston
Samuel Adams
Sally Ride
Seneca
Sioux
Socrates
Sojourner Truth
Susan B. Anthony
Theodore Roosevelt
Thomas Jefferson
Thomas Nast
Vasco da Gama
Vladamir Lenin
W. E. B. DuBois
William H. Taft
William the Conqueror

Winston Churchill
Woodrow Wilson

Middle School

Albert Einstein
Alfred Krupp
Anne Hutchinson
Bill Clinton
Calvin Coolidge
Catherine the Great
Charles Darwin
Charles Evans Hughes
Dorothea Lange
Dwight D. Eisenhower
Elizabeth I
Emmeline Pankhurst
Francis Bacon
Francis Townsend
Hiram Johnson
Huey Long
James Buchanan
James Madison
Jean Jaures
John Marshall
Jose Clemente Orozco
Joseph McCarthy
Karl Marx
Lucretia Mott
Mao Zedong
Mohandas Gandhi
Papacy/Pope
Peter Stolypin
Peter the Great
Ramsay MacDonald
Ramses II
Raymond Poincare
René Descartes
Robert La Follette
Rosa Luxemburg
Sigmund Freud

Stanley Baldwin

Warren G. Harding

High School

Adam Smith

Alexander the Great

Aristotle

Carrie Chapman Catt

Cyrus I

Czar Nicholas I

David Siqueiros

Diego Rivera

Emilio Aguinaldo

Erich Remarque

Ernest Hemmingway

George Orwell

James K. Polk

Jefferson Davis

Joan of Arc

John Collier

John Locke

John White

Joseph II

Machiavelli

Mark Hanna

Otto Von Bismarck

Plato

Roger Williams

Sun Yat-sen

Ulysses S. Grant

Upton Sinclair

William Jennings Bryan

William McKinley

William T. Sherman

Wilmot Proviso

10

WHERE AM I?

For lower elementary math and lower
and upper elementary social studies

Design

This game is named *Where Am I?* because its object is for students to find a specific location using relevant directional coordinates and landmarks. It can be used as both review and application at the elementary level in math or the elementary and middle school levels in social studies. Students should be familiar enough with the terms and phrases to apply them independently.

Materials

You will need a map for every student, or pair of students, in your class. The map you use depends on the vocabulary terms and phrases you select. For example, an elementary math teacher using terms such as *right, left, under,* and *above* would want a map that allows students to use these terms. That map might depict a school or a house. Conversely, a middle school social studies teacher who wants to use state names and terms such as *north, south, east,* and *west* would want a very different map, perhaps one depicting the entire country and all of its major highways.

Set Up

The major preparation for the game is the map. Once you have enough maps for every student (or pair of students), you may choose to make more specific preparations by writing out the directions to each location, but this is not absolutely necessary.

Play

Students can play this game individually or in pairs. Once every student or pair of students has been provided a map, begin play by telling them where the starting place on the map is. For example, the starting place might be in the state of Colorado on a map of the United States, or it might be the school on a map of the town. Every student begins in the same place, and they must follow your verbal step-by-step directions to find the location where you are hiding. For example, you might provide directions such as, "You are starting at the school. Go north on Vancouver Street until you get to Washington Avenue. Make a left turn and go east until you reach the Lawndale Park. I am hiding in the third house on the left. What is the address?"

You can choose to play in one of two ways. The first and simpler way to play (described in the preceding text) is that you provide the verbal step-by-step directions using the relevant vocabulary terms and phrases, and the students' only job is to follow those directions to find where you are hiding. For another example of this method, assume you have chosen to work with a map of the country. On the map, states, cities, and major highways and landmarks are identified. The starting place is the city of Denver in the state of Colorado, and you are hiding in Albany, New York. You might give the following directions: "We are starting in Denver where highway I-25 meets highway 225. Go north on highway 225 until it meets highway I-76. Go north on I-76 until you reach highway I-80. Head east on I-80 until you find I-90. Take I-90 east until you find US-9. This is where I am hiding. What state and city am I in?"

The second way to play is to have students take turns providing verbal-only directions to the class. In this case, you should give the student a list of the terms and phrases she can use to help her classmates find her. With younger students, you might even let them decide where they want to hide and write out the directions for them to read.

Vocabulary Words

As discussed previously, terms you choose may be prepositions or nouns (common or proper). The following terms and phrases we have provided are general (and only in the subjects of math and social studies) as this game needs to be tailored to each class.

Math

Lower Elementary

above
behind
below
beside
between
far
in front
inside
left
location
near
next to
outside
over
right
under
within

Social Studies

Lower Elementary

airport
America
body of water
Canada
city
city park
country
creek
dam
desert
direction
downtown
forest
highway
home
hospital
hotel
lake
location
map
mile
mountain
museum
nation

neighborhood
ocean
railroad
river
road
shopping center
sports stadium
state
stream
town
yard

Upper Elementary

Afghanistan
Africa
Americas
Andes
Antarctic Circle
Appalachian Mountains
Asia
Atlantic Basin
Atlantic Ocean
Australia
Baghdad
Balkans
Bering Land Bridge
Bering Sea
Black Sea
Brazil
Britain
British Isles
Buenos Aires
Cairo
Canada
cardinal directions
Caribbean

China
Cuba
Dominican Republic
East Coast
Eastern Hemisphere
Egypt
England
equator
Erie Canal
Europe
France
Ganges River Valley
Germany
hemisphere
India
Indian Ocean
Indonesia
Iran
Iraq
Ireland
Israel
Italy
Japan
Korea (North and South)
Latin America
latitude
London
longitude
Malaysia
Mali
Mexico
Middle East
Mississippi River
names of U.S. states
Netherlands

New Zealand
Nile Delta
Nile Valley
North Africa
North America
North Pole
ordinal/intermediate directions
Pacific Islands
Pacific Ocean
Pacific Rim
Palestine
Panama Canal
Paris
Peru
prime meridian
Puerto Rico
Rocky Mountains
Russia
Saudi Arabia
Scandinavia
Scotland
Siberia
Singapore
South Africa
South America
South Pole
Suez Canal
Tigris-Euphrates Valley
time zone
Tokyo
Turkey
Vietnam
Washington, D.C.
West Coast
Western Hemisphere

11

CREATE A CATEGORY

For upper elementary through high school language arts, math, science, and social studies

Design

Create a Category gets its name from its focus on categorization. The object is for students to create as many different categories of words as possible based on a given list of terms and phrases. It can be used in upper elementary through high school classes in all four major content areas (language arts, math, science, and social studies). It requires a working understanding of the relevant terms and phrases.

Materials

You will need a chalkboard or whiteboard.

Set Up

In advance, prepare word lists. Four to eight lists of fifteen to twenty words work well. The terms you choose should be similar enough to allow students to categorize them in ways discussed in class, but disparate enough for students to use creativity in creating categories as well.

Play

The game can be played by breaking students into teams, or each student can work alone. After you write or display the first list of words on the board, the students' job is to categorize three or more terms in as many ways as they can think of. At the end of an allotted period of time, each group shares what categories they came up with and what terms are in those categories. Points may be assigned based on the number of categories generated.

Vocabulary Words

The lists of terms you provide are the key to this game. They should be tailored, but not too tailored—you want to allow the students to use their creativity in coming up with categories. Terms from past units can be included as well. For example, consider a social studies teacher who has covered a unit on the Civil War, a unit on the American government, and a unit on the five major religions of the world. The following list of social studies terms might be provided:

Thomas Jefferson	monotheism	senator
Ulysses S. Grant	Union army	Judaism
freedom of speech	Supreme Court judge	Harriet Tubman
nirvana	election	emancipation

The students might categorize *Ulysses S. Grant*, *Harriet Tubman*, *senator*, and *Supreme Court judge* together under a category called "servants." They might pick out *monotheism*, *Judaism*, and *nirvana* as words associated with religion. The categories can be as predictable or as strange as the students like. You should review the list before handing it out to make sure there is adequate opportunity to create categories.

As category lists will be class-specific, no sample lists are provided. However, ideas for terms to use can be found in the appendix (page 203). In general, nouns (including proper nouns) work best for this game. If you want to use verbs or adjectives, it is best to create a list with those parts of speech exclusively. In other words, if you want to use verbs, create an entire list made of only verbs.

12

WHAT IS THE QUESTION?

For upper elementary, middle, and high school language arts, math, science, and social studies

Design

What Is the Question? is modeled after *Jeopardy!* It can be played in any of the four main content areas (language arts, math, science, and social studies) and is best for upper elementary, middle, and high school students. A working knowledge of relevant terms and phrases is necessary.

Materials

The material needs for this game vary. If you are taking a pencil-and-paper approach, you will need to design a creative game board. You can also use a chalkboard or whiteboard and tape sheets of paper over the answers, or you can create something more sophisticated. If you want a more authentic feel, you can download the *Classroom Jeopardy* software and customize your game items (www.classroomjeopardy.com). *Classroom Jeopardy* does have some pre-programmed game cartridges, but none of them focus specifically on vocabulary. Whatever you use, you will need a game board like the one on *Jeopardy!* (see figs. 12.1 and 12.2, page 92, for examples). Finally, you will need something for each team to signal your attention. Flags or small bells work well. Note that figure 12.1 displays what the game board for a self-contained classroom might look like, and figure 12.2 displays a sample board for a language arts class.

Set Up

In advance, prepare the questions and answers as well as the categories into which they fit. Because this preparation can be extensive, we have provided sample questions and answers at the upper elementary, middle, and high school levels for each of the four main content areas (language arts, math, science, and social studies; pages 96–126).

Note that we have not assigned point values to the items we have provided. This is because such designations are highly specialized to each class. You may wish to pick and choose among the items we have provided or modify them to suit the purposes of your class.

	Language arts	Math	Science	Social studies
100				
200				
300				
400				
500				

Figure 12.1: Sample game board for a self-contained classroom.

	Grammar	Literary analysis	Persuasive techniques	Speaking skills
100				
200				
300				
400				
500				

Figure 12.2: Sample game board for a language arts class.

Play

The game can be played in teams or by individual students. Whichever way you choose, be sure you have designated some way to keep track of points earned and lost. The game begins once you are sure students understand the directions. The first team or student chooses a category and a point value. Just like the game show, you read the answer, and the students formulate a question. For example, if you read an answer such as "He was the first official czar of Russia," the students should come up with the following question: "Who was Ivan the Great?" A variation on this game is simply to provide study with the vocabulary terms. Students then have to provide the definition of the word in the form of a question. For example, if the word is *crater*, a correct question would be, "What is a hole in the Earth caused by a meteorite?"

Once you read the answer, each team or student has ten or fifteen seconds to come up with the right question. If you are playing in teams, each team should designate a spokesperson to signal when they have the question. If the first question is wrong, the other students or teams have five seconds to come up with the correct question. On *Jeopardy!*, if a player gives the wrong question, points are taken away, but you may or may not choose to play that way. A simpler way to play is to designate every answer with the same point value. For example, instead of creating a game in which answers have 200-, 400-, 600-, and 800-point values (for simpler to more complex answers, respectively), you may elect to play using only a 200-point value.

Vocabulary Words

If you are choosing your own vocabulary terms, we recommend nouns (proper or common) and verbs. Ideally, the answers in an entire category would all be the same part of speech. For example, if the answer to one question in a category is a verb, then all of the other answers in that category would be verbs as well. Sample game items in all four content areas at the upper elementary, middle school, and high school levels follow. The vocabulary term that is the focus of each of the items appears in bold, and each of those terms appears in the appendix (page 203) as well. Note that some answers have examples (in parentheses). Where the answer lends itself to an example, you should present the example along with the answer for clarity.

Additionally, we have included multiple-choice hints you can use if your class is having trouble. You can offer students a list of either two or four terms (essentially changing the game item into alternative choice or multiple choice), one of which is the correct answer. Use the multiple-choice hints sparingly because they change the rigor of the game item. The items require students to independently recall an answer, and multiple-choice hints scaffold that requirement down to a recognition level. In other words, while you certainly want to make the game fun and encourage students' success, too much generosity with the hints will restrict the learning directly associated with the game.

Language Arts

Upper Elementary

Category: Parts of a word

ANSWER: the form of a word after all of its prefixes and suffixes have been removed (re*evaluate*, dis*qualify*, *manag*ing)

QUESTION: What are **root words**?

HINT: affix, syllable, comma, root word

ANSWER: the part of a word that comes before its base (pre, post, non, anti)

QUESTION: What is a **prefix**?

HINT: suffix, prefix, affix, capital letter

ANSWER: the part of a word that comes after its base (ing, ion, ly)

QUESTION: What is a **suffix?**

HINT: suffix, affix, apostrophe, colon

ANSWER: the letter that begins a sentence and/or a proper noun (*We* went to *Rosa's* house.)

QUESTION: What is a **capital letter?**

HINT: lowercase letter, vowel, consonant, capital letter

ANSWER: the individual sounds that words are made of (re/ne/go/ti/ate)

QUESTION: What are **syllables?**

HINT: vowels, roots, syllables, sentences

Category: Parts of speech

ANSWER: the use of two negative words when only one is needed (ain't never, don't need no)

QUESTION: What is a **double negative?**

HINT: double negative, auxiliary verb, compound word, noun phrase

ANSWER: a word, phrase, or sentence that gives an order (Sit down!)

QUESTION: What is a **command?**

HINT: quotation, command, exclamation, sentence fragment

ANSWER: a sentence that contains more than one main clause but is not separated by punctuation or a conjunction (Mary took her dog for a walk and then did laundry and then made dinner for her family Mary had a long day!)

QUESTION: What is a **run-on sentence?**

HINT: run-on sentence, sentence fragment, complex sentence, declarative sentence

ANSWER: a particular person, place, or thing (*Harry* took us to the *Smithsonian Institute.*)

QUESTION: What is a **proper noun?**

HINT: auxiliary verb, proper noun, linking verb, common noun

ANSWER: a pronoun that represents a person in a sentence (Marla and *I* went to *her* beach house.)

QUESTION: What is a **personal pronoun?**

HINT: root word, common noun, personal pronoun, preposition

Category: Punctuation

ANSWER: punctuation marks that show someone's exact words ("Don't hit your sister!" Mom yelled.)

QUESTION: What are **quotation marks?**

HINT: commas, semicolons, question marks, quotation marks

ANSWER: punctuation marks that put two words together to make a contraction or show possession (you're, Marty's, Mother's Day)

QUESTION: What are **apostrophes**?

HINT: periods, apostrophes, indexes, opinions

ANSWER: punctuation marks that make sentences into questions (Where did the cat go?)

QUESTION: What are **question marks**?

HINT: periods, pronouns, question marks, legends

ANSWER: a talk someone gives out loud to an entire class (a book report)

QUESTION: What is an **oral presentation**?

HINT: oral presentation, short story, cursive, myth

ANSWER: punctuation marks used to introduce lists or direct quotations (Gene needs these things for football practice: shoulder pads, a helmet, a mouth guard, and cleats.)

QUESTION: What are **colons**?

HINT: semicolons, apostrophes, colons, quotation marks

Category: Genre

(Note: Use texts from your reading list to use as examples in this category.)

ANSWER: a genre made up of books or stories that are about real people or real events

QUESTION: What is **nonfiction**?

HINT: fiction, poetry, nonfiction, cartoons

ANSWER: brief stories made up by an author

QUESTION: What is a **short story**?

HINT: poems, novels, short stories, picture books

ANSWER: a genre of stories made up by an author

QUESTION: What is **fiction**?

HINT: fiction, nonfiction, news, drama

ANSWER: a genre of stories that are intended to deliver a moral ("Hansel and Gretel")

QUESTION: What are **fairy tales**?

HINT: novel, fairy tale, letter, poem

ANSWER: a genre of stories that are intended to be performed

QUESTION: What are **plays**?

HINT: short stories, novels, letters, plays

Category: Story elements

ANSWER: the place in which a story happens (A story about the French Revolution takes place in *Paris.*)

QUESTION: What is **setting**?

HINT: mood, character, setting, drama

ANSWER: a story that is told through the eyes of the main character

QUESTION: What is **first person**?

HINT: third person, first person, director, encyclopedia

ANSWER: the technique an author uses to make readers feel like they know a character

QUESTION: What is **character development**?

HINT: proofreading, cueing, character development, role playing

ANSWER: descriptions of sounds, smells, tastes, sights, and textures (The room smelled like soap and perfume.)

QUESTION: What are **sensory details**?

HINT: first person, mood, context clues, sensory details

ANSWER: the technique an author uses to make readers feel excited about what will happen next in a story

QUESTION: What is **suspense**?

HINT: character, preface, suspense, theme

Middle School

Category: Grammar and punctuation

ANSWER: an adjective in its greatest form (biggest, softest, smartest)

QUESTION: What is a **superlative adjective**?

HINT: comparative adjective, superlative adjective, adjective phrase, pronominal adjective

ANSWER: words such as *and*, *or*, and *but* that connect two independent clauses (Julia got to go to the snow palace, *and* she told the class about it the next day.)

QUESTION: What is a **conjunction**?

HINT: periodical, simile, clue, conjunction

ANSWER: the origin of a word (The word *claustrophobia* comes from the Latin words *claustrum*, which means to close or shut, and the word *phobia*, which means to fear.)

QUESTION: What is **derivation**?

HINT: prefix, narration, derivation, projection

ANSWER: two or more verbs that belong to one subject in a sentence (The president *gave* a speech, *walked* to the White House, and *signed* a petition on Inauguration Day.)

QUESTION: What are **compound verbs**?

HINT: compound verbs, irregular verbs, proverb, verb phrase

ANSWER: a phrase or clause in a sentence that cannot stand alone as a complete sentence (Maria wanted Betsy to come over but *not Phillip*.)

QUESTION: What is a **dependent clause**?

HINT: verb phrase, dependent clause, independent clause, conjunction

Category: Literary analysis

ANSWER: giving an animal or object human feelings (The house sat, waiting to be purchased.)

QUESTION: What is **personification**?

HINT: hyperbole, metaphor, personification, exposition

ANSWER: language that departs from a literal meaning to achieve a certain effect (All the world's a stage.)

QUESTION: What is **figurative language**?

HINT: idiom, juxtaposition, descriptive language, figurative language

ANSWER: the act of performing a scene from a book or a play

QUESTION: What is **dramatization**?

HINT: compilation, dramatization, juxtaposition, facilitation

ANSWER: the point in the story where the main conflict plays out (The two countries that have been arguing throughout a story finally start a war.)

QUESTION: What is the **climax**?

HINT: climax, resolution, flashback, episode

ANSWER: the appearances, attitudes, and beliefs unique to a character in a story (Huck Finn is rebellious.)

QUESTION: What are **character traits**?

HINT: setting, dialogue, character traits, character development

Category: Revision and editing

ANSWER: this is what a confusing composition needs

QUESTION: What is **clarification**?

HINT: modifier, jargon, metaphor, clarification

ANSWER: information appearing in a research paper that does not fit or is not necessary

QUESTION: What is **extraneous information**?

HINT: relevant details, extraneous information, interjection, stress

ANSWER: opinions or constructive criticism intended to improve a work or skill

QUESTION: What is **feedback**?

HINT: interjection, feedback, exposition, intonation

ANSWER: the ability to read over your own work, catch mistakes, and improve your writing

QUESTION: What is **self-editing**?

HINT: self-editing, foreshadowing, salutation, synthesis

ANSWER: the process of stating a particular word or sentence in different words

QUESTION: What is **rephrasing**?

HINT: foreshadowing, intonation, rephrasing, metaphor

Category: Persuasive writing

ANSWER: the last paragraph of a persuasive composition in which the author summarizes his or her main points

QUESTION: What is a **closing**?

HINT: thesis statement, closing, footnote, projection

ANSWER: the aim or intention an author has when writing an essay or research paper

QUESTION: What is the author's **purpose**?

HINT: personification, purpose, report, perspective

ANSWER: reasonable or sound judgment

QUESTION: What is **logic**?

HINT: logic, slang, etymology, transition

ANSWER: a written address to a person or a corporation for professional purposes

QUESTION: What is a **business letter**?

HINT: personal letter, letter of request, business letter, invitation

ANSWER: the people whom authors or advertisers are trying to reach

QUESTION: What is a **target audience**?

HINT: public opinion trend, target audience, hostile audience, knowledge base

Category: Oral communication/media

ANSWER: a meeting at which one person is asked questions by another person

QUESTION: What is an **interview**?

HINT: feature story, narration, interview, skit

ANSWER: the act of speaking loudly enough to be heard by everyone in an audience when giving a speech

QUESTION: What is **projection**?

HINT: intonation, enunciation, projection, summarization

ANSWER: the act of looking at specific members of an audience while giving an oral presentation to engage them

QUESTION: What is **eye contact**?

HINT: projection, enunciation, eye contact, body language

ANSWER: an opinion about politics or people that is very popular for a brief period of time

QUESTION: What is a **public opinion trend**?

HINT: public audience, syntax, public opinion trend, viewpoint

ANSWER: a newspaper that focuses on gossip rather than news

QUESTION: What is a **tabloid**?

HINT: broadcast, periodical, tabloid, slang

High School

Category: Grammar and punctuation

ANSWER: adverbs or adjectives plus the noun they are modifying (The movie star is in the *last white limousine.*)

QUESTION: What is a **noun phrase**?

HINT: verb phrase, noun phrase, conjunctive adverb, indefinite adjective

ANSWER: two or more adjectives that work together to modify a noun (a *fifteen-minute* presentation)

QUESTION: What is a **compound adjective**?

HINT: compound adjective, conjunctive adverb, indefinite adjective, adjective phrase

ANSWER: a noun that appears in singular form but is plural in meaning (The *crowd* was restless.)

QUESTION: What is a **collective noun**?

HINT: noun phrase, reflexive noun, collective noun, singular noun

ANSWER: a pronoun used without an antecedent to ask a question (*Whose* house are we visiting?)

QUESTION: What is an **interrogative pronoun**?

HINT: reflexive pronoun, indefinite pronoun, interrogative pronoun, proper pronoun

ANSWER: a punctuation mark used informally to set off parenthetical statements (All four cats— Wiggles, Beatrice, Dr. Detroit, and Moose—had to go the vet at the same time.)

QUESTION: What is a **dash**?

HINT: couplet, diction, excerpt, dash

Category: Literary analysis

ANSWER: work that does not clearly belong in one genre or another (prose poems or historical fiction)

QUESTION: What is **blurring of genres**?

HINT: red herring, blurring of genres, false causality, logical fallacy

ANSWER: the broad term used to describe how an author makes his or her characters feel like real people

QUESTION: What is **characterization**?

HINT: diction, satire, characterization, persona

ANSWER: the literary movement that took place in the early nineteenth century and was defined by writers such as Wordsworth and Coleridge

QUESTION: What is the **romantic period**?

HINT: realism, romantic period, contemporary period, neoclassic period

ANSWER: the thoughts of a character in a book or play that are not said aloud

QUESTION: What is **interior monologue**?

HINT: dramatic dialogue, subvocalization, interior monologue, anecdote

ANSWER: the person who is telling the story in a book or movie

QUESTION: What is a **narrator**?

HINT: idiom, medium, narrator, reporter

Category: Revision and editing

ANSWER: the overall ease a person has understanding and reading a work

QUESTION: What is **readability**?

HINT: credibility, readability, emotional appeal, ambiguity

ANSWER: the process of improving a rough draft to create a polished final draft

QUESTION: What is **redrafting**?

HINT: deconstructing, negotiating, overstating, redrafting

ANSWER: a contextual error in logic that renders an argument invalid

QUESTION: What is a **logical fallacy**?

HINT: logical fallacy, red herring, faulty mode of presentation, exaggerated claim

ANSWER: the use of more words than necessary to complete a thought or make a point

QUESTION: What is **circumlocution**?

HINT: emphasis, circumlocution, context, memorandum

ANSWER: the common style used in our research papers

QUESTION: What is **Modern Language Association (MLA)**?

HINT: American Psychological Association (APA), Modern Language Association (MLA), Chicago Manual of Style (CMS), American Medical Association (AMA)

Category: Persuasive writing

ANSWER: an argument used in opposition to an originally presented argument

QUESTION: What is a **counterargument**?

HINT: attack ad hominem, thesis statement, deconstructive argument, counterargument

ANSWER: a persuasive technique designed to make consumers feel like everyone is using the advertised product (a sneaker commercial intended to entice young people by featuring a basketball court full of teenagers wearing the shoes and having a good time)

QUESTION: What is **bandwagon**?

HINT: bandwagon, testimonial, appeal to authority, incongruity

ANSWER: a sentence at the end of a paragraph or paper intended to leave the reader with a powerful impression

QUESTION: What is a **clincher sentence**?

HINT: thesis statement, understatement, overstatement, clincher sentence

ANSWER: a persuasive technique characterized by its focus on reason or fact (a public service announcement that warns against drunk driving by stating statistics about how many people died in drunk-driving accidents the previous year)

QUESTION: What is an **appeal to logic**?

HINT: appeal to emotion, appeal to authority, appeal to logic, attack ad hominem

ANSWER: a sentence in the introduction of an essay that clearly states the argument the essay will present

QUESTION: What is a **thesis statement**?

HINT: clincher sentence, analogy, thesis statement, bias statement

Category: Oral communication/Mass media

ANSWER: ideas or rumors spread to help or hurt a specific person or cause

QUESTION: What is **propaganda?**

HINT: bandwagon, bias, dictation, propaganda

ANSWER: any formal mode of communication or expression through which large numbers of people can be reached

QUESTION: What is a **medium**?

HINT: medium, visual text, censorship, hyperbole

ANSWER: a law that prevents the reproduction or use of an author's original work without permission

QUESTION: What is a **copyright law**?

HINT: copyright law, ethical ideals, FCC regulation, advertising law

ANSWER: the principle that advertising should not be intentionally misleading

QUESTION: What is **truth in advertising**?

HINT: attack ad hominem, appeal to logic, credibility, truth in advertising

ANSWER: an image that has been altered in order to sell a product or appeal to a specific audience

QUESTION: What is a **media-generated image**?

HINT: mass media, truth in advertising, media-generated image, allusion

Math

Upper Elementary

Category: Shapes

ANSWER:

QUESTION: What is a **rhombus**?

HINT: rhombus, rectangle, parallelogram, square

ANSWER: the measure of a straight line that passes through the center of a circle

QUESTION: What is the **diameter**?

HINT: radius, circumference, diameter, perimeter

ANSWER:

QUESTION: What is a **parallelogram**?

HINT: rhombus, parallelogram, rectangle, octagon

ANSWER: equilateral, isosceles, right, scalene

QUESTION: What are the types of **triangles**?

HINT: triangles, polygons, circles, prisms

ANSWER: the measure of a line that extends from the center of a circle to its edge

QUESTION: What is the **radius**?

HINT: hypotenuse, radius, circumference, perimeter

Category: Lines and angles

ANSWER: the tool used to measure angles

QUESTION: What is a **protractor**?

HINT: compass, ruler, protractor, scale

ANSWER: ═══════

QUESTION: What are **parallel lines**?

> **HINT:** parallel lines, perpendicular lines, intersecting lines, polygon

ANSWER: ⟋⟍

QUESTION: What are **perpendicular lines**?

> **HINT:** bar graph, perpendicular lines, intersecting lines, polygon

ANSWER: an angle that measures exactly 90°

QUESTION: What is a **right angle**?

> **HINT:** acute angle, obtuse angle, right angle

ANSWER: ✕

QUESTION: What are **corresponding angles**?

> **HINT:** acute angles, supplementary angles, complementary angles, corresponding angles

Category: Computation

ANSWER: the idea that a change in the grouping of addends does not change the sum, and a change in the grouping of factors does not change the quotient $[(a + b) + c = a + (b + c)]$

QUESTION: What is the **associative property**?

> **HINT:** identity property, associative property, distributive property, commutative property

ANSWER: the idea that no matter how you move numbers or variables around in an addition or multiplication problem, the sum or quotient will not change $(a + b = b + a)$

QUESTION: What is the **commutative property**?

> **HINT:** identity property, associative property, distributive property, commutative property

ANSWER: the idea that multiplication will distribute through an addition equation in parentheses $[3(a + b) = 3a + 3b]$

QUESTION: What is the **distributive property**?

> **HINT:** identity property, associative property, distributive property, commutative property

ANSWER: a denominator two or more fractions have in common

QUESTION: What is a **common denominator**?

> **HINT:** improper fraction, common denominator, unlike denominator, reduced form

ANSWER: an educated guess about a quantity or measurement

QUESTION: What is an **estimation**?

> **HINT:** rounding, rotation, estimation, remainder

Category: Measurement units

ANSWER: inches, feet, and miles

QUESTION: What is the **U.S. system of measurement**?

> **HINT:** U.S. system of measurement, metric system

ANSWER: centimeter, meter, and kilometer
QUESTION: What is the **metric system?**
HINT: U.S. system of measurement, metric system

ANSWER: the act of changing 3.67 to 3.7 to 4
QUESTION: What is **rounding?**
HINT: division, measuring, factoring, rounding

ANSWER: the process of calculation that determines 5 kilometers = 3.2 miles
QUESTION: What is **unit conversion?**
HINT: unit division, unit extension, unit conversion, unit clustering

ANSWER: a formal and detailed examination of something
QUESTION: What is a **survey?**
HINT: data, median, survey, horizontal axis

Category: Data and data display methods

ANSWER:
QUESTION: What is a **bar graph?**
HINT: bar graph, line graph, scatter plot, pie chart

ANSWER:
QUESTION: What is a **line graph?**
HINT: scatter plot, pie chart, line graph, Venn diagram

ANSWER:
QUESTION: What is a **Venn diagram?**
HINT: Venn diagram, line graph, pie chart, median

ANSWER: the number that appears most frequently in a data set
QUESTION: What is the **mode?**
HINT: mean, mode, median, measurement

ANSWER: the average value for a set of numbers
QUESTION: What is the **mean?**
HINT: mean, median, mode, tally

Middle School

Category: Algebra

ANSWER: $y = mx + b$

> **QUESTION:** What is a **linear equation**?

   HINT: algebraic step function, nonlinear equation, linear equation, enlarging transformation

ANSWER: an unlimited or immeasurable quantity

> **QUESTION:** What is **infinite**?

   HINT: exponential, infinite, conjecture, maximum

ANSWER: a linear function with the specific domain of the natural numbers

> **QUESTION:** What is a **linear arithmetic sequence**?

   HINT: range of estimations, graphic representation of function, table representation of functions, linear arithmetic sequence

ANSWER: $3x^2 + 7y + 10xy - 6$

> **QUESTION:** What is an **algebraic expression**?

   HINT: scientific notation, algebraic expression, iterative sequence, nonlinear equation

ANSWER: x or y in an equation; a quantity you are trying to find

> **QUESTION:** What is an **unknown**?

   HINT: array, root, unknown, maximum

Category: Geometry

ANSWER: πr^2

> **QUESTION:** What is the formula for the **area of a circle**?

   HINT: formula for the area of a circle, formula for the area of a prism, formula for the area of a rectangle, formula for the area of a triangle

ANSWER: the common point of two rays or line sections (↘∠)

> **QUESTION:** What is a **vertex**?

   HINT: variable, root, vertex, bisector

ANSWER: two figures that have the same shape and size but lie in different positions (▼ ◣)

> **QUESTION:** What is **congruence**?

   HINT: similarity, dilation, congruence, dispersion

ANSWER: a line that divides a figure so that both halves match exactly (▮▮)

> **QUESTION:** What is **line of symmetry**?

   HINT: line asymmetry, line of symmetry, line bisector, linear geometric sequence

ANSWER: $\pi r^2 h$

QUESTION: What is the formula for the **volume of a cylinder**?

HINT: formula for the volume of a cylinder, formula for the volume of a cube, formula for the volume of a pyramid, formula for the volume of a sphere

Category: Measurement

ANSWER: $5:5$ or $10:10$

QUESTION: What is an **equal ratio**?

HINT: equal ratio, sequence, data set, networks

ANSWER: a quantity of one thing expressed in relation to another (60 miles per hour)

QUESTION: What is **rate**?

HINT: rate, proportion, odds, array

ANSWER: the number of times a particular value occurs in a set of data

QUESTION: What is **frequency**?

HINT: rate, frequency, dispersion, range

ANSWER: a statement of two equal ratios (3/4 = 6/8)

QUESTION: What is **proportion**?

HINT: congruence, proportion, integer, range

ANSWER: the units used to measure area ( )

QUESTION: What are **square units**?

HINT: linear units, square units, inches, centimeters

Category: Graphing

ANSWER:

QUESTION: What is a **box and whisker plot**?

HINT: scatter plot, stem and leaf plot, box and whisker plot, tree diagram model

ANSWER:

QUESTION: What is a **stem and leaf plot**?

HINT: scatter plot, stem and leaf plot, box and whisker plot, tree diagram model

ANSWER: a graph consisting of perpendicular number lines creating four quadrants ( )

QUESTION: What is a **coordinate plane**?

HINT: scatter plot, coordinate system, coordinate plane, planar cross section

ANSWER: the x and y points on a coordinate plane

QUESTION: What are **ordered pairs**?

HINT: ordered pairs, odds, range, place holders

ANSWER: a data point that is numerically distant from other points in a set
QUESTION: What is an **outlier**?
HINT: integer, minimum, outlier, slope

Category: Numbers and number systems

ANSWER: an integer greater than one that is not prime
QUESTION: What is a **composite number**?
HINT: composite number, cube number, rational number, linear number

ANSWER: mathematical notation that shows how many times a number is multiplied by itself
QUESTION: What is an **exponent**?
HINT: vertex, exponent, tessellation, base 10

ANSWER: a number that can be expressed as a quotient of two integers (.75, 3/4, 1, 1/1)
QUESTION: What is a **rational number**?
HINT: composite number, cube number, rational number, linear number

ANSWER: any number raised to its third power
QUESTION: What is a **cube number**?
HINT: cube number, cube root, cubic unit, three-dimensional

ANSWER: a number generated from a data set entirely by chance
QUESTION: What is a **random number**?
HINT: random number, composite number, reference set, root number

High School

Category: Algebra

ANSWER: the distance of x from zero, which is expressed as $|x|$
QUESTION: What is **absolute value**?
HINT: absolute error, absolute function, absolute value, absolute distance

ANSWER: $4! = 4 \times 3 \times 2 \times 1$
QUESTION: What is **factorial notation**?
HINT: function notation, natural log, factorial notation, exponential notation

ANSWER: in terms of x, the power to which e would have to be raised to equal x
QUESTION: What is a **natural log**?
HINT: log function, natural log, negative log, limit

ANSWER: $\begin{bmatrix} 9 & 8 & 6 \\ 1 & 2 & 7 \\ 4 & 9 & 2 \\ 6 & 0 & 5 \end{bmatrix}$

QUESTION: What is a **matrix**?

HINT: bivariate distribution, range of function, matrix, Richter scale

ANSWER: a polynomial equation with polynomial coefficients
QUESTION: What is an **algebraic function**?

HINT: absolute function, algebraic function, direct function, exponential function

Category: Geometry

ANSWER: a line that links two points on a circle or curve ( )
QUESTION: What is a **chord**?

HINT: chord, tangent, transversal, pi

ANSWER: the angle below the horizon that you would have to look to see an object below you
QUESTION: What is the **angle of depression**?

HINT: area under a curve, angle of depression, angle of ascension, slope

ANSWER: a quantity that possesses magnitude and direction ( )
QUESTION: What is a **vector**?

HINT: vector, vertex, variance, transversal

ANSWER: $\sin\theta = o/h$
QUESTION: What is the **sine** of a right triangle?

HINT: sine, cosine, tangent, limit

ANSWER: the point at which a line meets the edge of a circle or curve ( )
QUESTION: What is the **point of tangency**?

HINT: chord, arc, point of tangency, scalar

Category: Numbers and number systems

ANSWER: real numbers that are uncountable
QUESTION: What are **irrational numbers**?

HINT: rational numbers, irrational numbers, composite numbers, zero

ANSWER: an irrational number estimated at 3.14 and expressed as π
QUESTION: What is **pi**?

HINT: absolute value, pi, limit, sine

ANSWER: $1, 1, 2, 3, 5, 8 \ldots$
QUESTION: What is the beginning of the **Fibonacci sequence**?
HINT: asymptote of function, function composition, Fibonacci sequence, vector sequence

ANSWER: a real number and an imaginary number
EXAMPLE: $3 - 4i$
QUESTION: What is a **complex number**?
HINT: $4i$, 8, –12, 10^2

ANSWER: a complex number with a squared value equal to or less than zero
QUESTION: What is an **imaginary number**?
HINT: irrational number, imaginary number, pi, conjugate number

Category: Laws and theorems

ANSWER: any set of weak convergence results in probability theory
QUESTION: What is the **central limit theorem**?
HINT: law of large numbers, law of probability, central limit theorem, Pythagorean theorem

ANSWER: $\Pr(A) = E[\Pr(A \mid N)]$
QUESTION: What is the **law of probability**?
HINT: law of probability, law of large numbers, successive approximations, standard deviation

ANSWER: $a^2 + b^2 = c^2$
QUESTION: What is the **Pythagorean theorem**?
HINT: slope formula, Pythagorean theorem, recurrence equation, central limit theorem

ANSWER: a statement that can be proven on the basis of what we already know
QUESTION: What is a **theorem**?
HINT: statistic, validity, series, theorem

ANSWER: the law that proves long-term stability in results of random events
QUESTION: What is the **law of large numbers**?
HINT: law of probability, law of large numbers, Pythagorean theorem, theorem direct proof

Category: Statistics and experimentation

ANSWER: the party in an experiment that is designed to minimize unintended influences in a single variable scientific experiment
QUESTION: What is the **control group**?
HINT: control group, experimental group, sample, population

ANSWER: all information-gathering exercises used to discover the effects of x on y

QUESTION: What is **experimental design**?

   HINT: statistical probability, experimental design, variance, expected value

ANSWER: a test that has multiple possible outcomes, each of which depends on chance (flipping a coin)

QUESTION: What is a **statistical experiment**?

   HINT: random number, empirical verification, statistical experiment, independent trial

ANSWER: one half of the difference between the third and first quartiles; $QD = 1/2(Q_3 - Q_1)$

QUESTION: What is **quartile deviation**?

   HINT: standard deviation, quartile deviation, quartile analysis, spurious correlation

ANSWER: the ratio of the number of times a particular event occurs to the total number of trials

QUESTION: What is **experimental probability**?

   HINT: statistic, empirical verification, experimental design, experimental probability

Science

Upper Elementary

Category: Earth sciences

ANSWER: the process of water turning to vapor

QUESTION: What is **evaporation**?

   HINT: condensation, precipitation, evaporation, drought

ANSWER: the element that makes up 21 percent of the Earth's atmosphere and that we need in order to breathe

QUESTION: What is **oxygen**?

   HINT: oxygen, nitrogen, helium, water

ANSWER: the element that makes up 78 percent of the Earth's atmosphere and plays an important role in our DNA

QUESTION: What is **nitrogen**?

   HINT: oxygen, nitrogen, helium, water

ANSWER: harmful or toxic substances in the air, water, or on land

QUESTION: What is **pollution**?

   HINT: minerals, nutrients, pollution, population

ANSWER: the systematic rise and fall of the ocean according to the changing positions of the Earth and moon

QUESTION: What is the **tide**?

HINT: water cycle, weathering, migration, tide

ANSWER: the second planet from the sun

QUESTION: What is **Venus**?

HINT: Mars, Mercury, Venus, Earth

ANSWER: something neither animal nor vegetable

QUESTION: What is a **mineral**?

HINT: nitrogen, organism, environment, mineral

ANSWER: the planet closest to the sun

QUESTION: What is **Mercury**?

HINT: Mars, Jupiter, Mercury, Earth

ANSWER: a tool you can use to better see celestial objects in the sky at night

QUESTION: What is a **telescope**?

HINT: microscope, periscope, telescope, protractor

Category: Life sciences

ANSWER: the struggle between species in the same environment for resources that are needed for survival such as food and space

QUESTION: What is **competition**?

HINT: extinction, competition, friction, carnivore

ANSWER: an internal or external cause for infection or sickness (cancer)

QUESTION: What is **disease**?

HINT: drought, erosion, disease, pitch

ANSWER: the children any plant or animal produces

QUESTION: What are **offspring**?

HINT: planets, predators, vapor, offspring

ANSWER: an animal who hunts other animals

QUESTION: What is a **predator**?

HINT: herbivore, predator, prey, bird

ANSWER: a tool that magnifies small things such as cells so you can see them more easily

QUESTION: What is a **microscope**?

HINT: telescope, periscope, microscope, camera lens

ANSWER: the way plants eat and breathe
QUESTION: What is **photosynthesis?**
HINT: pollination, precipitation, photosynthesis, population

ANSWER: the stage in the water cycle where water that has collected in clouds falls in the form of rain, hail, or snow
QUESTION: What is **precipitation?**
HINT: precipitation, evaporation, condensation, reflection

ANSWER: a species of animal or plant that no longer exists on the Earth
QUESTION: What is **extinct?**
HINT: fossil, recycle, migration, extinct

ANSWER: the traits transferred to a child through DNA provided from one or both parents
QUESTION: What are **inherited traits?**
HINT: inherited traits, acquired traits, reproduction, food web

Category: Physical sciences

ANSWER: the ability of a substance to dissolve in water
QUESTION: What is **solubility?**
HINT: constellation, astronomy, solubility, friction

ANSWER: any observable property of an object or organism
QUESTION: What is a **physical property?**
HINT: invisible property, imaginary property, mental property, physical property

ANSWER: a force resistant to motion between two objects
QUESTION: What is **friction?**
HINT: solubility, conduction, electricity, friction

ANSWER: stored energy that is waiting to be used
QUESTION: What is **potential energy?**
HINT: kinetic energy, potential energy, sound, force

ANSWER: a material that has a moveable electric charge
QUESTION: What is a **conductor?**
HINT: insulator, conductor, reflector, refractor

ANSWER: the way unlike charges interact
QUESTION: What is **charge attraction?**
HINT: charge repulsion, charge attraction, charge neutralization, charge isolation

ANSWER: the fundamental and unchangeable measure of the amount of matter in an object

QUESTION: What is **mass**?

HINT: mass, speed, friction, density

Middle School

Category: Earth sciences

ANSWER: a large object that orbits a sun and has a tail made of dust and gas that is illuminated by the sun

QUESTION: What is a **comet**?

HINT: comet, planet, asteroid, moon

ANSWER: the force of attraction between all masses in the universe

QUESTION: What is **gravitational force**?

HINT: gravitational force, magnetic force, electrical force, unbalanced force

ANSWER: the short- or long-term weather patterns created by the interaction between the atmosphere and the ocean or land

QUESTION: What are **climactic patterns**?

HINT: ecosystems, inertia, air mass circulation, climactic patterns

ANSWER: all of the fossils (discovered and undiscovered) and the rock in which they are buried

QUESTION: What is the **fossil record**?

HINT: extinction record, fossil record, carrying capacity, fungus

ANSWER: the combination of the water under, on, and over the surface of the Earth

QUESTION: What is the **hydrosphere**?

HINT: lithosphere, atmosphere, hydrosphere, ocean

ANSWER: the inner core, outer core, mantle, and crust

QUESTION: What are **Earth's layers**?

HINT: layers of the atmosphere, layers of the moon, layers of soil, Earth's layers

ANSWER: a system of stars, planets, dust, and gas held together by the force of gravity

QUESTION: What is a **galaxy**?

HINT: moon, solar system, galaxy, comet tail

ANSWER: gas, liquid, and solid

QUESTION: What are the three **forms of matter**?

HINT: parts of a cell, forms of matter, forms of energy, forms of sedimentation

Category: Life sciences

ANSWER: traits that have evolved in a species over time that help the species survive

QUESTION: What are **adaptive characteristics**?

HINT: adaptive characteristics, physical characteristics, muscular system, physiological change

ANSWER: reproduction that requires only one parent

QUESTION: What is **asexual reproduction**?

HINT: sexual reproduction, reproduction, photosynthesis, asexual reproduction

ANSWER: the behaviors exhibited by a species for the purpose of reproduction

QUESTION: What is the **continuation of species**

HINT: continuation of species, physiological change, mutualism, competition

ANSWER: the cell in a woman that must be fertilized in order to reproduce

QUESTION: What is an **egg cell**?

HINT: sperm cell, egg cell, red cell, white cell

ANSWER: a blueprint for the body of an organism

QUESTION: What is a **body plan**?

HINT: celestial body, circulatory system, body plan, host

ANSWER: the system in the human body that contains the ovaries in a woman and the testicles in a man

QUESTION: What is the **reproductive system**?

HINT: circulatory system, muscular system, digestive system, reproductive system

ANSWER: the complex processes of an organism that maintain equilibrium

QUESTION: What is **homeostasis**?

HINT: homeostasis, climate, body plan, fungus

ANSWER: any cell that is created to serve a specific purpose and combines with more of the same cells to make tissues and organs

QUESTION: What is a **specialized cell**?

HINT: red cell, white cell, divided cell, specialized cell

ANSWER: the number of species in an area and their relative abundance

QUESTION: What is **species diversity**?

HINT: species diversity, peer review, taxonomy, tolerance of ambiguity

Category: Physical sciences

ANSWER: the resistance of an object to any change in its state of motion
QUESTION: What is **inertia**?
HINT: friction, inertia, deceleration, climate

ANSWER: a force that does not cause change in direction
QUESTION: What is a **balanced force**?
HINT: balanced force, unbalanced force, gravitational force, displacement

ANSWER: distance divided by time
QUESTION: What is **speed**?
HINT: velocity, direction, diversity, acceleration

ANSWER: light that travels in wavelengths within the spectrum we can see
QUESTION: What is **visible light**?
HINT: infrared light, gamma rays, visible light, ultraviolet light

ANSWER: a simple machine used for lifting or lowering heavy objects
QUESTION: What is a **pulley**?
HINT: wedge, lever, pulley, bridge

ANSWER: the line a moving object follows
QUESTION: What is **direction**?
HINT: velocity, acceleration, force, direction

ANSWER: a force that can change the direction of an object's motion
QUESTION: What is an **unbalanced force**?
HINT: gravitational force, balanced force, unbalanced force, pure force

ANSWER: a material that resists the flow of an electric current
QUESTION: What is an **insulator**?
HINT: conductor, insulator, inertia, homeostasis

High School

Category: Earth sciences

ANSWER: the age of the universe
QUESTION: What is estimated at **13.5 to 14 billion years**?
HINT: age of the Earth, age of the moon, age of the universe, age of the sun

ANSWER: ninety percent of all stars are of this type, also known as dwarf stars; the sun is one of them

QUESTION: What are **main sequence stars**?

HINT: main sequence stars, giant stars, binary stars, variable stars

ANSWER: the migration of elements between the lithosphere, hydrosphere, and atmosphere during geologic changes

QUESTION: What is the **geochemical cycle**?

HINT: advection, geochemical cycle, flow of energy, exothermic reaction

ANSWER: a wave that travels through the Earth's interior

QUESTION: What is a **seismic wave**?

HINT: transverse wave, sound wave, seismic wave, heat wave

ANSWER: matter that comes from something that was once alive and/or is made from organic compounds

QUESTION: What is **organic matter**?

HINT: live matter, organic matter, fossil fuel, food

ANSWER: the sunlight zone, the twilight zone, the midnight zone, the abyss, the trenches

QUESTION: What are the **ocean's layers**?

HINT: Earth's layers, layers of the atmosphere, soil layers, ocean's layers

ANSWER: the argument that the universe spontaneously sprang into existence roughly 13.7 billion years ago

QUESTION: What is the **big bang theory**?

HINT: flow of energy, big bang theory, advection, theory of relativity

Category: Life sciences

ANSWER: generational inherited trait-changes in a population of organisms

QUESTION: What is **biological evolution**?

HINT: adaptation, gene mutation, biological evolution, organic matter

ANSWER: the process of cell division in which a single parent cell produces two identical daughter cells

QUESTION: What is **mitosis**?

HINT: meiosis, mitosis, asexual reproduction, duplication reproduction

ANSWER: the living organisms that make up an environment

QUESTION: What is a **biotic factor**?

HINT: biotic factor, abiotic factor

ANSWER:

QUESTION: What is a **cell nucleus**?

HINT: cell nucleus, cell wall, vacuole, organelle

ANSWER: biomolecules (mostly proteins) that speed up chemical reactions

QUESTION: What are **enzymes**?

HINT: amino acids, enzymes, blood cells, cytoplasm

ANSWER: the influential theory that microorganisms may be the cause of disease and the spreading of disease

QUESTION: What is **germ theory**?

HINT: plague theory, cell theory, theory of relativity, germ theory

ANSWER: the process by which a species makes generational adaptations that increase chances of survival

QUESTION: What is **natural selection**?

HINT: gene encoding, neurotransmission, Mendelian genetics, natural selection

Category: Physical sciences

ANSWER: the transport of any material by a fluid

QUESTION: What is **advection**?

HINT: advection, convection, insulation, distribution

ANSWER: he is best known for his theories of relativity

QUESTION: Who is **Albert Einstein**?

HINT: Ernest Rutherford, Charles Lyell, Gregor Mendel, Albert Einstein

ANSWER: the number of protons found in the nucleus of an atom

QUESTION: What is the **atomic number**?

HINT: atomic weight, atomic number, atomic mass, atomic theory

ANSWER: this has the highest energy and the shortest wavelength in the electromagnetic spectrum

QUESTION: What is a **gamma ray**?

HINT: X-ray, sound wave, infrared light, gamma ray

ANSWER: the measure of the disorder in a system

QUESTION: What is **entropy**?

HINT: entropy, endothermic reaction, drag, ionic motion

ANSWER: the energy produced by atoms

QUESTION: What is **atomic energy**?

HINT: atomic heat, atomic energy, atomic entropy, chemical energy

ANSWER: a way to measure the mass of molecules and atoms without using standard units by comparing them to carbon 12

QUESTION: What is **relative mass**?

HINT: carbon mass, relative mass, atomic mass, simple mass

ANSWER: an SI base unit measuring the amount of substance

QUESTION: What is a **mole**?

HINT: isotope, ion, mole, rate of nuclear decay

ANSWER: the laboratory techniques used to separate complex mixtures in order to measure proportions of analytes

QUESTION: What is **chromatography**?

HINT: experimental technique, empirical techniques, chromatography, big bang theory

Category: Scientific inquiry

ANSWER: scientifically based research that includes observation

QUESTION: What is **empirical evidence**?

HINT: empirical evidence, mathematical evidence, hypothesis testing, theoretical evidence

ANSWER: the controlled manipulation of one variable to see if there are changes in another variable

QUESTION: What is the **experimental method?**

HINT: empirical standards, Bernoulli's principle, Avogadro's hypothesis, experimental method

Social Studies

Upper Elementary

Category: U.S. history

ANSWER: the war that made the United States an independent nation

QUESTION: What was the **Revolutionary War**?

HINT: Civil War, Revolutionary War, Mexican American War, Korean War

ANSWER: the first major battle of the Civil War

QUESTION: What was the **Battle of Bull Run**?

HINT: Battle of Gettysburg, Battle of Bull Run, Trail of Tears, Antietam, the Alamo

ANSWER: the forced relocation of Native Americans to reservations in the Midwest

QUESTION: What was the **Trail of Tears**?

HINT: Constitutional Convention, Emancipation Proclamation, Trail of Tears, New Deal

ANSWER: the event that forced the United States into World War II

QUESTION: What was the bombing of **Pearl Harbor**?

HINT: bombing of Pearl Harbor, D day, Watergate, Boston Tea Party

ANSWER: the speech given by Dr. Martin Luther King Jr. on the steps of the Lincoln Memorial in 1963

QUESTION: What was the **"I have a dream" speech**?

HINT: Nobel Prize acceptance speech, "Our God is marching on" speech, "I have a dream" speech, "I've been to the mountaintop" speech

Category: World history

ANSWER: the land between the Tigris and Euphrates rivers where the Sumerians began building cities in 3500 BC

QUESTION: What was **Mesopotamia**?

HINT: Angel Island, Afro-Eurasia, Mesoamerica, Mesopotamia

ANSWER: the middle leg of the triangular trade route where African people were taken by force and sent by boat to America where they would become slaves

QUESTION: What was the **Middle Passage**?

HINT: Sugar Stretch, Middle Passage, Gin Run, the Hypotenuse

ANSWER: the empire that fell in 1453 when the Ottoman Turks invaded and captured Constantinople

QUESTION: What was the **Eastern Roman Empire**?

HINT: Western Roman Empire, Eastern Roman Empire, Ottoman Empire, British Empire

ANSWER: the arrangement of stones in Great Britain constructed more than five thousand years ago for largely unknown purposes

QUESTION: What is **Stonehenge**?

HINT: the pyramids, Stonehenge, Cincinnatus, Confucius

ANSWER: the gods of Mt. Olympus, including Zeus and Hera

QUESTION: Who are **Greek gods and goddesses**?

HINT: Roman gods and goddesses, Latin gods and goddesses, American gods and goddesses, Greek gods and goddesses

Category: Government/Civics

ANSWER: the branch of government made up of the president of the United States

QUESTION: What is the **executive branch**?

HINT: executive branch, legislative branch, judicial branch, constitutional branch

ANSWER: the acts of voting, participation in the community, paying taxes, and obeying the law

QUESTION: What are **civic responsibilities**?

HINT: Bill of Rights, civic responsibilities, civil rights, peaceful demonstrations

ANSWER: the concept of a citizen's love of his or her country

QUESTION: What is **patriotism**?

HINT: campaigning, democracy, patriotism, diplomacy

ANSWER: the use of a political or government position to harm or take advantage of people

QUESTION: What is **abuse of power**?

HINT: compromise, discrimination, invasion of privacy, abuse of power

ANSWER: the Senate and the House of Representatives

QUESTION: What two bodies make up the **U.S. Congress**?

HINT: U.S. Congress, U.S. Supreme Court, U.S. labor union, U.S. democracy

Category: Economics

ANSWER: a system of commerce based on trades of goods and services rather than currency

QUESTION: What is the **barter system**?

HINT: currency system, barter system, communism, petition system

ANSWER: what every working U.S. citizen pays to fund national and state programs, pay government employees, and help keep up highways and bridges

QUESTION: What is **income tax**?

HINT: income tax, principle tax, treaty, welfare

ANSWER: a person who creates, organizes, and manages a company

QUESTION: What is an **entrepreneur**?

HINT: reformer, representative, entrepreneur, consumer

ANSWER: the money made beyond the cost of production

QUESTION: What is a **profit?**

HINT: credit, debt, contract, profit

ANSWER: the pay one receives for work

QUESTION: What is a **wage**?

HINT: credit, savings, wage, class

Category: Geography

ANSWER: a handmade object that is characteristic of an ancient culture

QUESTION: What is an **artifact**?

HINT: aqueduct, site, compass, artifact

ANSWER: Asia, Africa, Australia, North America, South America, Europe, and Antarctica

QUESTION: What are **continents**?

HINT: countries, continents, states, cities

ANSWER: a resource created by nature and used by humans for energy

QUESTION: What is a **natural resource?**

HINT: man-made resource, solar power, natural resource, water

ANSWER: the key at the bottom of a map that translates all of the symbols used

QUESTION: What is a **legend**?

HINT: legend, compass, cardinal direction, artifact

ANSWER: the large-scale production of crops or livestock

QUESTION: What is **agriculture**?

HINT: economics, Afghanistan, irrigation, agriculture

Middle School

Category: U.S. history

ANSWER: the period of time in the United States preceding the Civil War

QUESTION: What is **antebellum**?

HINT: Reconstruction, Great Depression, antebellum, progressive movement

ANSWER: the section of the Bill of Rights that guarantees freedom of speech

QUESTION: What is the **First Amendment?**

HINT: First Amendment, Second Amendment, Fourth Amendment, Sixth Amendment

ANSWER: the first land expedition to the Pacific Coast during the years of 1803 to 1806

QUESTION: What was the **Lewis and Clark expedition**?

HINT: Oregon Territory expedition, Lewis and Clark expedition, Little Rock expedition, Alaskan expedition

ANSWER: the proposed amendment regarding the rights of women that has been debated since 1972 but not fully ratified

QUESTION: What is the **equal rights amendment?**

HINT: civil rights amendment, equal rights amendment, separate but equal amendment, suffrage amendment

ANSWER: the wife of the president of the United States

QUESTION: Who is the **First Lady**?

HINT: Speaker of the House, congresswoman, First Lady, Mrs. President

Category: World history

ANSWER: the religiously motivated military campaigns that took place at the end of the eleventh century and went on for nearly two hundred years

QUESTION: What were the **Crusades**?

HINT: Holocaust, Crusades, French Revolution, Middle Ages

ANSWER: the conference attended in 1814–1815 by (primarily) representatives from Austria, the United Kingdom, Russia, France, and Prussia that served as a model to the League of Nations and the United Nations because of its goal of satisfying all nations after the downfall of Napoleon I

QUESTION: What was the **Congress of Vienna**?

HINT: Treaty of Versailles, Congress of Vienna, New Deal, Potsdam Agreement

ANSWER: the 1989 protest for democracy in Beijing that led to a massacre

QUESTION: What was **Tiananmen Square?**

HINT: Tiananmen Square, Bloody Sunday, Stalin's Purge, Crusades

ANSWER: on April 4, 1949, the United States joined this treaty in which all parties agreed that an attack on any of them would be considered an attack on all of them

QUESTION: What is **North Atlantic Treaty (NATO)**

HINT: North American Free Trade Agreement, United Nations, North Atlantic Treaty, Potsdam Agreement

ANSWER: an ancient and sacred city used for astronomical purposes in Peru

QUESTION: What is **Machu Picchu?**

HINT: Stonehenge, Tulum, Machu Picchu, Tijuana

Category: Government/Civics

ANSWER: the first step in the process of removing an American president from power

QUESTION: What is **impeachment?**

HINT: due process, ex post facto, impeachment, habeas corpus

ANSWER: the rights not defined by the U.S. Constitution, nor forbidden by individual states

QUESTION: What are **states' rights?**

HINT: civil rights, states' rights, right to free speech, right of appeal

ANSWER: the principle stating that every citizen should be afforded access to all rights granted by the government

QUESTION: What is **due process?**

HINT: ex post facto, habeas corpus, right of appeal, due process

ANSWER: the power the president has to initially disallow a law passed by Congress

QUESTION: What is **veto power?**

HINT: separation of powers, veto power, welfare sovereignty

ANSWER: the process an alien must go through to become an American citizen

QUESTION: What is **naturalization?**

HINT: emigration, preamble, public trial, naturalization

Category: Economics

ANSWER: the steady rise in costs because of an increase in the volume of money and the resulting decrease of its value

QUESTION: What is **inflation?**

HINT: inflation, income, deflation, equilibrium

ANSWER: the total market value of all goods and services produced within a country during a year

QUESTION: What is **gross domestic product**?

HINT: gross international product, net domestic product, gross domestic product, greatest common cost

ANSWER: a product made in our country that we ship internationally to be sold

QUESTION: What is an **export**?

HINT: export, import, trade, finance

ANSWER: a financial term that specifies what one country's currency is worth in terms of the currency of another country

QUESTION: What is the **exchange rate**?

HINT: human capital, exchange rate, international market, opportunity cost

ANSWER: the basic economic principle that outlines the relationship between how many people want a product (and how much they want it) and how much a supplier makes (and how much they charge)

QUESTION: What is the **law of supply and demand**?

HINT: gross domestic product, law of goods and services, law of supply and demand, pooled resources

Category: Geography

ANSWER: the consistent destruction of the Earth's forests without regrowth efforts

QUESTION: What is **deforestation**?

HINT: crop rotation, acid rain, extractive mining, deforestation

ANSWER: an embankment designed to prevent the flooding of a river or the flooding from a hurricane

QUESTION: What is a **levee**?

HINT: delta, levee, aqueduct, adaptation

ANSWER: a term that refers to the number of children under one year of age who die during a calendar year divided by the total number of infants born in a calendar year

QUESTION: What is **infant mortality rate**?

HINT: life expectancy rate, death rate, infant mortality rate, population density

ANSWER: the global sum of all ecosystems

QUESTION: What is the **biosphere**?

HINT: microclimate, biology, envirosphere, biosphere

ANSWER: the coldest and only treeless climate

QUESTION: What is the **tundra**?

HINT: tropical, grassland, tundra, desert

High School

Category: U.S. history

ANSWER: June 6, 1944

QUESTION: When was **D day?**

HINT: bombing of Pearl Harbor, D day, Bay of Pigs, V-Day

ANSWER: the failed U.S.-funded invasion of Cuba that led to the Cuban Missile Crisis

QUESTION: What is the **Bay of Pigs?**

HINT: Bay of Pigs, Iran-Contra Affair, Red Scare, Boer War

ANSWER: five days of riots that began over the Emancipation Proclamation and the newly instituted draft for all men considered citizens of the Union

QUESTION: What were the **New York City draft riots of 1863?**

HINT: Texas Revolution, Desert Storm, New York City draft riots of 1863, New York City draft riots of 1895

ANSWER: the 1896 court case that upheld racial segregation in the United States using the "separate but equal" concept

QUESTION: What was *Plessy v. Ferguson?*

HINT: *Dartmouth College v. Woodward, Plessy v. Ferguson, Gibbons v. Ogden, Roe v. Wade*

ANSWER: segregation that exists because of cultural practice and not because of law

QUESTION: What is **de facto segregation?**

HINT: de facto segregation, de jure segregation

Category: World history

ANSWER: the agreement that made possible Germany's annexation of a portion of Czechoslovakia

QUESTION: What was the **Munich Agreement of 1938?**

HINT: Geneva Accords, October Manifesto, Nazi-Soviet Non-Aggression Pact, Munich Agreement of 1938

ANSWER: the sickness that is reported to have killed between 20 and 40 million people in a single year

QUESTION: What was the **world influenza pandemic of 1918 to 1919?**

HINT: Black Death, Decembrist uprising, world influenza pandemic of 1918 to 1919, world influenza pandemic of 1818 to 1819

ANSWER: the two major Islamic groups in the Middle East

QUESTION: Who are the **Sunni** and the **Shiite** factions?

HINT: Israel and Palestine, Sunni and Shiite, Hutu and Tutsi, Tamil and Sinhalese

ANSWER: the war that took place in South Africa between 1899 and 1902

QUESTION: What was the **Boer War**?

HINT: Franco-Prussian War, Great War, Boer War, Sino-Japanese War

ANSWER: the notorious 1972 event that strengthened the IRA

QUESTION: What was **Bloody Sunday**?

HINT: Bloody Sunday, Black Legend, Black Death, May Fourth Movement

Category: Government/Civics

ANSWER: policies that attempt to promote racial diversity in employment practices and public education

QUESTION: What is **affirmative action**?

HINT: double jeopardy policies, free enterprise, Helsinki Accord, affirmative action

ANSWER: the subjecting of the defendant of a crime to a second trial despite having been exonerated or punished according to the outcome of a first trial

QUESTION: What is **double jeopardy**?

HINT: writ of habeas corpus, clear and present danger rule, exclusionary rule, double jeopardy

ANSWER: the government agency that tests pharmaceutical drugs before allowing them on the market

QUESTION: What is the **Food and Drug Administration**?

HINT: Federal Communications Commission, Food and Drug Administration, Federal Bureau of Investigation, Drug Enforcement Agency

ANSWER: the help the United States often provides to poor or war-torn countries

QUESTION: What is **humanitarian aid**?

HINT: humanitarian aid, statue laws, excise taxes, vigilantism

ANSWER: the voters in one district who are all represented by the same elected officials

QUESTION: What is a **constituency**?

HINT: distribution of power, body politic, conservation, constituency

Category: Economics

ANSWER: a study of economics in terms of individual areas of activity, such as firms, households, or prices

QUESTION: What is **microeconomics**?

HINT: macroeconomics, Reaganomics, microeconomics, pre-economics

ANSWER: a person who owns stock in a corporation and therefore receives dividends

QUESTION: Who is a **shareholder**?

HINT: cooperative, proprietor, shareholder, expenditure

ANSWER: a limit, determined by the government, on how much a price can go up on certain goods

QUESTION: What is **price control**?

HINT: price floor, price control, price stability, deregulation

ANSWER: the situation when there is more expenditure than there is revenue

QUESTION: What is a **budget deficit**?

HINT: budget surplus, budget deficit, fraud, depression

ANSWER: the central banking system of the United States created in 1913

QUESTION: What is the **Federal Reserve System**?

HINT: gross domestic product, federal tax revenue, Wall Street, Federal Reserve System

Category: Geography

ANSWER: this can be seen from space and is the largest single structure made of and by living organisms

QUESTION: What is the **Great Barrier Reef**?

HINT: Great Wall of China, Great Barrier Reef, Rocky Mountains, Polynesian Islands

ANSWER: the much-debated model designed to explain distribution of social groups in urban cities

QUESTION: What is the **concentric zone model**?

HINT: central place theory, concentric zone model, comparative advantage, eutrophication

ANSWER: the nearly extinct form of farming designed to feed only the family or families that work the land

QUESTION: What is **subsistence farming**?

HINT: subsistence farming, center-pivot irrigation, commercial farming, agribusiness

ANSWER: where roughly 75 percent of the world's active and dormant volcanoes are found

QUESTION: What is the **Ring of Fire**?

HINT: South African coastline, Ring of Fire, equator, equinox

ANSWER: data that are systematically collected regarding population, economy, industry, and geography

QUESTION: What is **census data**?

HINT: mortality rate, crude data, census district, census data

13

CLASSROOM FEUD

For lower and upper elementary, middle, and high school language arts, math, science, and social studies

Design

Classroom Feud, modeled after the game show *Family Feud*, can be used as review in any of the four major content areas (language arts, math, science, and social studies) at the lower and upper elementary, middle, and high school levels.

Materials

The material needs for this game vary. If you are using a pencil-and-paper approach, you will need note cards. If you want to display the game questions, you will need an overhead projector or something similar.

Set Up

As with *What Is the Question?*, prepare the game questions ahead of time. Make sure there are at least as many questions as there are students in the class. You can use multiple-choice, short-answer, or fill-in-the-blank formats for your questions, but make sure you have approximately an even number of questions using each format. For example, if you have five multiple-choice questions, it is best to have five fill-in-the-blank questions as well. Also keep in mind that fill-in-the-blank items are more difficult because they require the student to recall the answer, while multiple-choice and alternative-choice items require only that students recognize the correct answer. Students will have a very limited period of time to answer, so if you are using a short-answer format, make sure your questions allow for complete answers to be given quickly.

Play

Split the class into two teams and tell each team to identify an initial spokesperson. The spokesperson's job is to confer with his or her team during the time allotted (usually fifteen seconds) and either deliver the agreed-upon answer, or make the ultimate decision in the case of a disagreement. Each time the team gets a turn, a new student acts as the spokesperson.

To begin the game, flip a coin to see which team goes first. You will act as the mediator, giving the first team a question. You can say it out loud and/or display it on an overhead projector. The team has fifteen seconds (or some set amount of time) to confer and decide on an answer, which is delivered aloud by the spokesperson. If the answer is right, the team gets a point, and you give them another question. If they are wrong, the other team gets a chance to answer the question and steal the point. If neither team has answered correctly, you can provide a hint and give both teams another chance. Whoever comes up with the correct answer first (within the allotted time) wins the point and the next turn.

If you wish, you can modify the game by categorizing the terms and announcing the category as a clue before you read off the question. You can also get creative by offering bonus rounds. Finally, instead of preparing questions for each term, you might simply present terms to students who are then required to provide the correct definition. The simpler rules of *Classroom Feud* allow you to easily make fun or appropriate modifications as you see fit.

Vocabulary Words

Guidelines for choosing terms for this game are much the same as the guidelines for *What Is the Question?* You should modify the game and the sample items provided to suit your purposes. In the following text, we have provided twenty to thirty sample *Classroom Feud* questions at the lower and upper elementary, middle, and high school levels in each of the four major content areas. The terms in bold are those that appear in the appendix (page 203); they are the vocabulary words compiled from extensive research with various schools, districts, and states. Because this game is about recall, you should use the fill-in-the-blank format for the majority of your game items. To show a variety of question formats, however, we have also included a few alternative-choice and true/false items; the proportion of fill-in-the-blank to these less-rigorous formats should be similar to what we have provided here. Because fill-in-the-blank items do require recall, we have also provided multiple-choice hints if your class is having difficulty. You can offer students a list of either two or four terms, one of which is correct. With the multiple-choice hints, students must only recognize the correct answer instead of recalling it. The less-rigorous question formats—alternative-choice and true/false items—require only recognition, so these items do not need hints.

As mentioned previously, use the multiple-choice hints sparingly as they change the rigor of the game item. While you certainly want to make the game fun and encourage students' success, too much generosity with the multiple-choice hints will restrict the learning directly associated with the game.

Language Arts

Lower Elementary

"Little Miss Muffet" is an example of _____.

A. an author
B. a **poem**
C. a date
D. a sign

If two things are not alike, they are _____.

A. the same
B. between
C. **different**
D. cartoons

When two people are talking, they are having a _____.

A. **conversation**
B. vocabulary
C. chapter
D. fairy tale

The person a story is about is called the _____.

A. symbol
B. **main character**
C. theater
D. villain

The blank spaces at the top and bottom and on both sides of a page are called _____.

A. **margins**
B. typings
C. front covers
D. rhymes

Someone who comes to school to talk about something he or she does for a living is a _____.

A. main idea
B. sentence
C. **guest speaker**
D. photographer

Putting the right letters together to make a word is called _____.

A. drawing
B. **spelling**
C. mapping
D. signing

To see a movie or a play, you would go to a _____.

A. conversation

B. map

C. **theater**

D. gym

? $ * & % These are _____.

A. **symbols**

B. words

C. letters

D. none of the above

Reading a story you have read before is called _____.

A. rhyming

B. cheating

C. **rereading**

D. none of the above

Letters that are not vowels are called _____.

A. syllables

B. characters

C. nouns

D. **consonants**

The bad guy in a book or movie is called the _____.

A. main character

B. cowboy

C. consonant

D. **villain**

A book used for classroom assignments and reading is called a _____.

A. fairy tale

B. magazine

C. **textbook**

D. title page

The name of a book is called its _____.

  A. **title**
  B. illustrator
  C. cover
  D. author

Jotting down writing ideas, creating idea webs, and creating outlines are all examples of _____.

  A. retelling
  B. **prewriting** (or **prewriting strategies**)
  C. keyboarding
  D. spelling

Sentences are made of individual _____.

  A. vowels
  B. characters
  C. **words**
  D. pictures

English is the _____ we speak in the United States.

  A. alphabet
  B. **language**
  C. letter
  D. magazine

To make sure everyone gets what they need while using class supplies, it is important that we all _____.

  A. read
  B. **share**
  C. pout
  D. draw

The collection of all of the words you know is called your _____.

  A. **vocabulary**
  B. author
  C. title
  D. last name

To figure out where you are going when in an unfamiliar place, you would look at a _____.

A. picture book
B. letter
C. **map**
D. movie

Making a guess about what will happen in a book or movie is called making a _____.

A. character
B. title
C. rule
D. **prediction**

The first word in the beginning of a sentence needs a _____.

A. vowel
B. **capital letter**
C. lowercase letter
D. date

These are all examples of _____.

A. **signs**
B. mirrors
C. letters
D. sentences

A person who risks his or her life to save someone else is called a _____.

A. mom
B. teacher
C. student
D. **hero**

The **initial** letter in the word *lizard* is _____.

> A. *l*
>
> B. *z*
>
> C. *r*
>
> D. *d*

ANSWER: A

When you start reading a book, you start at the _____.

> A. middle
>
> B. **beginning**
>
> C. end
>
> D. none of the above

When an author has something specific he or she wants to say, he or she has a _____.

> A. title
>
> B. word
>
> C. question
>
> D. **purpose**

Upper Elementary

Finding similarities and differences between two or more things is called _____.

> A. cause and effect
>
> B. **comparing**
>
> C. listing
>
> D. satire

A person who performs a play or script for an audience is called _____.

> A. an author
>
> B. a tyrant
>
> C. a sibling
>
> D. an **actor**

Artists used _____ to create *Kung Fu Panda* and *Toy Story*.

> A. comparison
>
> B. **animation**
>
> C. summary
>
> D. none of the above

In the sentence, "Lindsay has written a letter to her pen pal," the word *has* is _____.

  A. an **auxiliary verb**
  B. a subject
  C. a proper noun
  D. a common verb

The part of an essay that sums up the argument and the main points is called the _____.

  A. **conclusion**
  B. resolution
  C. quiz
  D. outline

Which of the following is an example of a **custom**?

  A. Every year at Christmas, Uncle Foster puts on his Santa suit and falls off the roof.
  B. Socks are the dumbest Christmas present.
  C. Last year my brother broke one of his presents before he even unwrapped it.
  D. Don't tell anyone, but Santa kind of scares me.

ANSWER: A

The person who films, alters, and edits a movie or play is called _____.

  A. the **director**
  B. Stephen Spielberg
  C. the producer
  D. the actor

Character, setting, and plot are all examples of _____.

  A. rules of grammar
  B. supporting details
  C. **story elements**
  D. multi-meaning words

When writing a research paper, you give credit to ideas and exact quotes from outside sources by providing _____.

  A. a summary
  B. an editor
  C. a period
  D. a **citation**

A short paper that informs or persuades is called _____.

A. bossy

B. an **essay**

C. a novel

D. a parody

Which of the following sentences uses **third-person** narration?

A. Angela didn't know that Perry was really an alien.

B. You should always put your elbow in your ear.

C. We played "Ring Around the Rosie" until we all fell down.

D. My dog Pooches likes to bark at the bird.

ANSWER: A

Which of the following is an example of **literature**?

A. the Mario Brothers video game

B. a commercial for soap

C. the book *Oliver Twist* by Charles Dickens

D. the Boy Scouts' handbook

ANSWER: C

When you check your work to make sure your sentences are complete, and you are using correct punctuation, you are paying attention to _____.

A. **grammar**

B. citation

C. story elements

D. none of the above

Which of the following is a **how question**?

A. Why can't all cars be bumper cars?

B. Are the London bridges really falling down?

C. Is the moon made of cheese?

D. How much wood would a woodchuck chuck if a woodchuck could chuck wood?

ANSWER: D

In the sentence, "Everyone feels sleepy after eating Thanksgiving dinner," the word *feels* is a
_____.

A. comma
B. proper noun
C. **linking verb**
D. adjective

Most sentences end with a _____.

A. comma
B. prefix
C. colon
D. **period**

If you have done something to hurt someone's feelings, you should _____.

A. brag
B. **apologize**
C. stand in line
D. draw

"How come Annie won't go to sleep?" is an example of a _____ question.

A. **why**
B. who
C. where
D. what

A section in the back of the book that defines all relevant terms used in the text is called _____.

A. a map
B. an index
C. a **glossary**
D. a mistake

Name a **minor character** in any book we have read in class this year. (Note: Create four choices
from books your class has read.)

Fiction, nonfiction, and poetry are all examples of different _____.

A. checklists

B. citations

C. myths

D. **genres**

What type of punctuation should end the following sentence: Where did you get that sweater

_____

A. **question mark**

B. comma

C. semicolon

D. plus sign

"At what time will the parade begin?" is an example of a _____ question.

A. where

B. how

C. **when**

D. who

"Is the statue in the same place?" is an example of a _____ question.

A. when

B. **where**

C. how

D. who

A book that contains facts about many subjects listed alphabetically is called _____.

A. a glossary

B. an almanac

C. an **encyclopedia**

D. a dictionary

"Ack" words like *tack*, *bracket*, and *knack* are all part of the same _____.

A. reading strategy

B. story map

C. **word family**

D. verb

The reason a character has for doing something is called his or her _____.

A. **motivation**

B. prop

C. rating

D. cue

Middle School

Which of the following is an example of **body language**?

A. Frank getting Lucia's attention by yelling out her name

B. Lucia flirting with Ira by making eye contact and smiling

C. Lucia asking Margaret to join her dance class

D. Margaret getting Frank's attention by pushing him down

ANSWER: B

Words appearing at the beginning of a sentence such as *although*, *when*, *before*, and *unless* signify the presence of what?

A. an independent clause

B. a **dependent clause**

C. a complete clause

D. an incomplete clause

In the United Kingdom, different words, phrases, and accents are used in writing and in speech. This is an example of what?

A. different religions

B. different populations

C. different points of view

D. different **dialects**

A film intended to provide information or insight into real people or a real issue is called _____.

A. a play

B. a **documentary**

C. literature

D. none of the above

Which of the following is not a **proverb**?

   A. between a rock and a hard place
   B. from the frying pan into the fire
   c. apple of my eye
   D. two sides of the same coin

ANSWER: C (an idiom)

Which of the following is not an example of a **contract**?

   A. the promise Emily made to Kristin to return the sweater she borrowed
   B. a marriage license
   c. the papers James signed when he bought a car
   D. a lease Penny signed when she moved into an apartment

ANSWER: A

Which of the following is not an example of good **etiquette**?

   A. putting your napkin in your lap at the beginning of a meal
   B. saying *please* and *thank you*
   c. cutting in line
   D. chewing with your mouth closed

ANSWER: C

What is the name of the genre in which play or movie actors sing instead of speak?

   A. radio
   B. **musical**
   c. songstress
   D. documentary

Name the italicized portion of the following sentence: "*Carl wanted to go to the concert,* but Ben didn't."

   A. the **independent clause**
   B. the dependent clause
   c. the adjective
   D. the noun phrase

If you are writing a paper to try to convince a reader about something, you are trying to be _____.

   A. hostile
   B. **persuasive**
   c. cool
   D. personified

To **synthesize** is to _____.

> A. add music to a piece of writing or video
> B. determine the irrelevant elements of an idea or an argument
> C. form an idea or argument by combining specific elements
> D. create an outline for a research paper

ANSWER: C

Many cultures have passed stories down through generations without ever writing them down. This is called _____.

> A. an **oral tradition**
> B. a verbal contract
> C. a viewpoint
> D. a dialect

Which of the following is not a **visual aid**?

> A. a diorama picturing a scene from a book and used for an oral book report
> B. a bar graph showing data being discussed by a presenter
> C. the bald eagle a guest speaker brings in when talking about wildlife conservation
> D. the photograph of his children that Keith keeps in his wallet

ANSWER: D

Writing for the purpose of explanation or to convey information is called _____.

> A. narrative writing
> B. scientific method
> C. **expository writing**
> D. summary

Which of the following defines **interpretation**?

> A. a conception of the meaning of an artistic or creative expression
> B. insight an author gives into a specific world or character
> C. modern performances of classic plays
> D. an accurate summary of events in a story or play

ANSWER: A

The opening of a letter is called the _____.

> A. closing
> B. body
> C. **salutation**
> D. complaint

A person who creates the dialogue for a play, movie, or television show is called the _____.

A. main character
B. director
C. **scriptwriter**
D. audience

A newspaper article in which the author states his viewpoint is called _____.

A. an **editorial**
B. a crawler
C. an exposé
D. a short story

The way a story ends is called the _____.

A. climax
B. **resolution**
C. projection
D. commencement

Memorizing the exact words of a poem or passage and reading them aloud is called _____.

A. proverb
B. dialogue
C. interior monologue
D. **recitation**

Using the exact language or ideas of another author in your work without proper citation is called _____.

A. personification
B. **plagiarism**
C. perspective
D. parallel structure

The process of forming overall ideas, opinions, or rules about something based on specific instances is called _____.

A. juxtaposition
B. etymology
C. **generalization**
D. specification

The rate at which the events in a text happen is called _____.

A. mood
B. tone
C. diction
D. **pacing**

A writer who raises the reader's anticipation level in a story about what will happen next is using _____.

A. tone
B. diction
C. **tension**
D. dialogue

To convey excitement in a sentence, you might end it with _____.

A. a question mark
B. an **exclamation mark**
C. a dash
D. a backslash

The basic rhythm structure of a poem is called its _____.

A. rhyme
B. conjunction
C. **meter**
D. syllabication

The slanted font style used for book titles or to put *emphasis* on a word or phrase is called _____.

A. Times New Roman
B. **italics**
C. caps lock
D. Arial

The specific group of people an advertisement is trying to appeal to is called the _____.

A. public audience
B. mass media
C. editorial audience
D. **target audience**

High School

A fictional character or a fictional act a person puts on to impress others is called the _____.

A. **persona**
B. couplet
C. irony
D. diction

Dictation can be defined as _____.

A. an author's word choice
B. the physical act of writing down what someone says
C. a fictional conversation between two or more characters
D. a persuasive technique used in advertising campaigns

ANSWER: B

A conversation between two or more people that is performed instead of read is called _____.

A. diction
B. a soliloquy
C. **dramatic dialogue**
D. an assembly

A long poetic composition about the journey of a hero is called _____.

A. a sonnet
B. a genre
C. a persona
D. an **epic**

A main character in a play who is acting on misinformation or on a lack of information while the audience has full access to the play's reality is an example of _____.

A. verbal irony
B. situational irony
C. **dramatic irony**
D. tragic irony

The variety of props and decorations used in a play are called _____.

A. **set designs**
B. anecdotes
C. red herrings
D. analogies

Making a counter argument based on a personal attack rather than on fact is called _____.

A. **attack ad hominem**
B. a fallacy
C. transparency
D. an overgeneralization

A short and ordinary story told only for amusement is called an _____.

A. **anecdote**
B. antagonist
C. epic
D. ode

A poem that expresses great admiration or exaltation is called _____.

A. a lyrical poem
B. a sonnet
C. an epic
D. an **ode**

A bibliography that contains brief notes regarding each reference is called _____.

A. an **annotated bibliography**
B. a summary bibliography
C. a citation
D. none of the above

A person who has very clear motives or is obvious in what he or she wants is being _____.

A. ethical
B. **transparent**
C. credible
D. coherent

A standard or rule by which something or someone will be judged is called _____.

A. an artifact
B. an excerpt
c. an allusion
D. **criteria**

The set of circumstances or events of the text that precedes a particular situation, sentence, or word is called _____.

A. credit
B. inflection
c. **context**
D. persona

The written document that summarizes someone's personal work history and is given to a prospective employer at the time of an interview is _____.

A. a thesis
B. a redraft
c. an idiom
D. a **résumé**

A narrator who is not part of the story, but can be present in the story at all times and know everything about what each character is thinking and feeling is referred to as _____.

A. **omniscient**
B. omnibenevolent
c. second person
D. first person

Man vs. man, man vs. environment, man vs. himself, and man vs. the supernatural are all examples of _____.

A. climaxes
B. **conflicts**
c. chronologies
D. exposition

A formal event in which two people argue different sides of an issue is called a _____.

A. fight
B. mediation
C. **debate**
D. lecture

A meaning or intention that is open to multiple interpretations is said to be _____.

A. objective
B. elaborate
C. juxtaposed
D. **ambiguous**

An example of a **credible source** would be _____.

A. *Newsweek*
B. *US Weekly*
C. a commercial
D. a brochure

ANSWER: A

Creating a story and character through exclusive use of nonlinear interior monologue is called

_____.

A. **stream of consciousness**
B. flashback
C. personal narrative
D. memoir

The atmosphere or mood created in an environment is called _____.

A. setting
B. ambiguity
C. **ambience**
D. intonation

The standard or pattern of behaviors viewed as normal by society is called the _____.

A. logic

B. **norm**

C. logo

D. law

A short poem that expresses thought or feeling and is sometimes set to music is called a _____.

A. haiku

B. sonnet

C. **lyric poem**

D. couplet

The commercial industry dedicated to luring customers into buying products and services is called the _____ industry.

A. economic

B. genre

C. mass

D. **marketing**

Humor that uses irony to make fun of something is called _____.

A. **sarcasm**

B. slapstick

C. a documentary

D. projection

An idea that appears to contradict itself but is actually true is called _____.

A. irony

B. juxtaposition

C. a **paradox**

D. italic

Math

Lower Elementary

If you are second in line, you are _____ the first person.

- **A.** in front of
- **B. behind**
- **C.** between
- **D.** above

Can you **tell** what **time** it is?

- **A.** 7:00
- **B. 7:15**
- **C.** 7:30
- **D.** 7:45

ANSWER: B

What is this shape?

- **A.** square
- **B.** circle
- **C. triangle**
- **D.** rectangle

Draw a line you **estimate** to be an **inch** long.

- **A.** ━━━━━━
- **B.** ━━━━━━━━━
- **C.** ━━━━
- **D.** ━━━━━━━

ANSWER: A

True or false: 5 > 3
ANSWER: true (term is **greater than**)

True or false: 10 < 3
ANSWER: false (term is **less than**)

Name an object that is a **circle**.

> A. a book
> B. a television
> C. a quarter
> D. a cat

ANSWER: C

Name an item you **estimate** to be about a **foot** long.

> A. a fingernail
> B. a car
> C. a piece of copy paper
> D. your shadow

ANSWER: C

A **square** and a **rectangle** both have _____ corners.

> A. 0
> B. 2
> C. 3
> D. 4

ANSWER: D

Is the pen in the teacher's **left** or **right** hand?
ANSWER: right or **left** (Note: Requires a teacher's demonstration.)

In an Oreo cookie, the cream is _____ the two cookies.

> A. over
> B. to the left of
> C. to the right of
> D. **between**

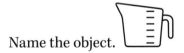

Name the object.

> A. a **measuring cup**
> B. a measuring spoon
> C. a saucepan
> D. a bottle

How long would you **estimate** it takes to brush your teeth?

A. 3 seconds
B. 3 **minutes**
C. 3 hours
D. 3 days

Are you most likely **outside** or **inside** when you go sledding?
ANSWER: outside

When kids go to bed on school nights, are they most likely **inside** or **outside**?
ANSWER: inside

Write a **subtraction** problem on the board.

A. $3 + 5 = 8$
B. $6 < 8$
C. $8 - 4 = 4$
D. none of the above

ANSWER: C

When you put your dinner on a plate, is the plate **under** or **over** your meal?
ANSWER: under

If there are five pieces of gum and I take two of them, what is the **difference**?

A. 2
B. 3
C. 4
D. 0

ANSWER: B

An airplane you build out of styrofoam is _____ of a real airplane.

A. a **model**
B. an estimate
C. a year
D. none of the above

If you have three peanuts and I have three peanuts, what is the **sum**?

A. 0
B. 2
C. 6
D. 10

ANSWER: C

If you are making a guess about how something will turn out, what are you doing?

A. **predicting**
B. adding
C. measuring
D. none of the above

If you are measuring how much water a glass can hold, you are measuring _____.

A. weight
B. length
C. **volume**
D. size

If you are in the driver's seat of a car, are you on the **left** or **right** side?
ANSWER: **left**

3, 7, 17, and 25 are all _____.

A. letters
B. **numbers**
C. sums
D. shapes

If you are measuring how tall you are, you are measuring your _____.

A. weight
B. **height**
C. shape
D. strength

Upper Elementary

Write a number that has 2 as its **denominator**.

A. 1/2
B. 2/3
C. 1.25
D. none of the above

ANSWER: A

∠ ∠ ＼ ∟   These are _____.

A. **angles**

B. rectangles

C. parallel lines

D. none of the above

The number of square units needed to cover a surface is referred to as _____.

A. **area**

B. perimeter

C. radius

D. circumference

"This pencil is six inches long" is an example of _____.

A. an estimate

B. a perimeter

C. a **measurement**

D. a number sentence

Name a **multiple** of 3.

A. 0

B. 1

C. 5

D. 9

ANSWER: D

Create an example of a **number sentence**.

A. 1, 4, 7

B. 50%

C. 3 + 5 = 8

D. 7 − 2

ANSWER: C

Write a number that has 3 in the **thousands place**.

A. 350

B. .035

C. 3,500

D. .0035

ANSWER: C

Name a set of **corresponding sides**.

A. BC and FE

B. AD and EH

C. CD and FG

D. BA and GH

ANSWER: B

The number to be divided in a division problem is _____.

A. the **dividend**

B. the divisor

C. the minuend

D. the addend

The amount a container can hold when filled is called its _____.

A. volume

B. **capacity**

C. density

D. data

If two numbers are equal in value, they are said to be _____.

A. median

B. similar

C. opposites

D. **equivalent**

Which property states that any number multiplied by one equals the original number?

A. inverse property

B. transitive property

C. **identity property**

D. reciprocal property

Write two **equivalent fractions**.

A. 2/3 and 4/12
B. 1/2 and 4/6
C. 4/7 and 5/10
D. 3/9 and 1/3

ANSWER: D

The following lines are _____.

A. parallel
B. perpendicular
C. vertices
D. **intersecting**

The **mean** of 0, 5, 4, 6, 9 is (rounded to the nearest whole number) _____.

A. 10
B. 8
C. 5
D. 4

ANSWER: C

A line extending from an inside edge of a circle to a point in the circle's center is called the _____.

A. circumference
B. perimeter
C. diameter
D. **radius**

True or false: A shape measured in length and width is **two-dimensional**.
ANSWER: true

True or false: **Probability** refers to the likelihood of an event happening.
ANSWER: true

True or false: The result or answer to a multiplication problem is the **product**.
ANSWER: true

True or false: The **remainder** of 16 ÷ 3 is 2.
ANSWER: false

In the number 178.60, the 6 is in the _____ place.

A. tens place

B. hundreds place

C. **tenths place**

D. hundredths place

The number that appears most often in a set of data is called the _____.

A. mean

B. median

C. **mode**

D. measure

True or false: Numbers with quantities less than zero are called **negative numbers**.

ANSWER: true

The number 2.36 **rounded** to the nearest whole number is _____.

A. 2.4

B. 3

C. 2

D. 2.3

ANSWER: C

Middle School

What is the definition of a **composite number**?

A. a number that can be divided evenly by numbers other than 1 or itself

B. a number that can be divided evenly only by 1 or itself

C. a number that can be used for counting

D. a number that can be expressed as a ratio of two integers

ANSWER: A

In mathematics, a **conjecture** is _____.

A. a special formula that can be used to solve an equation

B. a special classification for geometric shapes

C. a mathematical statement that has been formally proven to be true

D. a mathematical statement that appears likely to be true

ANSWER: D

In mathematics, **evaluate** means _____.

> A. to substitute values in a formula
> B. to substitute variables in an equation
> C. to calculate the algebraic value
> D. to calculate the numerical value

ANSWER: D

Write an example of a **function**.

> A. $d = rt$
> B. $x + 2 - 4x$
> C. $f(x) = 2x + 6$
> D. $42 > 35 - 7$

ANSWER: C

The **additive inverse** of 10 is _____.

> A. 100
> B. −10
> C. .1
> D. .5

ANSWER: B

Your chance of rolling a three on a single six-sided die is referred to as _____.

> A. perimeter
> B. an inequality
> C. a simulation
> D. **probability**

What is the **reciprocal** for 2/3?

> A. 1/3
> B. 3/2
> C. 2 : 3
> D. 6

ANSWER: B

What is a **scale drawing**?

 A. a drawing that is a reduction of the original in exact proportions
 B. a drawing that is an enlargement of the original in exact proportions
 C. a drawing that is a copy of the original
 D. both a and b

ANSWER: D

Simplify 8/12.

 A. 4/6
 B. 2/3
 C. 1 4/12
 D. 12/8

ANSWER: B

A numerical value that provides information about the sample or population is called a _____.

 A. composite
 B. **statistic**
 C. scale
 D. tendency

A _____ is created when a shape is repeated over and over again without any gaps or overlaps.

 A. **tessellation**
 B. composite
 C. sample
 D. measure of central tendency

The best way to calculate the **area of a complex/irregular shape** is to _____.

 A. multiply the lengths of all the sides
 B. add the lengths of all the sides
 C. multiply the length of the longest side by the shortest angle
 D. break the complex shape into simpler shapes and add the areas of these shapes together

ANSWER: D

Representing the number 500,000,000 as 5×10^8 is referred to as _____.

A. standard notation
B. decimal notation
C. expanded notation
D. exponential notation

$2 \times 2 \times 2 \times 2$ written as an **exponent** is _____.

A. 2×10^4
B. 2^4
C. 16
D. 0

ANSWER: B

Name an instance in which you might find a **percent greater than 100**.

A. eating an entire pizza
B. getting all of the answers on a test correct as well as the extra credit question
C. staying awake for twenty-three hours
D. hitting a home run

ANSWER: B

The ratio of any circle's circumference to its diameter is _____.

A. its radius
B. 3/5
C. 1/2
D. pi

True or false: 5/4 is a **rational number.**
ANSWER: true

A diagram with both a horizontal and vertical axis used to show a positive or negative correlation is called _____.

A. a scatter plot
B. the x and y axes
C. **a coordinate plane**
D. a triangular plane

True or false: Two angles are **complementary** if they add up to 90°.
ANSWER: true

True or false: **Cost per unit** can be calculated by dividing the total cost by the total number of units.
ANSWER: true

$d = rt$ is a formula that can be used to calculate _____.

  A. pi
  B. slope
  C. speed
  D. distance

$y = mx + b$ is the _____.

  A. y axis formula
  B. slope-intercept formula
  C. quadratic equation formula
  D. linear arithmetic sequence

A number that has a square root without decimals is _____.

  A. a prime factor
  B. an even number
  C. unknown
  D. a **perfect square**

Two angles with measures that add up to 180° are called _____.

  A. complementary angles
  B. supplementary angles
  C. congruent angles
  D. acute angles

Name this shape: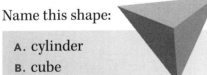

  A. cylinder
  B. cube
  C. tetrahedron
  D. octahedron

High School

True or false: $f(x) = 4(x) + 9$ is a **function notation**.
ANSWER: true

What is the definition for an **inverse function**?

- **A.** The domain of f is equal to the range of f, and the domain of f^{-1} and the range of f is equal to the range of f^{-1}.
- **B.** Each ordered pair in a function is placed in reverse order.
- **C.** Each positive number in the domain and the range becomes negative and each negative number becomes positive.
- **D.** The domain of f is equal to the range of f^{-1}, and the range of f is equal to the domain of f^{-1}.

ANSWER: D

True or false: $3x + 4y = 18$ is an example of a **linear system**.
ANSWER: false

What does the **midpoint formula** find?

- **A.** the average length of a line on a graph
- **B.** the average length of any two lines on a graph
- **C.** the point exactly in the middle of two other points on a Cartesian plane
- **D.** the point exactly in the middle of two lines

ANSWER: C

Equations of the second degree, such as $ax^2 + bx + c = 0$ are called _____.

- **A.** permutations
- **B.** linear systems
- **C.** the slope
- **D. quadratic equations**

A quadratic equation that doesn't factor can be solved by _____.

- **A.** setting the equation equal to zero
- **B. completing the square**
- **C.** using a radical equation
- **D.** using factorials

Any number using a real number as well as an imaginary number, noted with "i" is referred to as _____.

A. an **irrational number**

B. a complex number

C. a factorial

D. none of the above

The intersection of a plane and a cone that creates shapes such as circle, ellipse, parabola, and hyperbola is called _____.

A. a Cartesian plane

B. a complex number

C. a **conic section**

D. a function

True or false: $(a + bi) + (a - bi)$ is a **complex conjugate**.
ANSWER: false ($\bar{z} = a - bi$ is a complex conjugate)

To **bisect** an angle is to _____.

A. divide it into two congruent angles

B. add a supplementary angle

C. add a complementary angle

D. divide it into two 90° angles

ANSWER: A

Reaching a conclusion that is true by finding a set of related premises that are true is called _____.

A. **inductive reasoning**

B. deductive reasoning

C. a proof

D. a theorem

A figure that is completely contained within another figure, with as many points on each shape touching each other as possible is _____.

A. **inscribed**

B. an irregular figure

C. reflexive

D. symmetric

A logical proposition that has been demonstrated to be true in all situations is called _____.

A. a bisect
B. a **theorem**
C. a proof
D. similarity

A line that passes through two parallel lines at different points is called a _____.

A. chord
B. vector
C. **transversal**
D. tangent

True or false: A line that touches a curve at a point without crossing over is called a **secant**.
ANSWER: false

True or false: The **transitive property** can be stated as: if $a = b$ and $b = c$, then $a = c$.
ANSWER: true

Any of the methods for measuring variability of data (including standard deviation) are _____.

A. measures of central tendency
B. **measures of dispersion**
C. measures of standard deviation
D. indirect measures

Total surface area includes _____ while lateral surface area does not.

A. the **area of the bases**
B. the area of reflection
C. the area of the inside
D. the volume

The sum of a series is represented by the _____ notation.

A. Σ (**sigma**)
B. Δ (delta)
C. Ξ (xi)
D. Ω (omega)

```
          1
        1   1
      1   2   1
    1   3   3   1
  1   4   6   4   1
1  5  10  10   5   1
```
Identify the following: 1 6 15 20 15 6 1

A. Fibonacci sequence
B. Pythagorean theorem
C. **Pascal's triangle**
D. Bernoulli's triangle

An example of a **monomial** is _____.

A. $3x$
B. $16/x$
C. $4x^2 + 3b$
D. $5xy - y$

ANSWER: A

True or false: The **factorial** for 4 is $4 \times 4 \times 4 \times 4 = 4!$
ANSWER: false

True or false: The **reflexive property** can be stated as $a = a$.
ANSWER: true

A quantity that defines the characteristics of a function is called the _____.

A. **parameter**
B. permutation
C. postulation
D. phase shift

Science

Lower Elementary

Birds and reptiles are hatched from _____ when they are born.

A. clouds
B. **eggs**
C. pebbles
D. none of the above

Fish breathe underwater, but we breathe _____.

A. food

B. soil

C. **air**

D. water

A campfire is an example of which kind of reaction?

A. **burning**

B. freezing

C. running

D. none of the above

If you are using your nose, you are using your **sense** of _____.

A. sight

B. hearing

C. smell

D. skin

ANSWER: C

We are walking on the ground instead of floating in the air because of _____.

A. water

B. gas

C. **gravity**

D. the weather

Name a **machine**.

A. a dog

B. a computer

C. the sun

D. a year

ANSWER: B

All of outer space and everything in it is called the _____.

A. Earth

B. moon

C. sun

D. **universe**

To measure the length of your shoelace, you might use _____.

A. a **ruler**
B. a scale
C. a thermometer
D. none of the above

Snow, rain, and wind are all different types of _____.

A. stars
B. **weather**
C. mixtures
D. colors

When water turns to ice, does it **freeze** or **melt**?
ANSWER: freeze

Trees have roots that grow deep into the _____.

A. sky
B. shelter
C. **soil**
D. ocean

Does an engine move a train by pushing or pulling it?
ANSWER: **pulling** it

If you kick a ball, have you pushed it or pulled it?
ANSWER: **pushed** it

Our sun is an average _____.

A. moon
B. planet
C. **star**
D. cloud

Name something that can **vibrate**.

A. hula hoop
B. basketball
C. guitar string
D. sunglasses

ANSWER: C

Name an object that contains a simple or complex **computer**.

A. a car
B. a wall calendar
C. a book
D. a song

ANSWER: A

When a living being stops living, it _____.

A. is born
B. grows
C. **dies**
D. heats up

Put the following animals in order of **size**, biggest to smallest: bird, person, snail, whale.

A. snail, person, bird, whale
B. whale, person, bird, snail
C. person, whale, snail, bird
D. bird, whale, person, snail

ANSWER: B

Name a kind of **dinosaur**.

A. tyrannosaurus rex
B. iguana
C. tiger
D. rattlesnake

ANSWER: A

One **similarity** between birds and snakes is that they both _____.

A. have feathers
B. live in the water
C. lay eggs
D. live in cold environments

ANSWER: C

Where would you expect to find **sand**?

A. in a hotel room
B. in a forest
C. in a desert
D. none of the above

ANSWER: C

Our bodies use the food we eat to create _____.

A. rain
B. sound
C. **energy**
D. a magnet

When you mix Kool-Aid into water, the powder disappears because it _____.

A. **dissolves**
B. freezes
C. burns
D. none of the above

When animals and plants get bigger, they are _____.

A. being born
B. **growing**
C. dying
D. vibrating

The object that circles the Earth is called the _____.

A. sun
B. **moon**
C. magnet
D. machine

A very small rock is called a _____.

A. parent
B. **pebble**
C. ruler
D. night

Upper Elementary

The material that any physical object is made of is called _____.

A. an organism
B. photosynthesis
C. matter
D. **mass**

A plant's process of turning the energy from the sun into the food it needs to survive is called _____.

A. the life cycle
B. pollution
C. **photosynthesis**
D. photography

The Earth rotates in a circle by spinning on its _____.

A. orbit
B. lunar
C. **axis**
D. calendar

Rocks become smaller by a process known as _____.

A. evaporation
B. rotation
C. **weathering**
D. pollution

Bar graphs, scatter plots, and pie charts are all ways to display _____.

A. validity
B. **data**
C. temperature
D. mass

What is the **Earth's average temperature**?

A. 55 °F
B. 0 °F
C. 89 °F
D. 100 °F

ANSWER: A

When you use the raw materials of one object to make another object, the process is called
_____.

A. conservation
B. **recycling**
C. global warming
D. secondhand shopping

The naturally occurring water on the Earth that is free of salt is called _____.

A. ocean water
B. river water
C. **fresh water**
D. bottled water

When a parent passes on certain traits to a child, it is called _____.

A. a renewable resource
B. a mammal
C. **heredity**
D. a characteristic

What are the three major parts of **the water cycle**?

A. birth, growth, reproduction, death
B. mammals, reptiles, birds, fish
C. precipitation, evaporation, condensation
D. digestion, circulation, excretion

ANSWER: C

The **magnifying** device people use to see the objects in outer space more clearly is called _____.

A. a microscope
B. a telescope
C. an axis
D. a satellite

ANSWER: B

What is an example of a **technological advancement**?

A. the invention of penicillin
B. the Hubble space telescope
C. germ theory
D. Halley's comet

ANSWER: B

What is an example of **precipitation**?

A. a dry riverbed
B. a tornado
C. a rainstorm
D. a plant absorbing water for survival

ANSWER: C

Two like charges will _____.

A. remain neutral
B. attract
C. combine
D. **repel**

Gold, silver, and copper are all examples of _____.

A. alloys
B. **metals**
C. bases
D. circuits

Two or more cells that have been connected so that they can work together to independently create electric energy are called _____.

A. thermometers
B. **batteries**
C. remote controls
D. ice cubes

The largest planet in our solar system is _____.

A. Neptune
B. Mars
C. Earth
D. **Jupiter**

The eighth planet from the sun is _____.

A. **Neptune**
B. Mars
C. Earth
D. Jupiter

Taking scientific principles and advancements and applying them to society through things like bridge building and city planning is called _____.

A. biology
B. chemistry
C. physics
D. **engineering**

Is a body in motion using **kinetic energy** or **potential energy**?
ANSWER: kinetic energy

Creating a hypothesis, collecting data to test the hypothesis, recording results, and making a conclusion are all steps in a _____.

A. scientific cycle
B. **scientific experiment**
C. scientific reproduction
D. scientific observation

A substance that provides your body with the vitamins and minerals it needs is called a _____.

A. banana
B. metal
C. **nutrient**
D. disease

All of the members of one species in a particular place are called a _____.

A. **population**
B. offspring
C. tide
D. competition

The process of mature members of a species creating new members of the same species is called _____.

A. digestion
B. recycling
C. **reproduction**
D. migration

Is energy that is limitless in supply, like wind or solar energy, called **renewable energy** or **nonrenewable energy**?
ANSWER: renewable energy

Middle School

The body system made up of your bones is called the _____.

A. muscular system
B. **skeletal system**
C. respiratory system
D. immune system

Is the form of reproduction that requires one male parent and one female parent **asexual reproduction** or **sexual reproduction**?
ANSWER: sexual reproduction

Two species that are beneficial to each other in the same environment are engaging in _____.

  A. commensalism
  B. classification
  C. extinction
  D. **mutualism**

Bacteria are _____ organisms.

  A. **unicellular**
  B. complex
  C. abiotic
  D. decomposing

Any natural or man-made object that orbits a planet is called _____.

  A. an asteroid
  B. a moon
  C. a celestial body
  D. a **satellite**

The body system that allows you to move is the _____.

  A. excretory system
  B. **muscular system**
  C. respiratory system
  D. circulatory system

The process by which one body emits energy that travels through space and is then absorbed by another body is called _____.

  A. fission
  B. oxidation
  C. **radiation**
  D. convection

Electricity that comes from fission creates _____.

  A. gravitational power
  B. mechanical power
  C. renewable power
  D. **nuclear power**

True or false: **Sedimentary rock** is made of dirt that settles at the bottom of riverbeds.
ANSWER: false

Picking a person for your flag-football team because you like him and not because he is a good player is an example of _____.

A. birth
B. friction
C. the life cycle
D. **bias**

Name an **energy source**.

A. oil
B. bedrock
C. plastic
D. aluminum

ANSWER: A

Planets, stars, comets, and asteroids are all _____.

A. made of gas
B. orbiting the Earth
C. moons
D. **celestial bodies**

The energy stored in the covalent bonds between atoms in a molecule is known as _____.

A. sound
B. **chemical energy**
C. electrical energy
D. infrared radiation

The energy in electromagnetic waves is known as _____.

A. chemical energy
B. mechanical energy
C. **radiant energy**
D. nuclear energy

Chromosomes carry _____.

A. cytoplasm
B. **genes**
C. osmosis
D. lysosome

Sand and dirt settling to the bottom of a riverbed is an example of _____.

A. **sedimentation**
B. radiation
C. rusting
D. none of the above

Heat, pressure, and fluid can change one kind of rock into _____ rock.

A. igneous
B. sedimentary
C. **metamorphic**
D. limestone

True or false: Body tissues that form a unique structure and serve a specific purpose are called **organs**.
ANSWER: true

_____ made the first discovery of nuclear energy.

A. Isaac Newton
B. **Pierre Curie**
C. Marie Curie
D. Stephen Hawking

_____ is also known as "the father of modern science."

A. Stephen Hawking
B. Pierre Curie
C. **Galileo Galilei**
D. Nicolaus Copernicus

The system responsible for taking in oxygen and releasing carbon dioxide is the _____ system.

A. reproductive
B. circulatory
C. digestive
D. **respiratory**

The system responsible for getting rid of the body's waste is called the _____ system.

A. **excretory**
B. digestive
C. nervous
D. circulatory

An apple turning brown and a car fender rusting are both examples of _____.

A. homeostasis
B. **oxidation**
C. filtering
D. percolation

True or false: Examples of simple machines include **pulleys**, **levers**, and **wedges**.
ANSWER: true

High School

ATP or an electrochemical gradient used to transport molecules across a cell membrane is called _____.

A. **active transport**
B. passive transport
C. cellular respiration
D. homeostasis

One member of a pair that creates the gene for a given trait is called _____.

A. DNA replication
B. an organelle
C. a karyotype
D. an **allele**

The term used to describe the life cycle of plants, fungi, and protists is _____.

A. **alternation of generations**
B. biomass pyramid
C. DNA replication
D. evolution

The man who originally proposed the theory of plate tectonics was _____.

A. Charles Lyell
B. Copernicus
C. **Alfred Wegener**
D. Charles Darwin

A **biomolecule** can be made of any of the following: _____.

A. carbon, hydrogen, nitrogen, oxygen, phosphorous, sulfur
B. protons, electrons, neutrons
C. aerobic respiration, anaerobic respiration, fermentation
D. none of the above

ANSWER: A

_____ recognized and named oxygen and hydrogen and wrote the first list of elements.

A. Alfred Wegener
B. Pierre Curie
C. **Antoine Lavoisier**
D. none of the above

_____ states that equal volumes of perfect gasses contain the same number of particles or molecules when they are at the same temperature or pressure.

A. Bernoulli's principle
B. **Avogadro's hypothesis**
C. Coulomb's law
D. Doppler effect

The production of sex cells happens through the process called _____.

A. mitosis
B. **meiosis**
C. cellular respiration
D. none of the above

The reproduction of skin, hair, and heart cells happens through asexual reproduction known as

_____.

A. **mitosis**
B. meiosis
C. DNA replication
D. none of the above

The alternating high- and low-pressure areas caused by hot air rising and cold air sinking are called

_____.

A. acid rain
B. the **atmospheric cycle**
C. global warming
D. the tectonic cycle

_____ states that when there is a decrease in the pressure of a fluid, there is an increase in the speed of its flow.

A. Avogadro's hypothesis
B. **Bernoulli's principle**
C. theory of relativity
D. theory of plate tectonics

The tendency of certain minerals or rocks to break in a certain direction is called _____.

A. the geologic cycle
B. **fracture**
C. paleomagnetism
D. cleavage

Give an example of **geologic time**.

A. Precambrian
B. BC
C. AD
D. Iron Age

ANSWER: A

The principle that describes how waves will overlap and whether there will be constructive or destructive interference is known as _____.

A. **superposition**
B. inclination
C. pulsating theory
D. none of the above

When an unstable atomic nucleus loses energy by releasing ionizing particles and thus changes form, the process is known as _____.

A. a geo-chemical cycle
B. a solar flare
C. **radioactive decay**
D. uniform decay

The chemical element symbol of _____ is C.

A. chlorine
B. calcium
C. copper
D. **carbon**

Is a mixture with parts that can be mechanically separated (such as a salad) called a **heterogeneous mixture** or a **homogenous mixture**?
ANSWER: heterogeneous mixture

When two atoms share a pair of electrons, _____ bond is created.

A. an ionic
B. a **covalent**
C. a polar
D. a metallic

When a chemical bond is formed between two metallic elements in which electrons are able to move freely, the result is _____ bond.

A. an ionic
B. a covalent
C. a polar
D. a **metallic**

Is a wave with perpendicular particle displacement **longitudinal** or **transverse**?
ANSWER: transverse

The scientist best known for his theories of biological evolution and natural selection is _____.

A. Charles Lyell
B. Antoine Lavoisier
C. **Charles Darwin**
D. Enrico Fermi

An electrically charged (either positively or negatively) atom is called _____.

A. an isotope
B. an **ion**
C. a catalyst
D. a neutron

The geologist best known for influencing Charles Darwin was _____.

A. **Charles Lyell**
B. Antoine Lavoisier
C. Albert Einstein
D. Enrico Fermi

The first scientist to put forth a comprehensive heliocentric model was _____.

A. Ernest Rutherford
B. Johannes Kepler
C. Ptolemy
D. **Nicolaus Copernicus**

The process by which the like-charged nuclei of lighter atoms join to form nuclei of heavier atoms is called _____.

A. spontaneous nuclear reaction
B. nuclear fission
C. **nuclear fusion**
D. nuclear force

Social Studies

Lower Elementary

Where does the president of the United States live?

A. the **White House**
B. the Blue House
C. Mount Rushmore
D. Williamsburg

People go to work during the week to do their _____.

A. quarters
B. **jobs**
C. laws
D. decades

Dimes, nickels, quarters, and dollar bills are all examples of _____.

A. laws
B. holidays
C. **money**
D. none of the above

In the Revolutionary War, the United States fought against _____.

A. **England**
B. France
C. Germany
D. Italy

The total number of people who live in a town or city is called the _____.

A. capital
B. **population**
C. nation
D. none of the above

We elect our president by _____.

A. ruling
B. **voting**
C. starting a war
D. obeying

When you spend time helping other people or helping animals even though you don't have to, you are _____.

A. **volunteering**
B. transporting
C. racing
D. a citizen

You go to school so that you can get _____.

A. a cold
B. a law
C. an **education**
D. a vote

Telling the truth even when you don't want to is called _____.

A. religion
B. trading
C. volunteering
D. **honesty**

The U.S. national anthem is called _____.

A. the Pledge of Allegiance
B. **"The Star-Spangled Banner"**
C. the Statue of Liberty
D. the Sweet Land of Liberty

The study of the Earth and the populations on the earth is called _____.

A. **geography**
B. astronomy
C. history
D. democracy

A person who was born in a country is called _____ of that country.

A. a friend
B. an alien
C. a **citizen**
D. a family

The place where people keep their money is called the _____.

A. movies
B. debt
C. **bank**
D. none of the above

By doing your chores, you might _____ some money.

A. save
B. **earn**
C. spend
D. lose

Another word for the work a person does to make money is _____.

A. price
B. **labor**
C. business
D. advertising

The act of moving people or things from one place to another is called _____.

A. farming
B. a natural disaster
C. irrigation
D. **transportation**

People who lack material possessions and the money to buy necessities are _____.

A. **poor**
B. rich
C. dimes
D. buyers

Not spending your money so that you have more of it is called _____.

A. spending
B. **saving**
C. debt
D. selling

A very long trip can also be called a _____.

A. **journey**
B. prairie
C. town
D. week

Ancestors of the people who lived in North America before the arrival of Christopher Columbus are called _____.

A. Americans
B. Mexicans
C. Canadians
D. **Native Americans**

We know how hot or cold it is outside by measuring the _____.

A. miles
B. graphs
C. mountains
D. none of the above

ANSWER: D (The correct term is **temperature.**)

People who travel to places no one has been before are called _____.

A. **explorers**
B. policemen
C. ships
D. families

The idea that no one is better than anyone else and everyone should be treated the same is called

_____.

A. community
B. pioneering
C. **equality**
D. a myth

You can go to jail for breaking the _____.

   A. **law**
   B. crop
   C. job
   D. Liberty Bell

The products that are created and sold are called _____.

   A. **goods**
   B. services
   C. events
   D. beliefs

Name an example of a **monument**.

   A. Mount Rushmore
   B. the Grand Canyon
   C. Washington, D.C.
   D. the railroad

ANSWER: A

Activities you do just for fun are called _____.

   A. responsibilities
   B. ceremonies
   C. **hobbies**
   D. legends

When two countries use military force against each other they are in a _____.

   A. celebration
   B. **war**
   C. vote
   D. building

Giving a friend a granola bar because he or she gives you a sandwich is called a _____.

   A. **trade**
   B. debt
   C. loss
   D. profit

True or false: Events that haven't happened yet are in the **future**.
ANSWER: true

Upper Elementary

Provide an example of a **consumer**.

  A. a mother buying a dress for her daughter
  B. a mailman delivering mail
  C. a person grooming dogs for a fee
  D. a student creating a timeline

ANSWER: A

The fixed amount of money a person makes for regular work in a year is called _____.

  A. capital
  B. profit
  C. salary
  D. loan

The imaginary line over the Earth that separates two calendar days is called the _____.

  A. Antarctic circle
  B. equator
  C. North Pole
  D. international date line

A natural or man-made object that serves as a guide for travelers is called _____.

  A. an artifact
  B. a **landmark**
  C. a harbor
  D. a boundary

The imaginary lines such as the equator that run horizontally around the Earth measure _____.

  A. latitude
  B. longitude
  C. hemispheres
  D. timelines

The guide at the bottom of a map instructing the proper way to use the map is called the _____.

A. **legend**
B. population guide
C. color code
D. calculator

Name an example of a **product**.

A. electricity
B. a birthday party
C. a laptop computer
D. a weather forecast

ANSWER: C

The neighborhoods surrounding cities are commonly called the _____.

A. urban sprawl
B. rural areas
C. **suburbs**
D. construction sites

A city that is held sacred by the people of a particular religion is called a _____.

A. **holy city**
B. suburb
C. historic site
D. place of origin

The landmasses and the countries on the landmasses that surround the Pacific Ocean are called the _____.

A. Ring of Fire
B. Pacific route
C. **Pacific Rim**
D. Pacific waterway

The sections a city or town is divided into for election purposes are called _____.

A. **precincts**
B. provinces
C. plots
D. time zones

The imaginary lines such as the prime meridian that run vertically over the Earth measure _____.

A. latitude
B. **longitude**
C. hemispheres
D. timelines

Extreme hunger or starvation among a population of people is called _____.

A. crop failure
B. a drought
C. a plateau
D. a **famine**

A government in which power is invested in people or in elected officials is called _____.

A. a **democracy**
B. an autocracy
C. a mission
D. a constitution

An elected official who accepts bribes and spends public funds on himself or herself is an example of _____.

A. **corruption**
B. an empire
C. diplomacy
D. a motive

True or false: The United States was founded on the principles of **life, liberty, and the pursuit of happiness**.
ANSWER: true

The process by which the arriving immigrants from other countries explored and took ownership of the lands beyond the Mississippi River is called _____.

A. a trade route
B. the Seven Years' War
C. space exploration
D. **westward expansion**

A written request for something, often signed by many people who agree with the request, is called a _____.

   A. plague
   B. **petition**
   C. reform
   D. ritual

The group of eleven states that seceded from the United States was called the _____.

   A. Southern States of America
   B. **Confederate States of America**
   C. Slave States of America
   D. Union

The movement of African American literature and art that flourished in the years after World War I is called the _____.

   A. Black Reconstruction
   B. Prohibition
   C. Constitutional Convention
   D. **Harlem Renaissance**

The complaint of colonists that they still had to pay for a government in England that did not care about them was a major cause of the Revolutionary War. In protests, they chanted, "No _____ without _____!"

   A. **taxation without representation**
   B. draft without representation
   C. taxation without citizenship
   D. responsibility without freedom

The document written to detail the way the U.S. government would be structured is called the

_____.

   A. Declaration of Independence
   B. **U.S. Constitution**
   C. Articles of Confederation
   D. First Amendment

"We hold these truths to be self-evident, that all men are created equal, that they are endowed by their Creator with certain unalienable rights" is from the _____.

A. **Declaration of Independence**
B. U.S. Constitution
C. Articles of Confederation
D. First Amendment

A medication you receive to prevent getting a certain disease is called _____.

A. Tylenol
B. penicillin
C. a **vaccine**
D. a thermometer

A nation that takes land without permission is _____ it.

A. developing
B. **annexing**
C. employing
D. corrupting

The argument over the holy city of Jerusalem territory has caused much conflict between the _____ and _____.

A. **Israelis** and **Palestinians**
B. Jewish and Christians
C. Sunnis and Shiites
D. none of the above

During the late 1800s, most immigrants from Europe first stepped foot in the United States on _____ Island.

A. Angel
B. **Ellis**
C. Maui
D. Kodiak

We are living in the _____ century.

A. nineteenth
B. twentieth
C. **twenty-first**
D. twenty-second

A person who served in the military is known as _____.

A. a colonist
B. an immigrant
C. a **veteran**
D. a reformer

Middle School

Arms control is defined as _____.

A. any measure taken to restrict or reduce the number and type of weapons or armed forces a nation has
B. the attempt to disarm countries in the Middle East of their nuclear weapons
C. the law that states a person must have a license to possess a gun
D. the higher taxes people pay for owning weapons

ANSWER: A

Capital punishment is defined as _____.

A. a financial penalty paid in civil courts
B. a community service penalty for a small crime
C. a penalty of death for a crime
D. none of the above

ANSWER: C

The major religion that comes from the East and includes the idea of nirvana is called _____.

A. Hinduism
B. **Buddhism**
C. Islam
D. Judaism

The belief that you are reincarnated according to the kind of life you last lived belongs to which of the major world religions?

A. Christianity
B. Islam
C. **Hinduism**
D. Buddhism

Supplying land with water to grow crops is called _____.

A. **irrigation**
B. immigration
C. philosophy
D. drought

The farming system of varying which crops are planted on the same ground each year to avoid depleting the soil is called _____.

A. agricultural irrigation
B. **crop rotation**
C. subsistence farming
D. none of the above

The people who roam from place to place searching for work are called _____.

A. emigrants
B. **migrants**
C. pilgrims
D. citizens

The period of European history from roughly AD 476 to 1450 is called the _____.

A. Renaissance
B. **Middle Ages**
C. Ice Age
D. Punic Wars

The war that is rumored to have started over Helen of Troy is called the _____.

A. Punic Wars
B. Crimean War
C. Opium War
D. **Trojan War**

The clothing that is considered appropriate and inappropriate for school or work is determined by the _____.

   A. law

   B. code of conduct

   C. **dress code**

   D. honor code

Court decisions that spark a societal change are called _____.

   A. constitutional laws

   B. **landmark decisions**

   C. due process

   D. legislature

Betraying your country is known as _____.

   A. **treason**

   B. terrorism

   C. due process

   D. foreign aid

The preservation of natural resources to prevent destruction or exploitation of the environment is called _____.

   A. recycling

   B. **conservation**

   C. reforestation

   D. an embargo

Name an example of a **demographic.**

   A. a system of government

   B. a particular fact about a social society, such as level of education

   C. a model of the physical land in which a society lives

   D. a person who studies new inventions

ANSWER: B

Name an **Axis power.**

A. United States
B. Russia
C. Great Britain
D. Italy

ANSWER: D

The agreement ensuring free trade between Canada, the United States, and Mexico is called the _____.

A. North Atlantic Treaty Organization (NATO)
B. **North American Free Trade Agreement (NAFTA)**
C. United Nations (UN)
D. National Association for the Advancement of Colored People (NAACP)

The kind of mining that is most damaging to the environment because it destroys the Earth's surface above the product is called _____.

A. panning
B. immersion mining
C. **strip mining**
D. deep mining

The international organization founded after World War II with the intention of promoting world peace is called _____.

A. NATO
B. NAFTA
C. the **UN**
D. the NAACP

The unofficial war the United States engaged in between 1950 and 1953 is called the _____.

A. Trojan War
B. Crimean War
C. Vietnam War
D. **Korean War**

Violations of the established laws of war are called _____.

> A. a holocaust
> B. military tactics
> c. **war crimes**
> D. strikes

When two things are dependent on each other, they are _____.

> A. intradependent
> B. **interdependent**
> c. infrastructure
> D. federalism

The management of the resources of a community is called _____.

> A. a government
> B. an **economy**
> c. a religion
> D. a society

Reconstruction is defined as _____.

> A. the period of time before the Civil War
> B. the period of time after the Civil War
> c. the time during the Civil War
> D. the period of time after the Great Depression

ANSWER: B

The more than three billion people working in the world are collectively referred to as the _____.

> A. contract labor
> B. labor union
> c. labor market
> D. **labor force**

The money or other things of value given to a groom by the family of a bride at the time of marriage is called _____.

> A. interest
> B. tax
> c. a **dowry**
> D. a dissent

When a large group of people leave a place at once, it is known as _____.

A. a dissent

B. an **exodus**

C. a cosmos

D. an export

High School

The state of social and political disorder due to a complete lack of government is called _____.

A. communism

B. fascism

C. **anarchy**

D. civil disobedience

The total amount of goods and services demanded by a particular society in a particular time is called the _____.

A. compensatory demand

B. **aggregate demand**

C. aggregate supply

D. compensatory supply

A dispute can be resolved in a legally binding fashion outside of a court by _____.

A. meditation

B. **arbitration**

C. litigation

D. none of the above

When protestors refuse to buy products they find objectionable or products made by groups they find objectionable, they are _____.

A. arbitrating

B. using the business cycle

C. using Reaganomics

D. **boycotting**

When a union and an employer agree on the terms and conditions of employment in the name of all employees, this is called _____.

   A. collective reasoning
   B. **collective bargaining**
   C. Social Security
   D. deregulation

Change in the prices of goods and services is measured by _____.

   A. deregulation
   B. the standard of living
   C. vertical integration
   D. **the consumer price index**

Legally trying to influence the votes of elected officials is called _____.

   A. **lobbying**
   B. citizenry
   C. zoning
   D. bribery

Removing governmental controls, especially from an industry, is called _____.

   A. communism
   B. a business cycle
   C. entrepreneurship
   D. **deregulation**

Free enterprise is defined as _____.

   A. a market operating through the regulations of a federal government
   B. a market operating in a capitalist society based on supply and demand with little governmental intervention
   C. a market that dictates the rate of inflation through its investments
   D. a market that operates only in communist or socialist societies

ANSWER: B

Name something you might use **geographic information systems** for.

A. finding out the population of a country

B. tracing the roots of a major religion

C. trading one country's product with another

D. determining the response time for a natural disaster in a specific location

ANSWER: D

Indigenous is defined as _____.

A. foreign or imported

B. native or natural

C. growing or increasing

D. shrinking or decreasing

ANSWER: B

If you were studying the climate inside a cave you would be looking at _____.

A. a **microclimate**

B. a macroclimate

C. silting

D. a tectonic plate

A graph that represents the distribution of a population by factors such as age or sex is called _____.

A. a population slope

B. a **population pyramid**

C. a generation gap

D. a gross national product

Name an example of **regionalization**.

A. the signal distance of a radio station

B. the cultural differences of people in neighboring countries

C. the evening out of prices for trade between states

D. the lines drawn to dictate school districts

ANSWER: D

A _____ map shows geographical features such as elevation and vegetation.

A. physical
B. **topographical**
C. road
D. peripheral

A person who suffers torture or death rather than give up his or her religion is called a _____.

A. guerilla
B. mercenary
C. **martyr**
D. noble savage

Unverified or invalid information that cannot be proven as true is called _____.

A. circumstantial
B. **hearsay**
C. ideological
D. psyche

When one nation acts against another nation out of revenge, it is called _____.

A. secular ideology
B. wartime diplomacy
C. **retaliation**
D. nationalism

The man who created Wal-Mart is _____.

A. **Sam Walton**
B. Bill Gates
C. Warren Buffet
D. Clarence Thomas

The founder of Microsoft is _____.

A. Warren Buffet
B. Bernie Madoff
C. Joe Biden
D. **Bill Gates**

The empire that came to an end with the assassination of Franz Ferdinand and the onset of World War I was the _____.

A. Ghaznavid Empire
B. Iberian Empire
C. Mediterranean Empire
D. **Austrian/Hungarian Empire**

The custom practiced in China for nearly one thousand years that left many women and girls with severe deformities was _____.

A. Sufism
B. internment
C. **foot binding**
D. atonism

The idea that both geography and politics play a part in the fate of a nation is called _____.

A. **geopolitics**
B. agripolitics
C. national integrity
D. landmass politics

April 26, 1986, is the date of the _____ in the Soviet Union.

A. Bolshevik uprising
B. Red Scare
C. **Chernobyl nuclear disaster**
D. launch of the first space station

Giving someone money to influence his or her decision or change his or her behavior is called _____.

A. bait and switch
B. **bribery**
C. a warranty
D. Social Security

The power the government has to take private property for purposes of public use as long as compensation is given is called _____.

   A. free enterprise
   B. negative externality
   C. nonexclusion
   D. **eminent domain**

If you sue someone and go to court, you are engaging in _____.

   A. arbitration
   B. mediation
   C. **litigation**
   D. recitation

If you are called to the stand in a courtroom and you lie while under oath, you are committing _____.

   A. libel
   B. **perjury**
   C. referendum
   D. urban riot

APPENDIX

Table of Contents

The appendix contains academic terms only. It does not necessarily contain general vocabulary terms to be used for the games *Word Harvest*, *Name It!*, *Two of a Kind*, or *Opposites Attract*. For an extensive list of general vocabulary terms, consult *Teaching Basic and Advanced Vocabulary: A Framework for Direct Instruction* (Marzano, 2009). Each word is coded as a noun or noun phrase (n); a proper noun (pn); a verb (v); an adjective or adverb (adj/adv); or a preposition or prepositional phrase (p). Use these codes to help you choose terms for games. If a term or phrase can be used in more than one way, more than one code appears. Table A.1 is a reminder of the number of terms in each content area for lower elementary, upper elementary, middle school, and high school, and table A.2 is a reminder of the number of social studies terms in each category at the lower elementary, upper elementary, middle school, and high school levels.

Table A.1: Number of Terms by Content Area and Grade-Level Band

	Language arts	Math	Science	Social studies
Lower elementary	96	96	96	330
Upper elementary	251	190	179	1268
Middle school	253	204	218	1166
High school	217	218	299	1292

As table A.1 shows, social studies has more terms than the other three content areas. Because social studies is highly vocabulary oriented, we have split the terms at each grade-level band into the following categories: general history (applicable only to lower elementary), U.S. history, world history, civics, economics, and geography. This is shown in table A.2.

Table A.2: Number of Social Studies Terms by Category and Grade-Level Band

	General history	U.S. history	World history	Civics	Economics	Geography
Lower elementary	137	n/a	n/a	42	33	118
Upper elementary	n/a	265	358	182	100	363
Middle school	n/a	133	409	235	122	267
High school	n/a	156	392	233	224	286

Language Arts Terms

Lower Elementary

alphabet (n)

author (n)

back cover (n)

begin/beginning (v) (n) (adj)

beginning consonant (n)

blend (v) (n)

book (n)

capital letter (n)

cartoon (n)

chapter (n)

character (n)

compose/composition (v) (n)

complete sentence (n)

comprehend/comprehension (v) (n)

consonant/consonant blend (n)

converse/conversation (v) (n)

cover (v) (n)

date (n)

diary (n)

dictionary (n)

different (adj)

discuss/discussion (v) (n)

draw/drawing (v) (n)

end/ending (v) (n) (adj)

ending consonant (n)

everyday language (n)

fairy tale (n) (adj)

first name (n)

folk tale (n)

follow/give directions (v)

front cover (n)

group discussion (n)

guest speaker (n)

hero (n)

initial (n)

keyboard/keyboarding (v) (n)

language (n)

last name (n)

letter (n)

letter-sound relationship (n)

active listening/listening skill (n)

long vowel (n)

lowercase letter (n)

magazine (n)

main character (n)

main idea (n)

map (v) (n)

margin (n)

mental image (n)

menu (n)

message (n)

middle (n) (adj)

movie (n)

name (n)

newspaper (n)

number word (n)

order of events (n)

photograph (v) (n)

picture book (n)

picture dictionary (n)

poem (n)

predictable book (n)

prediction (n)

prewrite/prewriting strategies (v) (n)

print (v) (n)

publish (v)

purpose (n)

question (v) (n)

reread (v)

retell (v)

rhyme (v) (n)

same (adj)

short vowel (n)

sight word (n)

sign (v) (n)

speak/speech (v) (n)

spell/spelling (v) (n)

spelling pattern (n)

symbol (n)

table of contents (n)

take turns/share (v)

textbook (n)

theater (n)

title (n)

title page (n)

topic (n)

type (v) (n)

uppercase letter (n)

video/DVD (n)

villain (n)

vocabulary (n)

vowel (n)

vowel combination (n)

vowel sound (n)

webpage (n)

word (n)

Upper Elementary

abbreviate/abbreviation (v) (n)

action word (n)

act/actor (v) (n)

adjective (n)

adverb (n)

advertise/advertisement (v) (n)

affix (n)

animate/animation (v) (n)

antonym (n)

apologize/apology (v) (n)

apostrophe (n)

appendix (n)

ask permission (v)

audience (n)

audiotape (n)

auxiliary verb (n)

brainstorm (v)

capitalize/capitalization (v) (n)

card catalog (n)

cause-and-effect relationship (n)

central idea (n)

chapter title (n)

character development (n)

chart (v) (n)

checklist (n)

children's literature (n)

chronology (n)

cite/citation (v) (n)

closing sentence (n)

colon (n)

comma (n)

command (v) (n)

commercial (n)

common noun (n)

compare/comparison (v) (n)

complete sentence (n)

complex sentence (n)

compound word (n)

concluding statement (n)

conclude/conclusion (v) (n)

consonant substitution (n)

construct meaning (v)

content-area vocabulary (n)

context clue (n)

contraction (n)

contrast (v) (n)

cue (v) (n)

cursive (n)

custom (n)

declarative sentence (n)

decode (v)

define/definition (v) (n)

detail (v) (n)

diary (n)

directions (n)

direct/director (v) (n)

direct quote (n)

discussion/discussion leader (n)

double negative (n)

draft (v) (n)

drama (n)

edit (v)

email (v) (n)

encyclopedia (n)

end/ending (v) (n) (adj)

essay (n)

example (n)

explanation (n)

express/expression (v) (n)

fable (n)

fairy tale (n) (adj)

facial expression (n)

fact (n)

fantasy (n)

fiction (n)

first person (n)

form (v) (n)

friendly letter (n)

genre (n)

gesture (v) (n)

glossary (n)

grammar (n)

graphic artist (n)

graphic organizer (n)

graphics (n)

greet/greeting (v) (n)

guide word (n)

hardware (n)

heading (n)

headline (n)

host/hostess (v) (n)

how question (n)

humor (n)

illustrate/illustration (v) (n)

imagery (n)

indent/indentation (v) (n)

index (v) (n)

infer/inference (v) (n)

Internet (pn)

interrogative sentence (n)

introduce/introduction (v) (n)

investigate/investigation
  (v) (n)

invite/invitation (v) (n)

irregular plural noun (n)

journal (v) (n)

keyword (n)

learning log (n)

legend (n)

letter of request (n)

linking verb (n)

list (v) (n)

listening comprehension (n)

literature (n)

meaning clue (n)

memory aid (n)

minor character (n)

miscue (n)

mood (n)

motivate/motivation (v) (n)

multimeaning words (n)

multiple drafts (n)

multiple sources (n)

mystery (n)

myth (n)

negative (n) (adj)

news (n)

newspaper (n)

nonfiction (n)

note (v) (n)

noun (n)

novel (n)

numerical adjective (n)

object (v) (n)

opinion (n)

oral presentation (n)

organize/organization (v) (n)

outline (v) (n)

pamphlet (n)

paragraph (n)

passage (n)

past tense (n)

peer review (n)

pen pal (n)

period (n)

personal letter (n)

personal pronoun (n)

phone directory (n)

phonetic analysis (n)

phrase (v) (n)

pitch (v) (n)

play (v) (n)

plot (v) (n)

plot development (n)

plural (n) (adj)

point of view (n)

pose a question (v)

possessive noun (n)

possessive pronoun (n)

posture (n)

preface (v) (n)

prefix (n)

preposition (n)

prepositional phrase (n)

present/presentation (v) (n)

preview (v) (n)

prior knowledge (n)

pronoun (n)

pronounce (v)

proofread (v)

prop (v) (n)

proper noun (n)

punctuation (n)

question mark (n)

quote/quotation (v) (n)

rating (n)

r-controlled (n)

reading strategy (n)

reading vocabulary (n)

regular plural noun (n)

regular verb (n)

request (v) (n)

revise (v)

rhyming dictionary (n)

role-play (v)

root word (n)

rules of conversation (n)

run-on sentence (n)

scan (v) (n)

science fiction (n)

second person (n)

semicolon (n)

sensory details (n)

sentence fragment (n)

sentence structure (n)

sequential order (n)

set/setting (v) (n)

short story (n)

sign/signature (v) (n)

singular (n) (adj)

singular noun (n)

skim (v)

software (n)

sound effect (n)

source (n)

special effect (n)

spoken text (n)

stay on topic (v)

story elements (n)

story map (n)

story structure (n)

subject (n)

subject-verb agreement (n)

suffix (n)

summarize/summary (v) (n)

summary sentence (n)

supporting detail (n)

suspense (n)

syllabication (n)

syllable (n)

symbolism (n)

synonym (n)

table (n)

tall tale (n)

target language (n)

tense (n)

text (n)

thank-you letter (n)

theme (n)

theme music (n)

thesaurus (n)

third person (n)

timeline (n)

tone (n)

topic sentence (n)

typeface (n)

usage (n)

verb (n)

voice (n)

voice level (n)

volume (n)

website (n)

what question (n)

when question (n)

why question (n)

where question (n)

who question (n)

word choice (n)

word family (n)

word search (n)

written directions (n)

written exchange (n)

Middle School

action segment (n)

active listening/listener (n)

adjective clause (n)

adjective phrase (n)

adverb clause (n)

adverb phrase (n)

almanac (n)

Anglo-Saxon affix (n)

Anglo-Saxon root (n)

antagonist (n)

argue/argument (v) (n)

assume/assumption (v) (n)

atlas (n)

author's purpose (n)

autobiography (n)

background knowledge (n)

ballad (n)

bibliography (n)

biographical sketch (n)

biography (n)

body language (n)

body of the text (n)

broadcast (v) (n)

broadcast advertising (n)

business letter (n)

camera angle (n)

caption (n)

catalog (v) (n)

CD-ROM (n)

character trait (n)

children's program (n)

chronology (n)

clarify/clarification (v) (n)

climax (n)

close up (n) (p)

close (v) (adj) (p)

clue (n)

common feature (n)

comparative adjective (n)

compile (v)

composition structure (n)

compound sentence (n)

compound verb (n)

conjunction (n)

contract (v) (n)

convention (n)

coordinating conjunction (n)

criticize/criticism (v) (n)

cross-reference (v)

current affairs (n)

demonstrative pronoun (n)

dependent clause (n)

derive/derivation (v) (n)

descriptive language (n)

diagram (v) (n)

dialect (n)

dialogue (n)

document (v) (n)

documentary (n)

dramatize/dramatization (v) (n)

editorial (n)

elaborate (v) (adj)

electronic media (n)

enunciate/enunciation (v) (n)

episode (n)

etiquette (n)

etymology (n)

exclamation point (n)

exclamatory sentence (n)

explicit/implicit (adj)

expository writing/exposition (n)

extend invitation (v)

extraneous information (n)

eye contact (n)

facilitate/facilitator (v) (n)

fact (n)

familiar idiom (n)

feature story (n)

feedback (n)

figurative language (n)

figure of speech (n)

flashback (n)

fluency/fluent (n) (adj)

follow-up sentence (n)

footnote (n)

foreign word (n)

foreshadow (v)

formal language (n)

format (n)

future tense (n)

gender (n)

generalize/generalization (v) (n)

gerund/gerund phrase (n)

glittering generality (n)

grammatical form (n)

Greek affix (n)

Greek root (n)

haiku (n)

high-frequency word (n)

historical fiction (n)

historical theme (n)

homonym (n)

hyphen (n)

image/imagery (n)

imperative sentence (n)

inconsistency (n)

independent clause (n)

informal language (n)

information source (n)

interject/interjection (v) (n)

interpret/interpretation (v) (n)

interview (v) (n)

intonation (n)

irregular verb (n)

italics (n)

jargon (n)

juxtapose/juxtaposition (v) (n)

knowledge base (n)

language convention (n)

lay out/layout (v) (n)

lecture (v) (n)

line [in a play] (n)

literal phrase (n)

log (v) (n)

logic (n)

logical argument (n)

logo (n)

manner of speech (n)

mass media (n)

mechanics [of language] (n)

metaphor (n)

meter (n)

modify/modifier (v) (n)

monologue (n)

musical (n) (adj)

narrate/narration (v) (n)

native culture (n)

native speaker (n)

news broadcast (n)

news bulletin (n)

nonverbal cue (n)

object pronoun (n)

objective view (n)

opinion (n)

oral tradition (n)

pace/pacing (v) (n)

page format (n)

parallel episodes (n)

parallel structure (n)

paraphrase (v)

past tense (n)

peer-response group (n)

periodical (n)

personal narrative (n)

personify/personification
  (v) (n)

perspective (n)

persuade/persuasion (v) (n)

phrase grouping (n)

physical description (n)

physical gesture (n)

plagiarize/plagiarism (v) (n)

poetic element (n)

polite form (n)

political cartoonist (n)

political speech (n)

positive adjective (n)

predicate adjective (n)

present tense (n)

private audience (n)

problem-solution (n)

producer (n)

program/programming (v) (n)

project/projection (v) (n)

pronominal adjective (n)

proper adjective (n)

prose (n)

protagonist (n)

proverb (n)

public audience (n)

public opinion trend (n)

publication date (n)

pull-down menu (n)

quiz show (n)

recite/recitation (v) (n)

recurring theme (n)

reference source (n)

relative pronoun (n)

relevant detail (n)

rephrase (v)

report (v) (n)

represent/representation
  (v) (n)

research paper (n)

resolve/resolution (v) (n)

resource material (n)

restate/restatement (v) (n)

rhythm (n)

sales technique (n)

salutation (n)

saying (n)

scriptwriter (n)

self-edit (v)

sentence combining (n)

shades of meaning (n)

simile (n)

simple sentence (n)

sitcom (n)

skit (n)

slang (n)

slanted material (n)

small talk (n)

software (n)

sonnet (n)

sound system (n)

special interests (n)

specialized language (n)

speech pattern (n)

speed read (v)

stereotype (v) (n)

stress (v) (n)

stylistic feature (n)

subject pronoun (n)

subjective view (n)

subliminal message (n)

subordinate character (n)

subordinating conjunction (n)

subplot (n)

superlative adjective (n)

supernatural tale (n)

syllabic system (n)

syntax (n)

synthesize/synthesis (v) (n)

tabloid (n)

talk show (n)

target audience (n)

technical directions (n)

technical language (n)

tempo (n)

tension (n)

textual clue (n)

time lapse (n)

transition (v) (n)

translate/translation (v) (n)

trickster tale (n)

verb phrase (n)

verbal cue (n)

vernacular dialect (n)

viewer perception (n)

viewpoint (n)

visual aid (n)

voice inflection (n)

word borrowing (n)

word origin (n)

word play (n)

High School

acronym (n)

advertising code (n)

advertising copy (n)

aesthetic purpose (n)

aesthetic quality (n)

allegory (n)

alliteration (n)

allude/allusion (v) (n)

ambience (n)

ambiguous (n)

American literature (n)

American Psychological
　Association (pn)

analogy (n)

analyze/analysis (v) (n)

ancient literature (n)

anecdote (n)

annotated bibliography (n)

appeal to authority (v) (n)

appeal to emotion (v) (n)

appeal to logic (v) (n)

archetype/archetypal (n) (adj)

articulate/articulation (v) (n) (adj)

artifact (n)

assonance (n)

attack ad hominem (v)

autobiographical narrative (n)

bandwagon (n)

belief system (n)

bias (n)

biographical narrative (n)

blurring of genres (n)

British literature (n)

bylaw (n)

celebrity endorsement (n)

censor/censorship (v) (n)

characterize/characterization
　(v) (n)

cinematographer (n)

circumlocution (n)

clarity of purpose (n)

clincher sentence (n)

cognate (n)

coherence (n)

cohesion (n)

collective noun (n)

commercialize/
　commercialization (v) (n)

compound adjective (n)

compound noun (n)

compound personal pronoun (n)

compound-complex sentence (n)

computer-generated image (n)

concept (n)

conceptual map (n)

conflict [internal vs. external] (n)

conjunctive adverb (n)

connotative meaning (n)

consonance (n)

consumer document (n)

context (n)

contrasting expressions (n)

controlling idea (n)

copyright law (n)

correlative conjunction (n)

counterargument (n)

couplet (n)

credible source (n)

credit (v) (n)

criteria (n)

critical standard (n)

cultural agency (n)

cultural expression (n)

cultural influence (n)

cultural nuance (n)

cultural theme (n)

cutline (n)

dash (n)

debate (v) (n)

deconstruct (v)

deliver/delivery (v) (n)

denotative meaning (n)

dictate/dictation (v) (n)

diction (n)

digressive time (n)

direct address (n)

directionality (n)

divided quotation (n)

drama-documentary (n)

dramatic dialogue (n)

dramatic irony (n)

dramatic mood change (n)

emotional appeal (n)

emphasize/emphasis (v) (n)

epic poem (n)

ethics/ethical (n) (adj)

exaggerated claim (n)

excerpt (n)

expressive writing (n)

extended quotation (n)

false causality (n)

faulty mode of persuasion (n)

FCC regulation (n)

feature article (n)

fictional narrative (n)

field study (n)

film review (n)

filter [photography] (n)

friendly audience (n)

future perfect verb tense (n)

hierarchic structure (n)

Homeric Greek literature (n)

hostile audience (n)

hyperbole (n)

idiom (n)

incongruity (n)

indefinite adjective (n)

indefinite pronoun (n)

inflection (n)

interior monologue (n)

interrogative pronoun (n)

irony (n)

job application (n)

job interview (n)

Latin affix (n)

Latin root (n)

leave-taking (n)

limited point of view (n)

literary criticism (n)

literary device (n)

literature review (n)

logical fallacy (n)

logographic system (n)

lyric poem (n)

marketing (n)

media-generated image (n)

medieval literature (n)

medium (n) (adj)

memorandum (n)

methodology (n)

microfiche (n)

Modern Language Association (pn)

modern literature (n)

modulate/modulation (v) (n)

mythology (n)

narrate/narrator (v) (n)

negotiate/negotiation (v) (n)

neoclassic literature (n)

norm (n)

noun clause (n)

noun phrase (n)

nuance (n)

ode (n)

omniscient point of view (n)

onomatopoeia (n)

opening monologue (n)

overgeneralization (n)

overstate/overstatement (v) (n)

overview (n)

package (v) (n)

parable (n)

paradox (n)

parody (n)

past perfect verb tense (n)

pastoral (n)

performance review (n)

persona (n)

personal space (n)

personification (n)

philosophical assumption (n)

poise (n)

policy statement (n)

present perfect verb tense (n)

primary source (n)

production cost (n)

progressive verb form (n)

propaganda (n)

proposition of fact speech (n)

proposition of policy speech (n)

proposition of problem speech (n)

proposition of value speech (n)

questionnaire (n)

reaction shot (n)

readability (n)

red herring (n)

redraft (v)

reflexive pronoun (n)

repeat (v) (n)

résumé (n)

rhetorical device (n)

rhetorical question (n)

romantic period literature (n)

sarcasm/sarcastic (n) (adj)

satire/satirical (n) (adj)

secondary source (n)

set design (n)

sociocultural context (n)

soliloquy (n)

somber lighting (n)

speech action (n)

speed writing (n)

Standard English (pn)

status indicator (n)

stream of consciousness (n)

structural analysis (n)

style sheet format (n)

subvocalize (v)

text boundary (n)

text feature (n)

text structure (n)

thesis (n)

thesis statement (n)

transparent (adj)

truth in advertising (n)

understate/understatement (v) (n)

universal theme (n)

visual text (n)

warranty (n)

word processing (n)

word reference (n)

Mathematics Terms

Lower Elementary

above (p)

across (p)

add/addition (v) (n)

ahead (p)

area (n)

behind (p)

below (p)

beside (p)

between (p)

calendar (n)

cardinal number (n)

chance (n)

circle (v) (n)

clock (n)

close (v) (p)

coin (n)

corner (v) (n)

date (n)

day (n)

decreasing pattern (n)

diamond (n)

difference (n)

direction (n)

distance (n)

estimate (v) (n)

far (p)

foot (n)

gallon (n)

graph (v) (n)

greater than (adj)

group/grouping (v) (n)

guess and check (v)

height (n)

hour (n)

in front (p)

inch (v) (n)

increasing pattern (n)

inside (p)

left (p)

length (n)

less than (adj)

list (v) (n)

locate/location (v) (n)

measuring cup (n)

mile (n)

minute (n)

model (v) (n)

money (n)

near (p)

next to (p)

number (n)

number line (n)

numeral (n)

numerator (n)

numeric pattern (n)

ordinal number (n)

orientation (n)

outcome (n)

outside (p)

oval (n)

over (p)

pattern (n)

pattern extension (n)

pound (v) (n)

predict/prediction (v) (n)

rectangle (n)

right (p)

second [time] (n)

set (v) (n)

shape combination (n)

shape division (n)

shape pattern (n)

similarity (n)

size (n)

sound pattern (n)

standard measures of weight (n)

square (n)

subtract/subtraction (v) (n)

sum (n)

table (n)

tell time (v)

temperature (n)

temperature estimation (n)

temperature measurement (n)

time interval (n)

triangle (n)

under (p)

volume (n)

watch (v) (n)

week (n)

whole number (n)

width (n)

within (p)

yard (n)

year (n)

zero (n)

Upper Elementary

acute angle (n)

addend (n)

addition algorithm (n)

angle (n)

angle unit (n)

area (n)

associative property (n)

bar graph (n)

basic number combinations (n)

capacity (n)

centimeter (n)

certainty [probability] (n)

circumference (n)

cluster (v) (n)

common denominator (n)

common fractions (n)

commutative property (n)

conservation of area (n)

constant (n) (adj)

corresponding angle (n)

corresponding side (n)

cube (v) (n)

cylinder (n)

data (n)

data cluster (n)

decimal (n)

decimal addition (n)

decimal division (n)

decimal estimation (n)

decimal multiplication (n)

decimal subtraction (n)

denominator (n)

diagram (v) (n)

diameter (n)

distributive property (n)

divide/division (v) (n)

dividend (n)

divisibility (n)

divisor (n)

elapsed time (n)

equation (n)

equilateral triangle (n)

equivalent (n) (adj)

equivalent fractions (n)

equivalent representation (n)

estimate/estimation (v) (n)

estimation of fractions (n)

estimation of height (n)

estimation of length (n)

estimation of width (n)

even number (n)

event likelihood (n)

expanded notation (n)

extreme value (n)

faces of a shape (n)

factor (v) (n)

flip transformation (n)

fraction [proper/improper] (n)

fraction addition (n)

fraction division (n)

fraction multiplication (n)

fraction subtraction (n)

front-end digits (n)

front-end estimation (n)

function (v) (n)

geometric pattern (n)

geometric patterns extension (n)

gram (n)

greatest common factor (n)

growing pattern (n)

histogram (n)

horizontal axis (n)

identity property (n)

improbability (n)

inequality (n)

inequality solutions/statements (n)

intersection of shapes/lines (n)

invalid argument (n)

investigate/investigation (v) (n)

irrelevant information (n)

isosceles triangle (n)

least common multiple (n)

line graph (n)

linear pattern (n)

mass (n)

mean (n)

measure/measurement (v) (n)

measure of central tendency (n)

measures of length/height (n)

measures of weight (n)

measures of width (n)

median (n)

meter (n)

metric system (n)

midpoint (n)

mixed number (n)

mode (n)

multiple (n)

multiply/multiplication (v) (n)

negative number (n)

number of faces (n)

number pairs (n)

number sentence (n)

number triplet (n)

obtuse angle (n)

odd number (n)

open sentence (n)

order of operations (n)

parallel lines (n)

parallelogram (n)

parallelogram formula (n)

part to whole (n)

path (n)

pattern addition (n)

pattern subtraction (n)

percent (n)

perimeter (n)

perpendicular lines (n)

pie chart (n)

positive number (n)

prime factorization (n)

prime number (n)

prism (n)

probability (n)

process of elimination (n)

product (n)

proof (n)

protractor (n)

pyramid (n)

quart (n)

quotient (n)

radius (n)

rectangle formula (n)

rectangular prism (n)

reduced form (n)

relative distance (n)

relative magnitude (n)

relative magnitude of
    fractions (n)

relative size (n)

relevant information (n)

remainder (n)

repeating pattern (n)

restate a problem (v)

reversing order of operations (n)

rhombus (n)

right angle (n)

right triangle (n)

rotation (n)

round/rounding (v) (n)

ruler (n)

same size units (n)

sample (v) (n)

scale (n)

scalene triangle (n)

shape similarity (n)

shape symmetry (n)

shape transformation (n)

shrinking pattern (n)

sphere (n)

study (v) (n)

subset (n)

subtraction algorithm (n)

surface area (n)

survey (v) (n)

symbolic representation (n)

tablespoon (n)

tally (v) (n)

three-dimensional shape (n)

three-dimensional shape
    combination (n)

time zones (n)

trial and error (n)

triangle formula (n)

truncation (n)

two-dimensional shape (n)

two-dimensional shape
    combination (n)

two-dimensional shape
    decomposition (n)

two-dimensional shape slide (n)

two-dimensional shape turn (n)

two-dimensional space (n)

unit conversion (n)

unlike denominators (n)

U.S. system of measurement (n)

valid argument (n)

variability (n)

Venn diagram (pn)

verify/verification (v) (n)

vertical axis (n)

volume measurement (n)

volume of irregular shapes (n)

volume of rectangular solids (n)

Middle School

addition of fractions (n)

algebraic expression (n)

algebraic expression
    expansion (n)

algebraic representation (n)

algebraic step function (n)

alternate interior angles (n)

angle bisector (n)

approximate lines (n)

area model (n)

area of an irregular shape (n)

array (n)

axis of symmetry (n)

base 10 (n)

base 60 (n)

benchmark (v) (n)

biased sample (n)

blueprint (n)

box and whisker plot (n)

certainty of conclusions (n)

circumference formula (n)

combine like terms (v)

complementary angle (n)

complementary event (n)

complex problem (n)

composite number (n)

congruence (n)

conjecture (n)

constant difference (n)

constant rate of change (n)

constant ratio (n)

convert large number to small
    number (v)

convert small number to large
    number (v)

coordinate geometry (n)

coordinate plane (n)

coordinate system (n)

cost per unit (n)

counter example (n)

counting procedure (n)

cube number (n)

cube root (n)

cubic unit (n)

data display error (n)

data extreme (n)

data gap (n)

data set (n)

deductive argument (n)

deductive prediction (n)

defining properties of shapes/
    figures (n)

dilate/dilation (v) (n)

disperse/dispersion (v) (n)

distance formula (n)

enlarging transformation (n)

equal ratio (n)

equation system (n)

experiment (n)

exponent (n)

exponential notation (n)

fair chance (n)

formula for missing values (n)

frequency (n)

frequency distribution (n)

graphic representation of function (n)

graphic solution (n)

grid (n)

growth rate (n)

inductive reasoning (n)

input/output table (n)

integer (n)

infinite (n)

intercept (v) (n)

intersecting lines (n)

irrational number (n)

irregular polygon (n)

iterative sequence (n)

large sample (n)

limited sample (n)

line of symmetry (n)

linear arithmetic sequence (n)

linear equation (n)

linear geometric sequence (n)

linear units (n)

logic ALL (n)

logic AND (n)

logic IF/THEN (n)

logic NONE (n)

logic NOT (n)

logic OR (n)

logic SOME (n)

mathematical expression (n)

maximum (n)

measures of dispersion (n)

method selection (n)

minimum (n)

multiple problem-solving strategies (n)

multiple strategies for proofs (n)

multiplication algorithm (n)

mutually exclusive events (n)

network (n)

nominal data (n)

nondecimal numeration system (n)

nonlinear equation (n)

nonlinear function (n)

nonroutine versus routine problems (n)

number property (n)

number system (n)

number theory (n)

odds (n)

ordered pairs (n)

outlier (n)

overestimate/overestimation (v) (n)

parallel figures (n)

pattern division (n)

pattern multiplication (n)

pattern recognition (n)

percents greater than 100 (n)

percents less than 1 (n)

perimeter formula (n)

perfect square (n)

perpendicular bisector (n)

perspective (n)

pi (n)

pictorial representation (n)

placeholder (n)

planar cross-section (n)

plane (n)

plane figure (n)

polygon (n)

precision of measurement (n)

prime factor (n)

problem formulation (n)

problem space (n)

projection (n)

proportion (n)

proportional gain (n)

quadratic equation (n)

quadrilateral (n)

random number (n)

random sample (n)

random variable (n)

range (n)

range of estimations (n)

rate (n)

rate of change (n)

rational number (n)

rectangular coordinates (n)

recursive sequence (n)

reference set (n)

reflection transformation (n)

relative frequency (n)

relatively prime (n)

reliability (n)

Roman numeral (n)

root (n)

rotation symmetry (n)

sample selection techniques (n)

sample space (n)

sampling error (n)

scale drawing (n)

scale map (n)

scale transformations (n)

scatter plot (n)

scientific notation (n)

sequence (v) (n)

shrinking transformation (n)

significant digits (n)

similar proportions (n)

similarity (n)

simplification (n)

slide transformation (n)

slope (n)

slope-intercept formula (n)

solid figure (n)

solution algorithm (n)

solution probabilities (n)

spreadsheet (n)

square number (n)

square root (n)

square units (n)

statistic (n)

stem and leaf plot (n)

straight edge and compass (n)

substitution for unknowns (n)

supplementary angle (n)

table representation of functions (n)

table representation of probability (n)

tessellation (n)

tetrahedron (n)

theoretical probability (n)

thermometer (n)

three-dimensional shape cross-section (n)

three-dimensional space (n)

trapezoid formula (n)

tree diagram (n)

underestimation (n)

unit size (n)

unknown (n)

variable (n) (adj)

variable change (n)

vertex (n)

volume formula (n)

volume of a cylinder (n)

volume of a prism (n)

volume of a pyramid (n)

work backward (v)

written representation (n)

High School

absolute error (n)

absolute function (n)

absolute value (n)

acceleration (n)

add radical expressions (v)

addition counting procedure (n)

algebraic function (n)

angle of depression (n)

arc (n)

area under curve (n)

asymptote of function (n)

base *e* (n)

binary system (n)

bivariate data (n)

bivariate data transformation (n)

bivariate distribution (n)

Cartesian coordinates (pn)

categorical data (n)

central angle (n)

central limit theorem (n)

chord (n)

circle without center (n)

circular function (n)

classes of functions (n)

combination (n)

completing the square (v)

complex conjugates (n)

complex number (n)

compound event (n)

compound interest (n)

conditional probability (n)

confidence interval (n)

conjugate complex number (n)

continuity (n)

continuous probability distribution (n)

control group (n)

correlation (n)

cosine (n)

critical paths method (n)

curve fitting (n)

curve fitting median method (n)

decibel (n)

density (n)

dependent events (n)

derive/derivation (v) (n)

dilation of object in a plane (n)

direct function (n)

direct measure (n)

discrete probability (n)

discrete probability distribution (n)

divide radical expressions (v)

domain of function (n)

empirical verification (n)

equivalent forms of equations (n)

equivalent forms of inequalities (n)

expected value (n)

experimental design (n)

experimental probability (n)

exponent (n)

exponential function (n)

factorial (n)

factorial notation (n)

Fibonacci sequence (pn)

finite graph (n)

force (n)

formal mathematical induction (n)

fraction inversion (n)

function composition (n)

function notation (n)

geometric function (n)

imaginary number (n)

independent event (n)

independent trial (n)

indirect measure (n)

inflection (n)

inscribe/inscribed (v) (n)

interest (n)

inverse function (n)

irrational number (n)

isometry (n)

law of large numbers (n)

law of probability (n)

limit (v) (n)

linear (adj)

linear system (n)

line equation (n)

line segment (n)

line segment congruence (n)

line segment similarity (n)

line through point not on a line (n)

log function (n)

logarithm (n)

logarithmic function (n)

mathematical theories (n)

matrix (n)

matrix addition (n)

matrix division (n)

matrix equation (n)

matrix inversion (n)

matrix multiplication (n)

matrix subtraction (n)

midpoint formula (n)

minimum/maximum of function (n)

monitor progress of a problem (v)

monomial (n)

Monte Carlo simulation (pn)

multiply radical expressions (v)

natural log (n)

natural number (n)

nature of deduction (n)

negative exponent (n)

normal curve (n)

number subsystems (n)

parallel box plot (n)

parameter (n)

parameter estimate (n)

parameter equation (n)

Pascal's triangle (pn)

periodic function (n)

permutation (n)

phase shift (n)

pi (n)

point of tangency (n)

polar coordinates (n)

polynomial (n)

polynomial addition (n)

polynomial division (n)

polynomial function (n)

polynomial multiplication (n)

polynomial solution by bisection (n)

polynomial solution by sign change (n)

polynomial solution successive approximation (n)

polynomial subtraction (n)

population (n)

postulate (v)

powers (n)

precision of estimation (n)

probability distribution (n)

proof paragraph (n)

Pythagorean theorem (pn)

quartile deviation (n)

radical expression (n)

radical function (n)

random sampling technique (n)

range of function (n)

rational function (n)

real number (n)

real-world function (n)

reciprocal (n)

recurrence equation (n)

recurrence relationship (n)

recursive equation (n)

reflection in plane (n)

reflection in space (n)

regression coefficient (n)

regression line (n)

relative error (n)

representativeness of sample (n)

Richter scale (pn)

right-triangle geometry (n)

root and real numbers (n)

roots to determine cost (n)

roots to determine profit (n)

roots to determine revenue (n)

rotation in plane (n)

sample statistic (n)

sampling distribution (n)

scalar (n)

secant (n)

series (n)

series circuit (n)

sigma notation (n)

similar figures (n)

sine (n)

sinusoidal function (n)

smallest set of rules (n)

speed (n)

spurious correlation (n)

standard deviation (n)

statistical experiment (n)

statistical regression (n)

statistic (n)

step function (n)

strategy efficiency (n)

strategy generation technique (n)

subtract radical expressions (v)

successive approximations (n)

summary statistic (n)

surface-area cone (n)

surface-area cylinder (n)

surface-area sphere (n)

synthetic geometry (n)

systems of inequalities (n)

tangent (n)

term (n)

theorem (n)

theorem direct proof (n)

theorem indirect proof (n)

transversal (n)

treatment group (n)

trigonometric ratio (n)

trigonometric relation (n)

truth table proof (n)

two-way tables (n)

U.S. customary system (n)

unit analysis (n)

univariate data (n)

univariate distribution (n)

upper/lower bounds (n)

validity (n)

variance (n)

vector (n)

vector addition (n)

vector division (n)

vector multiplication (n)

vector subtraction (n)

velocity (n)

vertex edge graph (n)

Science Terms

Lower Elementary

air (n)

animal features (n)

balance (v) (n)

behavior pattern (n)

boulder (n)

burn (v) (n)

chart (v) (n)

circular motion (n)

cloud (v) (n)

color (v) (n)

compute/computer (v) (n)

daily weather pattern (n)

die/death (v) (n)

dinosaur (n)

dissolve (v)

distance (n)

diversity of life (n)

Earth (pn)

Earth's gravity (n)

Earth's materials (n)

Earth's rotation (n)

egg (n)

energy (n)

environment (n)

food (n)

freeze (v)

gas (n)

grow/growth (v) (n)

habitat (n)

hear/hearing (v) (n)

heat (v) (n)

insect (n)

light (v) (n) (adj)

liquid (n) (adj)

locate/location (v) (n)

machine (n)

magnet (n)

magnify/magnification (v) (n)

mammoth (n) (adj)

mix/mixture (v) (n)

month (n)

moon (n)

move/motion (v) (n)

night (n)

observe/observation (v) (n)

offspring (n)

parent (n)

parent/offspring similarity (n)

pebble (n)

plant (v) (n)

position (v) (n)

predict/prediction (v) (n)

prehistoric animals (n)

properties of light (n)

pull (v) (n)

push (v) (n)

reason/reasoning (v) (n)

requirements for life (n)

rock characteristics (n)

ruler (n)

saltwater (n)

sand (n)

science/scientist (n)

seasonal change (n)

see/sight (v) (n)

sense/senses (v) (n)

shape (v) (n)

shelter (v) (n)

similarities and differences among organisms (n)

size (n)

sky (n)

smell (v) (n)

soil (n)

solid rock (n)

sound (v) (n)

star (n)

star age (n)

star brightness (n)

states of matter (n)

straight-line motion (n)

sun's size (n)

taste (v) (n)

teamwork (n)

temperature (n)

thermometer (n)

touch (v) (n)

universe (n)

vibrate/vibration (v) (n)

water (n)

weather (n)

weather conditions (n)

weather patterns (n)

weigh/weight (v) (n)

wind (n)

year (n)

zigzag motion (n)

Upper Elementary

ability to support life (n)

accelerate/acceleration (v) (n)

air movement (n)

animal product (n)

apparent movement of the
    planets (n)

apparent movement of the stars
    (n)

apparent movement of the
    sun (n)

applied force (n)

astronomical distance (n)

astronomical object (n)

astronomical size (n)

astronomy (n)

atmosphere (n)

battery (n)

bedrock (n)

beneficial change (n)

birth (n)

boiling point (n)

bones (n)

calculate/calculator (v) (n)

carnivore (n)

cause and effect (n)

change of direction (n)

change of motion (n)

change of speed (n)

changes in the Earth's
    surface (n)

characteristics of air (n)

charge attraction (n)

charge repulsion (n)

compete/competition (v) (n)

composition of matter (n)

condense/condensation (v) (n)

conductor/conduction (n)

conserve (v)

conservation of mass (n)

conservation of matter (n)

constellation (n)

control of variables (n)

controlled experiment (n)

cool/cooling (v) (n) (adj)

core (n)

data (n)

data analysis (n)

data interpretation (n)

data presentation (n)

detrimental change (n)

disease (n)

drought (n)

Earth (pn)

Earth's axis (n)

Earth's orbit (n)

Earth's surface (n)

Earth's average temperature (n)

earthquake (n)

electrical charge (n)

electrical circuit (n)

electrical current (n)

electricity (n)

energy transfer (n)

engineering (n)

environment (n)

environmental changes (n)

environmental conditions (n)

erode/erosion (v) (n)

evaporate/evaporation (v) (n)

external cue (n)

extinct (adj)

food chain (n)

food web (n)

force strength (n)

formulate/formula (v) (n)

fossil (n)

fossil evidence (n)

fresh water (n)

friction (n)

generate/generator (v) (n)

glacial movement (n)

glacier (n)

graduated cylinder (n)

graph (v) (n)

ground water (n)

heat conduction (n)

heat transfer (n)

herbivore (n)

history of science (n)

ice (n)

inherited characteristic (n)

Jupiter (pn)

kinetic energy (n)

land form (n)

landslide (n)

life cycle (n)

light absorption (n)

light emission (n)

light reflection (n)

light refraction (n)

logical argument (n)

magnetic attraction (n)

magnetic repulsion (n)

Mars (pn)

mass (n)

measurement of motion (n)

melting point (n)

Mercury (pn)

metal (n)

microscope (n)

migrate/migration (v) (n)

mineral (n)

moon's orbit (n)

moon's phases (n)

naturalistic observation (n)

Neptune (pn)

nitrogen (n)

nutrient (n)

ocean's currents (n)

offspring (n)

oil (n)

omnivore (n)

organism (n)

outer space (n)

oxygen (n)

phase change (n)

photosynthesis (n)

photosynthetic plants (n)

physical property (n)

physical setting (n)

pitch (n)

planet (n)

plant organ (n)

plant product (n)

plant root (n)

Pluto (pn)

pollute/pollution (v) (n)

populate/population (v) (n)

population density (n)

position over time (n)

potential energy (n)

precipitation (n)

predator (n)

prehistoric environment (n)

prehistoric organisms (n)

prey (v) (n)

properties of soil (n)

properties of sound (n)

properties of water (n)

question formulation (n)

recycle (v)

relative position (n)

renewable/nonrenewable energy (n)

replicable experiment (n)

reproduce/reproduction (v) (n)

reproducible result (n)

resource availability (n)

rock breakage (n)

rock composition (n)

rock cycle (n)

saltwater (n)

Saturn (pn)

scientific equipment (n)

scientific evidence (n)

scientific experiment (n)

soil color (n)

soil composition (n)

soil texture (n)

solar system (n)

solubility (n)

stored energy (n)

survival of organisms (n)

technology/technological advancement (n)

telescope (n)

tide (n)

Uranus (pn)

vapor (n)

Venus (pn)

volcanic eruption (n)

water capacity (n)

water cycle (n)

weathering (n)

wind pattern (n)

Middle School

acquired trait (n)

adaptive characteristic (n)

air mass circulation (n)

alternative explanation of data (n)

asexual reproduction (n)

asteroid (n)

asteroid impact (n)

asteroid movement patterns (n)

atmosphere (n)

atmospheric pressure (n)

atom (n)

atomic arrangement (n)

balanced force (n)

behavioral change in organisms (n)

behavioral response to stimuli (n)

bias (n)

body plan (n)

carrying capacity (n)

celestial body (n)

cell (n)

cell division (n)

cell growth (n)

characteristics of life (n)

chemical change (n)

chemical compound (n)

chemical element (n)

chemical energy (n)

chemical reaction (n)

circulatory system (n)

climate (n)

climate change (n)

climactic pattern (n)

closed system (n)

color of light (n)

comet (n)

comet impact (n)

comet movement patterns (n)

common ancestry (n)

concentration of reactants (n)

confirmation by observation (n)

conflicting interpretation (n)

conservation of energy (n)

constant speed (n)

continuation of species (n)

crustal deformation (n)

crustal plate movement (n)

crystal (n)

debris (n)

decelerate/deceleration (v) (n)

decompose/decomposer/
    decomposition (v) (n)

digestive system (n)

direction (n)

direction of force (n)

direction of motion (n)

displacement of results (n)

Earth system (n)

Earth's age (n)

Earth's atmosphere (n)

Earth's climate (n)

Earth's crust (n)

Earth's layers (n)

eclipse (n)

ecological role (n)

ecosystem (n)

egg cell (n)

electrical current (n)

electrical energy (n)

element stability (n)

emergence of life forms (n)

energy source (n)

erosion resistance (n)

ethics in science (n)

excretory system (n)

experimental confirmation (n)

experimental control (n)

external feature (n)

faulty reasoning (n)

filter/filtering (v) (n)

food oxidation (n)

forms of matter (n)

fossil record (n)

fundamental unit of life (n)

fungus (n)

galaxy (n)

Galileo Galilei (pn)

gene (n)

geologic evidence (n)

geologic force (n)

geological shift (n)

gravitational force (n)

Greek basic four elements (n)

habits of mind (n)

heat convection (n)

heat emission (n)

heat energy (n)

heat radiation (n)

heat retention (n)

hereditary information (n)

homeostasis (n)

host (v) (n)

hydrosphere (n)

hypothesis (n)

igneous rock (n)

immune system (n)

inertia (n)

infection (n)

informed subject (n)

infrared radiation (n)

insulator/insulation (n)

intellectual honesty (n)

interdependence of organisms
    (n)

internal cue (n)

internal structure (n)

invertebrate (n)

lever arm (n)

life form change (n)

life-sustaining functions (n)

light scattering (n)

light transmission (n)

light wavelength (n)

light-year (n)

lithosphere (n)

logic (n)

Louis Pasteur (pn)

mantle (n)

Marie Curie (pn)

mathematical model (n)

mechanical energy (n)

mechanical motion (n)

metal reactivity (n)

metamorphic rock (n)

meteor (n)

meteor impact (n)

meteor movement patterns (n)

Milky Way galaxy (pn)

molecular arrangement (n)

molecular motion (n)

molecule (n)

multicellular organism (n)

muscular system (n)

mutualism (n)

nervous system (n)

Newton's laws of motion (pn)

nitrogen cycle (n)

nonreactive gas (n)

nuclear energy/reaction (n)

organ (n)

organ system (n)

organ system failure (n)

oxidize/oxidation (v) (n)

parasite (n)

particle ring (n)

peer review (n)

percolation (n)

physiological change (n)

Pierre Curie (pn)

planet composition (n)

planet orbit (n)

planet size (n)

planet surface features (n)

plant tissue (n)

polygenic trait (n)

predation/prey (n)

properties of elements (n)

pulley (n)

radiant energy (n)

radiation (n)

reaction rate (n)

recrystallization (n)

recycling of matter (n)

reproductive system (n)

research question (n)

respire/respiration (v) (n)

respiratory system (n)

right of refusal (n)

risk and benefit (n)

rock layer movement (n)

rust/rusting (v) (n) (adj)

satellite (n)

scientific interpretation (n)

scientific method (n)

scientific skepticism (n)

screen (v) (n)

sediment deposition (n)

sedimentary rock (n)

sedimentation (n)

separation method (n)

sexual reproduction (n)

simple machines (n)

skeletal system (n)

soil erosion (n)

soil fertility (n)

solar system formation (n)

sound energy (n)

specialized cell (n)

specialized organ (n)

specialized tissue (n)

species (n)

species diversity (n)

speed (n)

sperm (n)

sperm cell (n)

surface area of reactants (n)

surface runoff (n)

taxonomy (n)

theoretical model (n)

thermal energy (n)

tissue [plant and animal] (n)

tolerance of ambiguity (n)

unbalanced force (n)

unicellular organism (n)

unity of life (n)

universal solvent (n)

vertebrate (n)

visible light (n)

water cycle (n)

wavelength (n)

wedge (v) (n)

High School

abiotic/abiotic components (n)

accelerate/accelerator (v) (n)

acid/base reactions (n)

active transport (n)

actual mass (n)

advection (n)

age of the universe (n)

Albert Einstein (pn)

Alfred Wegener (pn)

allele (n)

alternation of generations (n)

amino acid sequence (n)

anatomical characteristic (n)

Antoine Lavoisier (pn)

atmospheric cycle/atmospheric change (n)

atomic bomb (n)

atomic bonding principles (n)

atomic configuration (n)

atomic energy (n)

atomic mass (n)

atomic motion (n)

atomic nucleus (n)

atomic number (n)

atomic reaction (n)

atomic theory (n)

atomic weight (n)

Avogadro's hypothesis (pn)

Bernoulli's principle (pn)

big bang theory (n)

biochemical characteristic (n)

biological adaptation (n)

biological evolution (n)

biological molecule/biomolecule (n)

breakdown of food molecules (n)

buoyancy (n)

carbon (n)

carbon atom (n)

carbon cycle (n)

carbon dioxide (n)

catalyst (n)

cell function (n)

cell membrane (n)

cell nucleus (n)

cell organelle (n)

cell wall (n)

cellular communication (n)

cellular differentiation (n)

cellular energy conversion (n)

cellular regulation (n)

cellular response (n)

cellular waste disposal (n)

charged object (n)

Charles Darwin (pn)

Charles Lyell (pn)

chemical bond (n)

chemical organization of organisms (n)

chemical properties of elements (n)

chemical reaction rate (n)

chlorophyll (n)

chloroplast (n)

chromatography (n)

chromosome (n)

chromosome pair (n)

composition of the universe (n)

convection (n)

convection current (n)

Copernican revolution (pn)

Nicolaus Copernicus (pn)

Coulomb's law (pn)

covalent bond (n)

criteria for acceptance (n)

crystalline solid (n)

cytoplasm (n)

data reduction (n)

decay rate (n)

degree of kinship (n)

derived characteristic (n)

disclosure of methods and procedures (n)

DNA (n)

DNA molecule (n)

DNA replication (n)

DNA sequence (n)

DNA structure (n)

DNA subunit (n)

dominant trait (n)

Doppler effect (pn)

drag (v) (n)

Earth's elements (n)

Earth's external energy sources (n)

Earth's formation (n)

Earth's internal energy sources (n)

elasticity (n)

electric force (n)

electric motor (n)

electric potential (n)

electrically neutral (n)

electromagnetic field (n)

electromagnetic force (n)

electromagnetic radiation (n)

electromagnetic spectrum (n)

electromagnetic wave (n)

electron (n)

electron configuration (n)

electron sharing (n)

electron transfer (n)

elementary particle (n)

elements of matter (n)

elimination of matter and energy (n)

elliptical orbits (n)

embryo formation (n)

empirical standards/evidence (n)

endothermic (adj)

endothermic reaction (n)

energy requirements of living systems (n)

Enrico Fermi (pn)

entropy (n)

enzyme (n)

equal and opposite force (n)

equilibrium of ecosystems (n)

Ernest Rutherford (pn)

evidence for the big bang theory (n)

evidence for the expansion of the universe (n)

evidence for the unity among organisms (n)

excitatory molecule (n)

exothermic (adj)

exothermic reaction (n)

experimental method (n)

Fahrenheit (pn)

filial generation (n)

flow of energy (n)

flow of matter (n)

fluid resistance (n)

foot-pound force (n)

formation of polymers (n)

fossil fuels (n)

fracture (v) (n)

frequency (n)

gamma ray (n)

gene encoding (n)

gene expression (n)

general theory of relativity (n)

genetic diversity (n)

genetic mutation (n)

genetic variation (n)

geochemical cycle (n)

geologic time (n)

geologic time scale (n)

geological dating (n)

germ theory (n)

Golgi apparatus (pn)

gravitational energy (n)

greenhouse gas (n)

Gregor Mendel (pn)

Halley's comet (pn)

harvesting of resources (n)

heterogeneous mixture (n)

history of the universe (n)

homogenous mixture (n)

human genetics (n)

human modification of
    ecosystems (n)

hydrogen bomb (n)

hydrogen ion (n)

inertial frame of reference (n)

infrared light (n)

inhibitory molecule (n)

inverse square law (n)

ion (n)

ionic bond (n)

ionic motion (n)

isotope (n)

Johannes Kepler (pn)

John Dalton (pn)

Kelvin [temperature] (pn)

Lise Meitner (pn)

longitudinal wave (n)

main sequence star (n)

mass-to-energy conversion (n)

meiosis (n)

Mendelian genetics (pn)

metallic bond (n)

metallic surface (n)

method of investigation (n)

microwave (n)

mitochondrion (n)

mitosis (n)

molar volume (n)

mole (n)

molecular energy (n)

molecular synthesis (n)

molten rock (n)

mountain building (n)

moving electrical charge (n)

moving magnet (n)

natural selection (n)

net force (n)

neuron (n)

neurotransmitter (n)

neutron (n)

Newtonian mechanics (pn)

nitrogen (n)

nitrogen cycle (n)

nuclear fission (n)

nuclear force (n)

nuclear fusion (n)

nuclear mass (n)

nuclear stability (n)

nucleated cell (n)

ocean layers (n)

ohm (n)

organic compound synthesis (n)

organic matter (n)

origin of life (n)

origin of the universe (n)

oxidation-reduction reactions (n)

ozone (n)

paradigm shift (n)

parental generation (n)

particle emission (n)

periodic table of elements (n)

photosynthesizing organism (n)

phylogenetics (n)

plate boundary (n)

plate collision (n)

plate tectonics (n)

potential energy (n)

pressure (v) (n)

properties of reactants (n)

properties of waves (n)

protein (n)

protein structure (n)

protein synthesis (n)

proton (n)

Ptolemy (pn)

quantum of energy (n)

radical reaction (n)

radio wave (n)

radioactive dating (n)

radioactive decay (n)

radioactive isotope (n)

rate of nuclear decay (n)

recessive trait (n)

recombination of chemical
    elements (n)

recombination of genetic
    material (n)

relative mass (n)

relative motion (n)

release of energy (n)

reproductive capacity (n)

reproductive value of traits (n)

revision of scientific theories (n)

rock sequence (n)

rules of evidence (n)

sea floor spreading (n)

segregation (n)

seismic wave (n)

selective gene expression (n)

semiconductor (n)

sex cell (n)

sex chromosomes (n)

sex-linked trait (n)

shared characteristic (n)

sound wave (n)

space probe (n)

special theory of relativity (n)

speciation (n)

speed of light (n)

spontaneous nuclear reaction (n)

star composition (n)

star destruction (n)

star formation (n)

star size (n)

star system (n)

star temperature (n)

star types (n)

stellar energy (n)

storage of genetic information (n)

sun's radiation (n)

superconductor (n)

superposition (n)

survival value of traits (n)

synthetic polymer (n)

thermal equilibrium (n)

torque (n)

transforming matter and/or energy (n)

transport of cell materials (n)

transport of matter and/or energy (n)

transverse wave (n)

ultraviolet light (n)

ultraviolet radiation (n)

unequal heating of air (n)

unequal heating of land masses (n)

unequal heating of oceans (n)

vacuole (n)

viscosity (n)

water wave (n)

wave amplitude (n)

wave packet (n)

wave source (n)

weight of subatomic particles (n)

X-ray (n)

Social Studies Terms

Lower Elementary

General History

Abraham Lincoln (pn)

America (pn)

American Revolution, 1776 (pn)

April (pn)

argue/argument (v) (n)

August (pn)

automobile (n)

begin/beginning (v) (n)

behave/behavior (v) (n)

believe/belief (v) (n)

Benjamin Franklin (pn)

bow and arrow (n)

cause-and-effect relationship (n)

celebration (n)

ceremony (n)

chariot (n)

Christmas (pn)

Christopher Columbus (pn)

colony (n)

common good (n)

computer (n)

cowboy (n)

dance (v) (n)

decade (n)

December (pn)

democracy (n)

disagreement (n)

domestic animal/pet (n)

education (n)

end/ending (v) (n) (adj)

equality (n)

event (n)

expand/expansion (v) (n)

explorer (n)

family (n)

family history (n)

family life (n)

father of our country (n)

February (pn)

Fourth of July (pn)

freedom (n)

Friday (pn)

future (n)

generation (n)

George Washington (pn)

group membership (n)

harvest festival (n)

heroism (n)

history (n)

hobby (n)

holiday (n)

house of worship (n)

human rights (n)

hunger (v) (n)

hunter/gatherer (n)

idea (n)

independence (n)

invention (n)

January (pn)

journey (n)

July (pn)

June (pn)

legend (n)

liberty (n)

Liberty Bell (pn)

lifestyle (n)

local history (n)

March (pn)

Martin Luther King Jr. (pn)

Martin Luther King Jr. Day (pn)

May (pn)

Memorial Day (pn)

middle (n) (adj)

Monday (pn)

monument (n)

myth (n)

national flag (n)

national holiday (n)

Native American (pn)

newcomer (n)

November (pn)

October (pn)

oral tradition (n)

origin (n)

past (n) (p) (adj) (adv)

photograph (v) (n)

picture time line (n)

pioneer (v) (n)

place-name (n)

Plymouth (pn)

pony express (n)

present (v) (n) (adj)

printing press (n)

radio (v) (n)

recreation (n)

region (n)

regional folk hero (n)

regional song (n)

religion (n)

resistance (n)

respect for others (n)

revolution (n)

role (n)

rule (v) (n)

satellite system (n)

Saturday (pn)

sculpture (n)

September (pn)

society (n)

soup kitchen (n)

steam engine (n)

Sunday (pn)

surplus food (n)

symbol (n)

tall tale (n)

team member (n)

telegraph (n)

temple (n)

territory (n)

Thanksgiving (pn)

today (n)

Thomas Jefferson (pn)

Thursday (pn)

time line (n)

tomorrow (n)

tool (n)

town (n)

trade (v) (n)

trail (n)

travel (v)

Tuesday (pn)

United States (pn)

war (v) (n)

Wednesday (pn)

wheel (n)

White House (pn)

yesterday (n)

Civics

agree/agreement (v) (n)

authority (n)

citizen (n)

control (v) (n)

duty (n)

election (n)

flag (n)

good law (n)

good rule (n)

government (n)

honesty (n)

individual (n)

individual rights (n)

justice (n)

law (n)

leader (n)

nation (n)

national anthem (n)

national symbol (n)

official (n) (adj)

open-mindedness (n)

order (v) (n)

personal responsibility (n)

Pledge of Allegiance (pn)

police authority (n)

power (v) (n)

privacy (n)

qualification (n)

race (v) (n)

respect for law (n)

respect for the rights of others (n)

responsibility (n)

right (n)

rule (v) (n)

symbol (n)

take turns (v)

territory (n)

trade (v) (n)

truth (n)

volunteer (v) (n)

vote (v) (n)

war (v) (n)

Economics

advertising (n)

bank (v) (n)

business (n)

buyer (n)

cash (n)

cent (n)

coin (n)

cost (v) (n)

debt (n)

dime (n)

dollar (n)

earn (v)

gain (v) (n)

goods (n)

job (n)

labor (v) (n)

lose/loss (v) (n)

money (n)

need (v) (n)

nickel (n)

penny (n)

poverty (n)

price (v) (n)

quarter (v) (n)

sale (n)

save/saving (v) (n)

sell (v)

seller (n)

service (v) (n)

skill (n)

spend (v)

want (v) (n)

worker (n)

Geography

air (n)

airplane (n)

airport (n)

America/Americas (pn)

apartment (n)

area (n)

autumn/fall (n)

barrier (n)

bay (n)

bicycle (n)

body of water (n)

bridge (n)

building (n)

bus (n)

city (n)

city park (n)

climate (n)

climate change (n)

coast (n)

cold climate (n)

community (n)

community project (n)

competition (n)

construction (n)

country (n)

creek (n)

crop (n)

custom (n)

dam (v) (n)

desert (n)

direction (n)

distance (n)

downtown (n)

east (p)

elevation (n)

England (pn)

environment (n)

factory (n)

farm (v) (n)

fish (v) (n)

flood (v) (n)

forest (n)

fuel (v) (n)

geography (n)

globe (n)

government (n)

graph (v) (n)

highway (n)

hill (n)

home (n)

hospital (n)

hotel (n)

house/housing (v) (n)

lake (n)

land (n)

library (n)

lightening (n)

local community (n)

location (n)

map (v) (n)

measure/measurement (v) (n)

mile (n)

mountain (n)

museum (n)

neighborhood (n)

north (p)

ocean (n)

park (v) (n)

pattern (v) (n)

pipeline (n)

place (v) (n)

plant cultivation (n)

plant population (n)

pond (n)

population (n)

position (v) (n)

prairie (n)

railroad (n)

rain/rainfall (n)

region (n)

river (n)

road/road system (n)

rural region (n)

school (n)

sea (n)

senior citizens' home (n)

settlement (n)

shelter/homeless shelter (n)

ship (v) (n)

shopping center (n)

snow (v) (n)

soil (n)

south (p)

sports stadium (n)

spring (n)

state (n)

steamship (n)

storm (v) (n)

stream (v) (n)

subway (n)

summer (n)

temperature (n)

timber (n)

thunder (v) (n)

town (n)

train (n)

transportation (n)

urban area (n)

vegetation (n)

village (n)

Washington, D.C. (pn)

weather (n)

west (p)

wildlife (n)

wind (n)

winter (n)

world (n)

yard (n)

Upper Elementary

U.S. History

1492 (n)

1896 election (n)

1920s (n)

Age of Exploration (pn)

abolition movement (n)

abolitionist (n) (adj)

African American (pn)

African slave trade (n)

Alamo (pn)

Alexander Graham Bell (pn)

Alexander Hamilton (pn)

Amelia Earhart (pn)

American Expeditionary Force (pn)

American Indian chief (n)

Andrew Jackson (pn)

Angel Island (pn)

Antietam (pn)

Articles of Confederation (pn)

Asian American (pn)

assembly line (n)

autobiography (n)

Barack Obama (pn)

Battle of Bull Run (pn)

Betty Zane (pn)

Billy the Kid (pn)

biography (n)

Black Hawk War (pn)

Black Reconstruction (pn)

Booker T. Washington (pn)

Boston Tea Party (pn)

Brown v. Board of Education (1954) (pn)

Cabeza de Vaca (pn)

Cayuga (pn)

Charles Finney (pn)

Cherokee Indians (pn)

Cherokee Trail of Tears (pn)

Chickasaw removal (n)

Chickasaw (pn)

Chocktaw removal (n)

Christopher Columbus (pn)

civil rights movement (n)

Civil War [U.S.] (pn)

Clara Barton (pn)

coal mine strike (n)

coal mining (n)

cold war (n)

colonial period (n)

colonist (n)

colonize (v)

colony (n)

Confederate Army (pn)

confederacy (n)

Connecticut Compromise (pn)

Constitutional Convention (pn)

cotton gin (n)

cowboy culture (n)

Cree removal (n)

Cuban Missile Crisis (pn)

Daniel Boone (pn)

Davey Crockett (pn)

December 7, 1941 (n)

dust bowl (n)

Eighteenth Amendment (pn)

Eleanor Roosevelt (pn)

Ellis Island (pn)

emancipate/emancipation (v) (n)

Emancipation Proclamation (pn)

equal rights (n)

escaped slave (n)

extended family (n)

eyewitness account (n)

Fifteenth Amendment (pn)

former master (n)

former slave (n)

Fort Sumter (pn)

Fourteen Points (pn)

Fourteenth Amendment (pn)

Francisco Vasquez de Coronado (pn)

Franklin D. Roosevelt (pn)

Frederick Douglass (pn)

Fredericksburg (pn)

Freedmen's Bureau (pn)

Freedom Ride (pn)

frontier (n)

frontiersman (n)

fur trade (n)

General Robert E. Lee (pn)

George H. W. Bush (pn)

George W. Bush (pn)

George Washington Carver (pn)

Gerald Ford (pn)

Geronimo (pn)

GI Bill (pn)

Golden Door (pn)

Great Awakening (pn)

Great Depression (pn)

Great Plains (pn)

Harlem Renaissance (pn)

Harriet Tubman (pn)

Harry S. Truman (pn)

Henry Ford (pn)

Herbert Hoover (pn)

Hispanic American (pn)

home country (n)

home front (n)

homeless (n) (adj)

Hopi (pn)

hymn (n)

"I have a dream" speech (pn)

immigrant (n)

immigrate/immigration (v) (n)

Industrial North (pn)

Industrial Revolution (pn)

Internet (pn)

internment of Japanese
    Americans (n)

interstate highway system (n)

Inuit (pn)

Iroquois (pn)

Jackie Robinson (pn)

Jacqueline Kennedy Onassis (pn)

James Armistead (pn)

James Monroe (pn)

Jedediah Smith (pn)

Jim Bowie (pn)

Jim Crow (n)

Jimmy Carter (pn)

Joe Magarac (pn)

John Adams (pn)

John F. Kennedy (pn)

John Glenn (pn)

John Hancock (pn)

John Henry (pn)

Jonas Salk (pn)

King James I (pn)

Know-Nothing Party (pn)

land owner (n)

land use (n)

Latino (pn)

Lexington and Concord (pn)

Lincoln Memorial (pn)

Louisiana Purchase (pn)

Lower South colony (pn)

Lydia Darragh (pn)

Lyndon B. Johnson (pn)

Manassas (pn)

manifest destiny (n)

Mary McLeod Bethune (pn)

Mayflower Compact (pn)

Mexican-American War (pn)

Mexican migrant worker (n)

mid-Atlantic colony (n)

mill (n)

mining town (n)

minority rights (n)

minstrel show (n)

Missouri Compromise (pn)

Monroe Doctrine (pn)

Mormon (pn)

Mary "Mother" Jones (pn)

mountain man (n)

Mount Rushmore (pn)

Nathan Beman (pn)

National Organization for
    Women (pn)

Native American ancestors (n)

Native American land holdings
    (n)

Native American tribe (n)

New Deal (pn)

New England (pn)

New England mill town (n)

New Federalism (pn)

New Frontier (pn)

New Jersey Plan (pn)

Nez Perce (pn)

Nineteenth Amendment (pn)

Oneida (pn)

Onondaga (pn)

Open Door policy (pn)

P. T. Barnum (pn)

parable (n)

patriot/patriotism (n)

Paul Bunyan (pn)

Pearl Harbor (pn)

Pecos Bill (pn)

Peter Cartwright (pn)

pictograph (n)

pilgrim (n)

plantation (n)

plantation colony (n)

post–Civil War period (n)

pre-Columbus (n)

primary source (n)

Prohibition (pn)

proverb (n)

rail construction (n)

rail transportation (n)

Reagan Revolution (pn)

ranch/ranching (v) (n)

rapid transit (n)

Reconstruction (pn)

reservation (n)

Revolutionary War (pn)

Richard Henry Lee (pn)

Richard Nixon (pn)

Ronald Reagan (pn)

Rosa Parks (pn)

Sally Ride (pn)

Sam Houston (pn)

Samuel Adams (pn)

secondary source (n)

Second Great Awakening (pn)

Seminole removal (n)

Seneca (pn)

separation of church and state (n)

separation of powers (n)

settlement (n)

settler (n)

Seventeenth Amendment (pn)

sharecropper (n)

Shays Rebellion (pn)

Shiloh (pn)

silent majority (n)

Sioux (pn)

Sixteenth Amendment (pn)

slave (n)

slave holder (n)

slave rebellion (n)

slave trade (n)

Sojourner Truth (pn)

Spanish-American War (pn)

spinning jenny (n)

Statue of Liberty (pn)

steam locomotive (n)

steel construction (n)

stock market crash of 1929 (n)

street gang (n)

suffrage movement (n)

Susan B. Anthony (pn)

taxation without representation (n)

Tecumseh (pn)

Texas War for Independence (pn)

Theodore Roosevelt (pn)

thirteen colonies (n)

Thirteenth Amendment (pn)

Thomas Nast (pn)

Trail of Tears (pn)

Treaty of Guadalupe Hildago (pn)

Treaty of Paris (pn)

Underground Railroad (pn)

Union Army (pn)

university (n)

U.S. territory (n)

Vicksburg (pn)

Vietnam War (pn)

Virginia Plan (pn)

War of 1812 (pn)

Warren Court (pn)

Watergate (pn)

W. E. B. Dubois (pn)

Westward expansion (n)

Whiskey Rebellion (pn)

William Taft (pn)

Williamsburg (pn)

women's movement (n)

Woodrow Wilson (pn)

yeoman farmer (n)

World History

1948 UN Declaration of Human Rights (pn)

Adolf Hitler (pn)

African heritage (n)

Afro-Eurasia (pn)

Age of Enlightenment (pn)

Alfred the Great (pn)

alliance (n)

Allied Powers (pn)

ancestor worship (n)

Ancient Greece (pn)

Ancient Rome (pn)

annex/annexation (v) (n)

AD/anno domini (adj)

Arab-Israeli crisis (n)

Arab/Palestinian (pn)

armed forces (n)

Ashikaga period (pn)

Ashoka (pn)

astrolabe (n)

Athenian democracy (pn)

Augustus (pn)

aviation (n)

Axis powers (pn)

Aztec Indians/Aztec Empire (pn)

Aztec "Foundation of Heaven" (pn)

Bantu migrations in Africa (n)

Bartholomew de las Casas (pn)

Battle of Hastings (pn)

BC/before Christ (adj)

BCE/before common era (adj)

Benito Mussolini (pn)

Berlin blockade (n)

Boxer Rebellion (pn)

Brahmanism (pn)

British East India Company (pn)

bronze tool-making technology (n)

Buddha (pn)

Buddhism (pn)

Byzantine Empire (pn)

Byzantium (pn)

camel (n)

Camelot image (n)

Canton (pn)

capture of Constantinople (n)

Carthage (pn)

caste system (n)

castle (n)

cavalry warfare (n)

celestial empire (n)

Cesar Chavez (pn)

Central Asia (pn)

Central Asian steppes (pn)

Central Iberia (pn)

Central Powers (pn)

century (n)

Charlemagne (pn)

Chinese New Year (pn)

chivalry (n)

Christian/Christianity (pn)

Christopher Columbus (pn)

chronology (n)

Cicero (pn)

Cincinnatus (pn)

Cinco de Mayo (pn)

civil war (n)

class system (n)

classical Greek art and architecture (n)

clay pottery (n)

coffee trade (n)

Columbian Exchange (pn)

Commodore Matthew Perry (pn)

CE/Common Era (adj)

communism (n)

Confucianism (pn)

Confucius (pn)

conquer/conquest (v) (n)

Constantine (pn)

convent (n)

corrupt/corruption (v) (n)

Cortes (pn)

country of origin (n)

Court of Heian (pn)

Cro-Magnon (pn)

cuneiform (n)

custom (n)

czar (n)

Czar Nicholas II (pn)

daily prayer [Salat] (n)

dharma (n)

Diderot (pn)

discovery (n)

discovery of diamonds (n)

discovery of gold (n)

disease (n)

Duchy of Moscow (pn)

dugout Phoenician ship (n)

Early Middle Ages (pn)

East Africa (pn)

Eastern Roman Empire (pn)

Edmund Cartwright (pn)

Egyptian time (n)

electricity (n)

elite status (n)

Elizabeth Blackwell (pn)

emperor (n)

empire (n)

English Civil War (pn)

English Revolution of 1688 (pn)

Enlightenment (pn)

era (n)

Eric the Red (pn)

ethnic diversity (n)

ethnic tradition (n)

Eurasia (pn)

Eurasian society (n)

European colonization (n)

European crusades (n)

European economic community (n)

European explorer (n)

European opium trade (n)

European settler (n)

European Theater (pn)

expedition (n)

factory (n)

famine (n)

father of modern Egypt (n)

Ferdinand Magellan (pn)

feudal society (n)

first inhabitant (n)

forced relocation (n)

foreign policy (n)

foreign trade (n)

founding of Rome (n)

Francisco Franco (pn)

French colony (n)

French East India Company (pn)

French invasion of Egypt in 1798 (n)

French Quarter (pn)

French Quebec (pn)

French Revolution (pn)

Galileo Galilei (pn)

Garibaldi (pn)

Garibaldi's nationalist redshirts (n)

Genghis Khan (pn)

Great Canal of China (pn)

Greek city-state (n)

Greek gods and goddesses (n)

Guangzhou (pn)

gunpowder (n)

Gupta Empire (pn)

Haitian Revolution (pn)

Hajj (pn)

Han Empire (pn)

Hanging Gardens of Babylon (pn)

Hebrew Torah (pn)

Hegira [Hirjah] (pn)

Hellenist culture (n)

Hellenistic art (n)

Henri Matisse (pn)

hieroglyphic (n)

Hinduism (pn)

historic figure (n)

historical document (n)

hominid (n)

Huang He [Yellow River] civilization (pn)

human community (n)

Hundred Years' War (pn)

Hungarian revolt (n)

imperial conquest (n)

Incan Empire (pn)

Inca highway (pn)

indentured servant (n)

independent lord (n)

Indian spice (n)

Indian time (n)

indigenous people (n)

Industrial Age (pn)

industrial development (n)

industrial society (n)

Indus Valley (pn)

infectious disease (n)

international conflict (n)

international trade routes (n)

invention of paper (n)

iron tools and weapons (n)

Islam (pn)

Islamic law (n)

Jacques Cartier (pn)

Jakarta tales (n)

James Hargreaves (pn)

James Watt (pn)

Japanese feudal society (n)

Japanese tea ceremony (n)

Jesus of Nazareth (pn)

Jew (pn)

Jewish civilization (n)

Jewish time (n)

John Kay (pn)

Joseph Stalin (pn)

Judaism (pn)

Julius Caesar (pn)

Justinian (pn)

Kaaba (pn)

Kilwa (pn)

King Affonso II of the Kongo and Po (pn)

King Alfred of England (pn)

kingdom (n)

knight (n)

knightly class (n)

Kush culture (n)

League of Nations (pn)

lesson of history (n)

Liberty, Equality, Fraternity (pn)

long-distance trade (n)

Louis Pasteur (pn)

maize cultivation (n)

Mali Empire (pn)

Marco Polo (pn)

Marcus Aurelius (pn)

Marie Curie (pn)

Maurya Empire (pn)

Mayan calendar (pn)

Mayan city-state (n)

Mayan pyramids (n)

Mayan religion (n)

medical advance (n)

Medieval Europe (pn)

Mediterranean region (n)

Meiji Japan (pn)

Mesoamerica (pn)

Mesopotamia (pn)

Middle Passage (pn)

migrant (n)

military power (n)

Ming Dynasty (pn)

missionary (n)

Moche civilization (n)

Mohenjo-Daro (pn)

monk (n)

Moslem (pn)

mother country (n)

Mughal Empire (pn)

Muhammad (pn)

Muhammad Ali of Egypt (pn)

mummification (n)

Muslim (pn)

Muslim time (n)

Mycenaean Greek culture (n)

Napoleon Bonaparte (pn)

Napoleonic period (pn)

naval warfare (n)

navigate/navigation (v) (n)

Nazi Holocaust (pn)

Neanderthal (pn)

Nero (pn)

New Kingdom (pn)

New Testament (pn)

Newton (pn)

Nicolaus Copernicus (pn)

nonviolent resistance (n)

Norse invasion (n)

Norse long ship (n)

nuclear technology (n)

Oceania (pn)

Olmec civilization (n)

Ottoman Empire (pn)

overland trade route (n)

overseas trade (n)

Pablo Picasso (pn)

Pacific Rim economy (n)

Pacific Theater (pn)

Pan-Arabism (pn)

peasant (n)

pharaoh (n)

Phoenicia (pn)

plague (v) (n)

Pompeii (pn)

post-war period (n)

pottery (n)

Pre-European life in the Americas (n)

Puritan (pn)

pyramids [Egyptian] (n)

Qur'an/Koran (pn)

Ramadan (pn)

Rasputin (pn)

Reformation (pn)

religious freedom (n)

religious revival (n)

Renaissance (pn)

revolutionary government (n)

Richard Arkwright (pn)

ritual (n)

Roman Empire [Eastern/ Western] (pn)

Roman Republic (pn)

Roman system of roads (n)

ruling class (n)

Russian peasantry (n)

Safavid Empire (pn)

samurai class (n)

scientific breakthrough (n)

scientific revolution (n)

Scipio Africanus (pn)

serf (n)

Seven Years' War (pn)

Shah Abbas I (pn)

Shang Dynasty (pn)

Sheba (pn)

siege of Troy (n)

silk roads (n)

Socrates (pn)

solar system (n)

Solomon (pn)

Song Dynasty (pn)

Songhai Empire (pn)

Southern Iberia (pn)

Soviet invasion of Czechoslovakia (n)

Soviet Union (pn)

space exploration (n)

Spanish Civil War (pn)

Spanish colony (n)

spice trade (n)

Stonehenge (pn)

Suleiman the Magnificent (pn)

Sunna (pn)

Sun Yat-sen (pn)

superstition/superstitious (n) (adj)

Swahili (pn)

Syria (pn)

Taj Mahal (pn)

Tang China (pn)

Tang Empire (pn)

Ten Commandments (pn)

Tenochtitlan (pn)

Teotihuacan civilization (n)

Tiberius Gracchus (pn)

tobacco (n)

Tokugawa Shogunate (pn)

tradition (n)

transatlantic slave trade (n)

Treaty of Versailles (pn)

Turkic Empire (pn)

twenty-first century (n)

unify/unification (v) (n)

vaccinate/vaccine (v) (n)

Vasco da Gama (pn)

Vietnamese boat people (n)

Vladimir Lenin (pn)

Western Roman Empire (pn)

William the Conqueror (pn)

Winston Churchill (pn)

World War I (pn)

World War II (pn)

written code (n)

written language (n)

written record (n)

Zapotec civilization (n)

Zheng He maritime expeditions (n)

Zulu Empire (pn)

Civics

absence of rules and laws (n)

abuse of power (n)

acceptable behavior (n)

alien (n) (adj)

American holiday (n)

American society (n)

American symbol (n)

attitude (n)

behavior consequence (n)

Bill of Rights (pn)

campaign (v) (n)

candidate (n)

chamber of commerce (n)

citizenship (n)

city council (n)

civic-mindedness (n)

civic responsibility (n)

civil liberty (n)

civil right (n)

clean air laws (n)

Columbus Day (pn)

common good (n)

community (n)

compromise (v) (n)

Congress (pn)

consent of the governed (n)

consider the rights and interests of others (v)

constitution (n)

Constitution of the United States (pn)

court (n)

credibility/credible (n) (adj)

Declaration of Independence (pn)

delegated power (n)

democracy (n)

democratic party (n)

democratic value (n)

diplomacy (n)

discriminate/discrimination (v) (n)

discrimination based on age (n)

discrimination based on disability (n)

discrimination based on ethnicity (n)

discrimination based on gender (n)

discrimination based on language (n)

discrimination based on religious belief (n)

diversify/diversity (v) (n)

elected representative (n)

equal opportunity (n)

equal pay for equal work (n)

evidence (n)

executive/executive branch (n)

Fourth of July (pn)

freedom of expression (n)

freedom of religion (n)

freedom of speech (n)

governor (n)

Great Seal (pn)

Greek democracy (n)

health services (n)

highest law of the land (n)

human rights (n)

individual liberty (n)

individual responsibility (n)

individual rights (n)

institution (n)

interest group (n)

interpret/interpretation (v) (n)

invasion of privacy (n)

jury duty (n)

justice (n)

Labor Day (pn)

labor union (n)

law and order (n)

law enforcement (n)

lawmaker (n)

leadership (n)

legislator (n)

liberty and justice for all (n)

life, liberty, and the pursuit of happiness (n)

local government (n)

majority rule (n)

Martin Luther King Jr. (pn)

mayor (n)

Memorial Day (pn)

military force (n)

military intervention (n)

modern democratic thought (n)

motive (n)

national origin (n)

national park (n)

national security (n)

negotiate/negotiation (v) (n)

nobility (n)

norm (n)

oath of office (n)

outlaw (v) (n)

patriotism (n)

peaceful demonstration (n)

peacekeeper (n)

personal responsibility (n)

petition (v) (n)

point of view (n)

policy issue (n)

political candidate (n)

political cartoon (n)

political office (n)

political party (n)

politics (n)

pollute/pollution (v) (n)

population growth (n)

poverty (n)

power by the people (n)

precinct (n)

prejudice (v) (n)

president (n)

presidential election (n)

Presidents' Day (pn)

principle (n)

private life (n)

privilege (n)

protest (v) (n)

Parent Teacher Association (pn)

public good (n)

public office (n)

public policy (n)

public servant (n)

public utilities (n)

pure food and drug laws (n)

quality of life (n)

racial discrimination (n)

racial diversity (n)

reform/reformer (v) (n)

refugee (n)

religious belief (n)

religious discrimination (n)

represent/representation (v) (n)

representative (n) (adj)

revolution (n)

right to a fair trial (n)

right to choose one's work (n)

right to criticize the government (n)

right to hold office (n)

right to join a political party (n)

right to public education (n)

right to vote (n)

right to work (n)

royalty (n)

rule by the people (n)

rule of law (n)

school attendance (n)

school board (n)

school prayer (n)

self-discipline (n)

self-governance (n)

senator (n)

slavery (n)

social class (n)

social reform (n)

special interest group (n)

state government (n)

statehood (n)

state legislature (n)

state senator (n)

Statue of Justice (pn)

Statue of Liberty (pn)

Supreme Court (pn)

tax/taxes (v) (n)

Thanksgiving (pn)

tolerate/tolerance (v) (n)

trade agreement (n)

treaty (n)

tribal council (n)

tribal government (n)

Uncle Sam (pn)

unemployment (n)

United States citizenship (n)

unlimited government (n)

veteran (n)

Veterans' Day (pn)

veterans' memorial (n)

volunteer/volunteerism (v) (n)

welfare (n)

world leader (n)

Economics

advantage (n)

barter system (n)

benefit (v) (n)

big business (n)

borrow (v)

business firm (n)

capital (n)

capital goods (n)

capital resource (n)

class (n)

commercial advertising (n)

commercial center (n)

competition (n)

competitive market (n)

consumer (n)

consumption (n)

contract (n)

contract negotiation (n)

credit (n)

currency (n)

customer service (n)

debt (n)

developing country (n)

development (n)

division of labor (n)

earn/earnings (v) (n)

economic interdependence (n)

economic system (n)

economy (n)

employer (n)

employment (n)

entertainment industry (n)

entrepreneur (n)

firm (n)

funds (n)

goods/services exchange (n)

household (n)

incentive (n)

income (n)

income tax (n)

innovation (n)

invention (n)

investment (n)

investor (n)

labor (v) (n)

labor movement (n)

limited budget (n)

limited resources (n)

loan (v) (n)

luxury good (n)

manufacture (v)

market (v) (n)

marketplace (n)

mass advertising (n)

mass media (n)

mass production (n)

media (n)

merchant (n)

middle class (n) (adj)

modernize/modernization
    (v) (n)

natural resource (n)

partnership (n)

payment (n)

penalty (n)

personal value (n)

poverty (n)

price decrease (n)

price increase (n)

produce/producer (v) (n)

product (n)

production (n)

profit (n)

profit opportunity (n)

property ownership (n)

purchasing power (n)

rent (v) (n)

resource (n)

resource scarcity (n)

revenue (n)

reward (v) (n)

risk (v) (n)

salary (n)

savings (n)

scarcity (n)

shortage (n)

slogan (n)

specialization (n)

surplus (n)

tax (v) (n)

tenant (n)

textile industry (n)

trade (v) (n)

trade barrier (n)

trade-off (n)

training (n)

value (v) (n)

wage (n)

working conditions (n)

workplace (n)

world economy (n)

Geography

accessibility (n)

aerial photograph (n)

Afghanistan (pn)

Africa (pn)

agricultural practice (n)

agriculture (n)

air conditioning (n)

air pollution (n)

Alabama (pn)

Alaska (pn)

Americas (pn)

Andes Mountains (pn)

Antarctic Circle (pn)

Appalachian Mountains (pn)

aqueduct (n)

archeology/archeologist (n)

architecture/architect (n)

Arizona (pn)

Arkansas (pn)

artifact (n)

Asia (pn)

Atlantic Basin (pn)

Atlantic Ocean (pn)

atmosphere (n)

Australia (pn)

Baghdad (pn)

Balkans (pn)

behavior pattern (n)

Bering Land Bridge (pn)

Bering Sea (pn)

Black Sea (pn)

boomtown (n)

boundary (n)

Brazil (pn)

Britain (pn)

British Isles (n)

Buenos Aires (pn)

Cairo (pn)

California (pn)

Canada (pn)

canal system (n)

capacity (n)

capital (n)

cardinal directions (n)

Caribbean (pn)

Central Africa (pn)

Central America (pn)

central business district (n)

chart (n)

China (pn)

city center (n)

climate change (n)

coal mining (n)

coastal area (n)

colonization (n)

Colorado (pn)

Colorado mining town
  [nineteenth century] (n)

communication route (n)

compass (n)

Connecticut (pn)

conservation issue (n)

contagious disease (n)

continent (n)

country (n)

crop failure (n)

crop yield (n)

Cuba (pn)

cultural tradition (n)

culture (n)

culture group (n)

Delaware (pn)

discovery (n)

Dominican Republic (pn)

downwind (n)

drought (n)

earthquake (n)

east (n)

East Asia (pn)

East Coast (pn)

Eastern Europe (pn)

Eastern Hemisphere (pn)

economic region (n)

education system (n)

Egypt (pn)

energy consumption (n)

England (pn)

environment (n)

environmental conditions (n)

equator (n)

Erie Canal (pn)

Europe (pn)

European colonialism (n)

expansion (n)

fall line (n)

famine (n)

farming method (n)

farmland (n)

fertile soil (n)

fertilizer (n)

fire station (n)

flash flood (n)

flooding pattern (n)

Florida (pn)

food chain (n)

food production (n)

food storage (n)

food supply (n)

food web (n)

force (v) (n)

forest cover (n)

forest fire (n)

forestry (n)

fossil fuel (n)

France (pn)

Ganges River Valley (pn)

geographic border (n)

geographical representation (n)

geology (n)

Georgia (pn)

Germany (pn)

ghost town (n)

grassland (n)

harbor (v) (n)

Hawaii (pn)

hemisphere (n)

Hindus (pn)

historic site (n)

historical map (n)

holy city (n)

houses on stilts (n)

humid tropical climate (n)

Idaho (pn)

Illinois (pn)

India (pn)

Indiana (pn)

Indian Ocean (pn)

Indonesia (pn)

inhabitants (n)

international date line (n)

invade/invasion (v) (n)

Iowa (pn)

Iran (pn)

Iraq (pn)

Ireland (pn)

iron (n)

iron ore (n)

irrigation (n)

Israel (pn)

Italy (pn)

Japan (pn)

Kansas (pn)

Kentucky (pn)

kilometer (n)

Korea (pn)

land clearing (n)

landform (n)

landlocked country (n)

landmark (n)

landscape (n)

landslide (n)

land use (n)

land-use regulation (n)

Latin America (pn)

latitude (n)

legend (n)

life cycle (n)

life expectancy (n)

lifestyle (n)

literacy (n)

literacy rate (n)

local resource (n)

local water (n)

log/logging (v) (n)

London (pn)

longitude (n)

Louisiana (pn)

low-income area (n)

manufacturing plant (n)

Maine (pn)

Malaysia (pn)

Mali (pn)

map grid (n)

map projection (n)

Maryland (pn)

Massachusetts (pn)

metropolitan area (n)

Mexico (pn)

Michigan (pn)

Middle East (pn)

migrate/migration (v) (n)

mineral resource (n)

mine (v) (n)

Minnesota (pn)

Mississippi (pn)

Mississippi River (pn)

Missouri (pn)

monsoon (n)

Montana (pn)

mountain pass (n)

mountain range (n)

mudslide (n)

Muslim trading vessel (pn)

national forest (n)

national park (n)

Native Americans (n)

natural disaster (n)

natural environment (n)

natural hazard (n)

natural resource (n)

Nebraska (pn)

Netherlands (pn)

Nevada (pn)

New Hampshire (pn)

New Jersey (pn)

New Mexico (pn)

New Orleans (pn)

New York (pn)

New Zealand (pn)

Nile Delta (pn)

Nile Valley (pn)

north (n)

North Africa (pn)

North America (pn)

North Carolina (pn)

North Dakota (pn)

Northeast (pn)

North Pole (pn)

Nubia (pn)

nuclear power plant (n)

ocean current (n)

Ohio (pn)

Oklahoma (pn)

Old Northwest (pn)

ordinal directions (n)

Oregon (pn)

Pacific Islands (pn)

Pacific Ocean (pn)

Pacific Rim (pn)

Palestine (pn)

Panama Canal (pn)

parallel (n) (adj)

Paris (n)

pattern of change (n)

Pennsylvania (pn)

Peru (pn)

Philadelphia (pn)

physical feature (n)

physical geography (n)

place of origin (n)

plain (n) (adj)

plantation agriculture (n)

plateau (v) (n)

plot (v) (n)

political geography (n)

pollute/pollution (v) (n)

populate/population (v) (n)

population growth (n)

port (n)

port city (n)

precipitation (n)

preservation (n)

prime meridian (n)

projection (n)

province (n)

Puerto Rico (pn)

rain forest (n)

recreation area (n)

recycle (v)

refrigerated railroad car (n)

refrigerated trucking (n)

reusable (adj)

Rhode Island (pn)

river system (n)

Riyadh (pn)

road development (n)

Rocky Mountains (pn)

Rome (pn)

Ruhr (pn)

running water (n)

rural area (n)

Russia (pn)

satellite image (n)

Saudi Arabia (pn)

scale (n)

Scandinavia (pn)

scarce resource (n)

scenic area (n)

school attendance zone (n)

Scotland (pn)

section (v) (n)

Siberia (pn)

Singapore (pn)

single household (n)

site (v) (n)

situation (n)

smog (n)

social class (n)

society (n)

soil conservation (n)

soil region (n)

solar energy (n)

south (n)

South Africa (pn)

South America (pn)

Southeast Asia (pn)

South Carolina (pn)

South Dakota (pn)

South Pacific (pn)

South Pole (pn)

Southwest Asia (pn)

Spain (pn)

storage (n)

Sub-Saharan Africa (pn)

suburb (n)

Suez Canal (pn)

technology (n)

Tennessee (pn)

territory (n)

Texas (pn)

Tigris-Euphrates Valley (pn)

timber cutting (n)

Timbuktu (pn)

time zone (n)

Tokyo (pn)

topographic map (n)

tornado (n)

tourist center (n)

township (n)

trade pact (n)

trade route (n)

trade wind (n)

transportation route (n)

transportation system (n)

Turkey (pn)

urban center (n)

urban community (n)

Utah (pn)

vegetation region (n)

Vermont (pn)

Versailles (pn)

Vietnam (pn)

Virginia (pn)

volcano (n)

volume (n)

Washington (pn)

Washington, D.C. (pn)

water availability (n)

water basin (n)

water crossing (n)

water pollution (n)

waterway (n)

west (n)

West Africa (pn)

West Coast (pn)

Western Europe (pn)

Western Hemisphere (pn)

West Virginia (pn)

wetland (n)

wind storm (n)

windward (adj)

Wisconsin (pn)

world population growth (n)

Wyoming (pn)

Middle School
U.S. History

1960 presidential campaign (n)

African American Union soldier (pn)

American dream (n)

American foreign policy (n)

American identity (n)

American West (pn)

Anne Hutchinson (pn)

antebellum (adj)

antifederalist (n)

anti-immigrant attitude (n)

antislavery ideology (n)

Article III of the Constitution (pn)

Atlantic slave trade (pn)

Bacon's Rebellion (pn)

Battle for Britain (pn)

Benjamin Franklin (pn)

Big Stick diplomacy (pn)

Bill Clinton (pn)

Calvin Coolidge (pn)

Camp David Accords (pn)

Charles Evans Hughes (pn)

Christian evangelical movement (n)

civil rights movement (n)

closed shop (n)

colony in Massachusetts (n)

Compromise of 1850 (pn)

Compromise of 1877 (pn)

congressional authority (n)

Continental Congress (pn)

Dawes Severalty Act of 1887 (pn)

Declaration of Sentiments (pn)

discriminate/discrimination (v) (n)

dollar diplomacy (n)

domestic policy (n)

domestic program (n)

Francis Townsend (pn)

Dred Scott decision (n)

Dwight D. Eisenhower (pn)

Eisenhower doctrine (pn)

election of 1880 (n)

election of 1912 (n)

Engel v. Vitale [1962] (pn)

equal rights amendment (n)

Fair Deal (pn)

family assistance program (n)

farm labor (n)

featherbedding (n)

federal Indian policy (n)

federalism (n)

feminism (n)

Filipino insurrection (n)

First Amendment (pn)

First Congress (pn)

First Lady (pn)

flawed peace (n)

free exercise clause (n)

French and Indian War (pn)

Garvey movement (n)

gentleman's agreement (n)

Glorious Revolution (pn)

Great Society (pn)

Hiram Johnson (pn)

Huey Long (pn)

immigration screening (n)

Industrial Workers of the World (pn)

Iranian hostage crisis (n)

James Buchanan (pn)

James Madison (pn)

Jay's Treaty (pn)

jazz (n)

John Marshall (pn)

Joseph McCarthy (pn)

Judiciary Act of 1789 (pn)

Kennedy assassination (n)

Korean War (pn)

Ku Klux Klan (pn)

"Letter From a Birmingham Jail" (pn)

Lewis and Clark expedition (pn)

Little Rock 1957 (pn)

Lost Generation (pn)

loyalist (n)

lynch/lynching (v) (n)

Malcolm X (pn)

Marbury v. Madison [1803] (pn)

Martin Luther King Jr's "I have a dream" speech (pn)

Mayflower Compact (pn)

McCarthyism (pn)

midnight judge (n)

migrant worker (n)

modern republicanism (n)

NAACP (pn)

Navigation Acts (pn)

new freedom (n)

new nationalism (n)

North American Free Trade Agreement (pn)

North American mound-building people (n)

North American plains society (n)

Northwest Ordinance of 1778 (pn)

Oregon Territory (pn)

pardon of Richard Nixon (n)

Paxton Boys Massacre (pn)

populism (n)

Populist Party (pn)

Progressive movement (pn)

Reconstruction (pn)

return to domesticity (n)

Robert La Follette (pn)

Roosevelt coalition (n)

Rust Belt (pn)

Scopes trial (pn)

Seneca Falls Convention (pn)

share the wealth (v)

shot heard round the world (n)

Soviet espionage (n)

stereotype (v) (n)

Sun Belt (pn)

temperance (n)

Tenure of Office Act (pn)

territorial expansion (n)

Thirteen Virtues (pn)

Townsend Plan (pn)

Transcendentalism (n)

trans-Mississippi region (pn)

triangular trade route (n)

Truman Doctrine (pn)

universal white male suffrage (n)

U.S. Supreme Court (pn)

U.S. v. Nixon [1974] (pn)

Warren G. Harding (pn)

Whig Party (pn)

Woodrow Wilson's Fourteen Points (pn)

women's suffrage (n)

Works Progress Administration (pn)

World History

Abbasid Empire (pn)

Abd al-Quadir (pn)

African resistance movement (n)

Agustin de Iturbide (pn)

Akbar (pn)

Albert Einstein (pn)

alchemy (n)

Alfred Krupp (pn)

American Indian nation (n)

Ammianus Marcellinus (pn)

Anasazi (pn)

Anatolia (pn)

antibiotics (n)

apartheid (n)

Arab Muslim (pn)

armed revolution (n)

arranged marriage (n)

Aryan culture (n)

Ashanti (pn)

Asian art form (n)

Assyria (pn)

Assyrian Empire (n)

astronomical discovery (n)

astronomy (n)

atomic bomb (n)

authoritarian rule (n)

Axis powers (pn)

Babylonian Empire (pn)

Baltic region (pn)

Bantu (pn)

Barbados (pn)

Benin (pn)

Berlin (pn)

Bismarck's "Blood and Iron" speech (pn)

bourgeois/bourgeoisie (n) (adj)

British rule (n)

Buddhism/Buddhist beliefs (pn)

Carolingian Empire (pn)

Catherine the Great (pn)

Catholic Christianity (pn)

Catholic Church (pn)

Catholic Reformation (pn)

Cecil Rhodes (pn)

Champa (pn)

Chandogya Upanishad (pn)

Chandragupta (pn)

chattel slavery (n)

Charles Darwin (pn)

child labor (n)

China's 1911 Republican Revolution (pn)

Christian religious art (n)

Christian soldier (n)

civilization (n)

classical civilization (n)

Cleisthenes (pn)

clergy (n)

Clothilde (pn)

Clovis (pn)

coerced labor (n)

Colonial Africa (pn)

colonize/colonization (v) (n)

commercial agriculture (n)

communal life (n)

communist country (n)

Communist Party (pn)

Communist Party in China (pn)

Conference of Versailles (pn)

Congress of Vienna (pn)

constitutional monarchy (n)

convert (v) (n)

Coptic Christians (pn)

courtly ideal (n)

courtly love (n)

creation myths of Babylon (n)

creation myths of China (n)

creation myths of Egypt (n)

creation myths of Greece (n)

creation myths of Sumer (n)

Creole (pn)

Creole-dominated revolt of 1812 (n)

Crete (pn)

Crimean War (pn)

cross-cultural contact (n)

Crusades (pn)

cultural exchange (n)

cultural heritage (n)

cultural integration (n)

cultural revolution (n)

Dahomey (pn)

Dai Vet (pn)

Daoism/Taoism (pn)

Darius I (pn)

Darius the Great (pn)

democratic despotism (n)

desegregation (n)

dissent (v) (n)

Dorothea Lange (pn)

dowry (n)

Dutch colonization (n)

Dutch Republic (pn)

dynastic politics (n)

Early Middle Ages (pn)

East India Company (pn)

Egyptian civilization (n)

Elizabeth I (pn)

Ellora (pn)

emigration (n)

Emmeline Pankhurst (pn)

empire-builder (n)

English Bill of Rights [1689] (pn)

English Common Law (pn)

epic (n) (adj)

Epic of Gilgamesh (pn)

epidemic disease (n)

Estates-General (pn)

ethnic art (n)

ethnic conflict (n)

ethnic identity (n)

ethnicity (n)

ethnic minority (n)

ethnic origin (n)

European imperialism (n)

European monarchy (n)

European resistance movement (n)

evolution/evolve (v) (n)

exodus (n)

fascism (n)

fascist aggression (n)

fascist regime (n)

Father Miguel Hidalgo (pn)

feudalism (n)

feudal lord (n)

fortify/fortification (v) (n)

Francis Bacon (pn)

Francisco Pizarro (pn)

Frankish Empire (pn)

French colonization (n)

French Revolution (pn)

Gangetic states (n)

Gangzhou [Canton] (pn)

Glorious Revolution of 1688 (pn)

gothic cathedral (n)

Great Leap Forward (pn)

Great Plague (pn)

great powers in Europe (n)

Great Reform Bill of 1832 (pn)

Greco-Roman antiquity (pn)

Greece (pn)

Greek art (n)

Greek Christian civilization (n)

Greek drama (n)

Greek rationalism (n)

Greenland (pn)

Grimke sisters (pn)

Griot "keeper of tales" (pn)

Haitian Revolution (pn)

Heian (pn)

Hellinistic period (pn)

Helsinki Accords (pn)

Herding societies (n)

Hermit Kingdom (pn)

hierarchy/hierarchical (n) (a)

High Middle Ages (pn)

High Renaissance (pn)

Hinduism (pn)

historical account (n)

Hittite people (n)

hoard/hoarder (v) (n)

Holocaust (pn)

Homo erectus (n)

Homo sapiens (n)

Iberia (pn)

Ibn Battuta (pn)

ice age (n)

imperial absolutism (n)

imperialism (n)

imperial policy (n)

Indian culture (n)

Indo-Aryan people (n)

Indo-European language (n)

Indo-Gangetic plain (n)

Indonesian archipelago (n)

industrialization (n)

international relations (n)

intervene/intervention (v) (n)

Iraq invasion of Kuwait [1991] (n)

Islam (pn)

Islamic beliefs (n)

Italian Renaissance (pn)

James Maxwell (pn)

Janissary Corps (pn)

Japanese modernization (n)

Japanese occupation of Manchuria [1930s] (n)

Jean Jaures (pn)

Jesus Christ (pn)

Jewish monotheism (n)

Jewish refugee (n)

Jewish resistance movement (n)

Jose Clemente Orozco (pn)

Kamakura period (pn)

Karl Marx (pn)

karma (n)

Kathe Kollwitz (pn)

Khans (pn)

Kingdom of Aksum (pn)

kinship group (n)

Korean culture (n)

Kulak (n)

Kuomintang (pn)

lateen sail (n)

Lenin's New Economic Policy (pn)

Leo Africanus (pn)

linguistic diversity (n)

Lucretia Mott (pn)

Lunda Kingdom (pn)

Macedonia (pn)

Machu Picchu (pn)

Magna Carta [1215] (pn)

Mahmud II (pn)

Malayo-Polynesia (pn)

Manchu Empire (pn)

Manchu (pn)

Mandate of Heaven (pn)

Manorialism (pn)

Mao Zedong (pn)

Mao's program (n)

marine transportation (n)

maritime technology (n)

maritime trade route (n)

Maroon society (n)

Marshall Plan (pn)

Mauryan-Buddhist power (n)

Medieval Christian society (n)

medieval theology (n)

megalithic stone building (n)

megalopolis (n)

Menelik II (pn)

Merotitic period (pn)

Middle Ages (pn)

Middle Kingdom (pn)

militant religious movement (n)

military mobilization (n)

military tactic (n)

military unit (n)

Minoan Crete (pn)

modern art (n)

Mohandas Gandhi (pn)

Mohandas Gandhi's call for nonviolent dissent (n)

Monarch Mansa Musa (pn)

monarchy (n)

monastery (n)

monasticism (n)

Mongol conquest of 1206 (pn)

moral reform (n)

Moroccan resistance movement (pn)

mosque (n)

Muhammad Ahmad (pn)

Muslim Empire (pn)

Napoleon's invasions (n)

national self-rule (n)

nation-state (n)

nativism (n)

Nazi (pn)

Nazi-Soviet Non-Aggression Pact of 1939 (pn)

Neolithic agricultural society (n)

neutrality (n)

neutral nation (n)

nirvana (n)

nobility (n)

nomadic people (n)

Normandy Invasion (pn)

North Atlantic Treaty Organization (pn)

nuclear politics (n)

Oaxaca (pn)

Old Kingdom (pn)

Old Regime France (pn)

opium war (n)

oracle bone inscription (n)

Paleolithic cave painting (n)

Panchatantra (pn)

pandemic disease (n)

papacy/pope (n)

pastoral nomadic people (n)

Paris Peace Accord of 1973 (pn)

participatory government (n)

pathogen (n)

patriarchal society (n)

Paulus Orosius (pn)

peasantry (n)

People's Republic of China (pn)

Persia (pn)

Persian Empire (pn)

Persian Gulf (pn)

perspective (n)

Peter Stolypin (pn)

Peter the Great (pn)

philanthropist/philanthropy (n)

Philippine annexation (n)

philosophical movement (n)

philosophy (n)

polis (n)

political alliance (n)

political border (n)

Portuguese caravel (n)

post-Mao China (n)

post–World War I (n)

post–World War II (n)

post-Vincennes (n)

Potsdam Agreement (pn)

Priscus (pn)

Protestant Christianity (pn)

Protestant Reformation (pn)

Punic Wars (pn)

Puritanism (pn)

Queen Hatshepsut (pn)

Quin Empire (pn)

racial minority (n)

Ramsay MacDonald (pn)

Ramses II (pn)

rapid industrialization (n)

ration/rationing (v) (n)

Raymond Poincaré (pn)

Reagan-Gorbachev summit
   diplomacy (n)

reconquest of Spain (n)

reincarnation (n)

religious dissenter (n)

removal policy (n)

renaissance humanism (n)

René Descartes (pn)

ritual sacrifice (n)

Robert Owen's New Lanark
   System (pn)

Roman Catholic Church (pn)

Roman occupation of Britain (n)

romanticism (n)

Rosa Luxemburg (pn)

royal court (n)

Rule of St. Benedict (pn)

Russian absolutism (n)

Russian Revolution of 1917 (pn)

saint (n)

Samarkand (pn)

Samori Ture (pn)

Sassanid Empire (pn)

Saxon peoples (n)

scientific method (n)

Scythian society (n)

secede/secession (v) (n)

Second Industrial Revolution
   (pn)

secular ruler (n)

secular state (n)

segregation (n)

seizure of Constantinople (n)

Selim III (pn)

Shiba Kokan (pn)

Shinto (pn)

Siam (pn)

Sigmund Freud (pn)

Solon (pn)

Sotabu Screen (pn)

Soviet bloc (n)

Soviet domination (n)

Soviet invasion of Afghanistan
   (n)

Soviet Union (pn)

Spanish Muslim society (n)

squire (n)

St. Petersburg, "window on the
   west" (n)

Stalin's purge (n)

Stanley Baldwin (pn)

steppe lands (n)

Story of Olaudah Equiano
   [Gustavus Vassa] (pn)

superpower rivalry (n)

Svetaketu (pn)

telecommunication (n)

terrorism (n)

theater of conflict (n)

Thutmose II (pn)

Tiananmen Square protest (pn)

Timur the Lame [Tamerlane]
   (pn)

Tippu Tip (pn)

Toltecs (pn)

Torah (pn)

totalitarian regime (n)

Toussaint L'Ouverture (pn)

trading triangle (n)

trench warfare (n)

trial of Galileo (n)

tribal identity (n)

Trojan War (pn)

Turkic migration (n)

Turkestan (pn)

unification of Germany (n)

unification of Italy (n)

Upanishad (pn)

Vedas (pn)

Vedic gods (n)

war crime (n)

warrior culture (n)

Warsaw Pact (pn)

weaponry (n)

Western and Eastern European
   societies (n)

Western art and literature (n)

World Council of Churches (pn)

world history (n)

world power (n)

world war (n)

Xiongnu society (pn)

Zagwé Dynasty (pn)

Zhou Dynasty (pn)

Zhu Xi (pn)

Civics

AFL-CIO (pn)

Aid to Families with Dependent Children (pn)

allegiance (n)

ambassador (n)

American citizenship (n)

American Revolution (pn)

American tribal government (n)

armed forces (n)

arms control (n)

bias (n)

binding agreement (n)

cabinet (n)

capital punishment (n)

central government (n)

charitable group (n)

charter document (n)

checks and balances (n)

citizenship by birth (n)

civil disobedience (n)

civil rights (n)

civil service examination (n)

civil service reform (n)

civilian (n)

civilian control of the military (n)

coining [money] (n)

colonial charters (n)

commander in chief (n)

common cause (n)

Confederate States of America (pn)

conflict management (n)

conservatism (n)

constitutional law (n)

contemporary democracy (n)

corrective justice (n)

court packing (n)

covert action (n)

criminal law (n)

curfew (n)

customs search (n)

debate (v) (n)

delegated powers (n)

democrat (n)

Democratic-Republican Party (pn)

demographics (n)

demonstration (n)

domestic policy (n)

dress code (n)

due process (n)

economic aid (n)

economic sanctions (n)

economic security (n)

English Parliament (pn)

enumerated powers (n)

Environmental Protection Act (pn)

environmental protection movement (n)

equal justice for all (n)

equal opportunity (n)

equal protection of the law (n)

equal rights under the law (n)

equity (n)

ethical belief (n)

ethical dilemma (n)

ethical system (n)

ex post facto (adj) (adv)

executive power (n)

fair notice of a hearing (n)

fair trial (n)

federal court (n)

federal income tax (n)

Federalist Papers (pn)

First Amendment (pn)

foreign aid (n)

foreign policy (n)

foreign relations (n)

form a more perfect union (v)

founder (n)

framer (n)

freedom of assembly (n)

freedom of association (n)

freedom of conscience (n)

freedom of petition (n)

freedom of press (n)

freedom of residence (n)

freedom to emigrate (n)

freedom to marry whomever one chooses (n)

freedom to travel (n)

fundamental value (n)

gender diversity (n)

general election (n)

Gettysburg Address (pn)

Greenpeace (pn)

gun control (n)

habeas corpus (n)

hate speech (n)

human nature (n)

immigration (n)

impeachment (n)

income tax (n)

indentured servitude (n)

informed citizenry (n)

inheritance law (n)

institution [political] (n)

interest group (n)

international law (n)

International Red Cross (pn)

interstate commerce (n)

interstate highways (n)

isolationism (n)

judicial branch (n)

judicial power (n)

just compensation (n)

juvenile (n) (adj)

labor movement (n)

landmark case (n)

Latin America (pn)

League of Women Voters (pn)

legal recourse (n)

legislative branch (n)

legislative power (n)

legislature (n)

letter to the editor (n)

liberal democracy (n)

license/licensing (v) (n)

limited government (n)

local election (n)

lower court (n)

loyal opposition (n)

majority rule (n)

mandate (v) (n)

Marbury v. Madison [1803] (pn)

marital status (n)

maritime rights (n)

Medicaid (pn)

Medicare (pn)

minimum wage (n)

minority rights (n)

moral responsibility (n)

moral value (n)

NAACP (pn)

national defense (n)

nationalism (n)

nation-state (n)

NATO (pn)

naturalization (n)

Nineteenth Amendment (pn)

nomination (n)

OAS (pn)

parliament (n)

parliamentary system (n)

party system (n)

picket (v) (n)

political appointment (n)

political life (n)

popular sovereignty (n)

prayer in public school (n)

preamble (n)

Preamble to the Constitution (pn)

president's cabinet (n)

press (n)

presumption of innocence (n)

prime minister (n)

principle (n)

private life (n)

private property (n)

property tax (n)

protest (v) (n)

public agenda (n)

public education (n)

public life (n)

public opinion (n)

public trial (n)

Pure Food and Drug Act (pn)

recall election (n)

reform government (n)

reform legislation (n)

representative democracy (n)

representative government (n)

Republican/Republican Party (pn)

revenue (n)

right of appeal (n)

right to acquire/dispose of property (n)

right to copyright (n)

right to counsel (n)

right to enter into a lawful contract (n)

right to equal protection of the law (n)

right to establish a business (n)

right to hold public office (n)

right to join a labor union (n)

right to join a professional association (n)

right to know (n)

right to patent (n)

right to privacy (n)

right to property (n)

Roman Republic (pn)

rule of men (n)

senate (n)

separation of church and state (n)

separation of powers (n)

shared power (n)

slander (v) (n)

Socialist Party (pn)

socialism/socialist (n)

Social Security (pn)

sovereign state (n)

sovereignty (n)

speedy trial (n)

state bureaucracy (n)

state constitution (n)

state court (n)

state election (n)

state sales tax (n)

states' rights (n)

strike (n)

suffrage (n)

suffrage movement (n)

supreme being (n)

tariff (n)

tax revenue (n)

terrorism (n)

third party (n)

totalitarian system (n)

trade union (n)

treason (n)

trial by jury (n)

union/Union (n) (pn)

United Nations (pn)

United Nations Charter (pn)

United States foreign policy (n)

United States isolationist policy (n)

Universal Declaration of Human Rights (pn)

veto power (n)

vote of no confidence (n)

voter registration (n)

welfare (n)

World Court (pn)

Economics

agribusiness (n)

agricultural economy (n)

average price level (n)

blue-collar sector (n)

business practice (n)

capitalism (n)

capitalist economy (n)

carrying money (v)

central authority (n)

cheap labor (n)

checking account (n)

command economic system (n)

commercial bank (n)

commercialization (n)

contract labor (n)

cost of production (n)

credit policy (n)

debtor class (n)

decentralization (n)

demographic shift (n)

depression (n)

disincentive (n)

earned income (n)

economic incentive (n)

economic indicator (n)

economic power (n)

economic specialization (n)

economy (n)

employment opportunity (n)

equilibrium (n)

exchange rate (n)

export (v) (n)

exporting firm (n)

fair employment practice (n)

finance (v) (n)

foreign capital investment (n)

foreign exchange market (n)

foreign trade (n)

free trade (n)

fringe benefit (n)

full-time employment (n)

funding (n)

global communication (n)

global market (n)

gross domestic product (n)

human capital (n)

human resource (n)

import (v) (n)

inflation (n)

inflation rate (n)

interest (n)

intermediary (n)

international market (n)

labor force (n)

labor market (n)

labor union (n)

large firm (n)

law of supply and demand (n)

market clearing price (n)

market economy (n)

market exchange (n)

mass consumer economy (n)

middle-class culture (n)

national bank (n)

national defense spending (n)

national economy (n)

negative incentive (n)

nonprofit organization (n)

nonrival product (n)

occupational specialization (n)

opportunity benefit (n)

opportunity cost (n)

organized labor (n)

output per hour (n)

output per machine (n)

output per unit of land (n)

output per worker (n)

part-time employment (n)

pooled resources (n)

positive incentive (n)

price war (n)

private market (n)

production (n)

productivity (n)

professional sector (n)

property rights (n)

protective tariff (n)

public project (n)

quota (n)

recession (n)

relative price (n)

rent control (n)

risk reduction (n)

sales tax (n)

savings account (n)

self-employment (n)

self-sufficiency (n)

service industry (n)

shared consumption (n)

side effect (n)

special interest group (n)

specialized economic institution (n)

spoils system (n)

standard currency (n)

standard of living (n)

storing money (n)

substitute product (n)

supplier (n)

supply and demand (n)

surcharge (n)

systems of weights and measures (n)

tariff (n)

tax deduction (n)

tax exemption (n)

tax reduction (n)

total benefit (n)

total cost (n)

total market value (n)

trade balance (n)

unemployment (n)

unemployment rate (n)

wage rate (n)

white-collar sector (n)

working-class culture (n)

Geography

acid rain (n)

adaptation (n)

agrarian society (n)

agricultural lifestyle (n)

agricultural technology (n)

Algeria (pn)

Alps (pn)

alphanumeric system (n)

alternative energy source (n)

Amsterdam (pn)

Andean region (pn)

anthropology/anthropologist (n)

architectural style of buildings (n)

arid climate (n)

assimilation (n)

Australia (pn)

average family size (n)

axis (n)

Barrier Island (pn)

Belgium (pn)

bicycle lane (n)

biome (n)

biosphere (n)

birth rate (n)

Boston (pn)

boundary dispute (n)

Brenner Pass (pn)

Burma Pass (pn)

Canberra (pn)

Capitol Hill (pn)

Central Europe (pn)

Chile (pn)

China (pn)

Chinatown (pn)

clearing of forests (n)

climate region (n)

Congo (pn)

conserve/conservationist (v) (n)

crop rotation (n)

Cumberland Gap (pn)

data set (n)

database (n)

death rate (n)

decentralization (n)

deforestation (n)

demographic change (n)

demographic information (n)

density (n)

density of population (n)

developed county (n)

developing country (n)

diamond trade (n)

diesel machinery (n)

dispersion (n)

division [of Earth's surface] (n)

domestic crop (n)

downstream (p)

drainage basin (n)

dry-land farming technique (n)

earth-moving machinery (n)

earthquake-resistant construction (n)

earthquake zone (n)

East Indies (pn)

Eastern Mediterranean (pn)

economic alliance (n)

ecosystem (n)

electric car (n)

energy-poor region (n)

energy industry (n)

energy source (n)

environmental change (n)

equilibrium (n)

Ethiopia (pn)

evacuation route (n)

everglade (n)

export (v) (n)

extractive mining (n)

fall line of the Appalachians (n)

fauna (n)

flat-map projection (n)

flood-control project (n)

floodplain (n)

flora (n)

fungi (n)

geographic factor (n)

Ghana (pn)

global impact (n)

global warming (n)

Great American Desert (pn)

grid (n)

Hague, The (pn)

Haiti (pn)

hemisphere (n)

historic preservation (n)

Holland (pn)

Hong Kong (pn)

housing development (n)

Huang Ho (pn)

human process (n)

hurricane (n)

hurricane shelter (n)

hurricane tracks (n)

hydroelectric power (n)

imported resource (n)

Indians (pn)

Indonesia (pn)

industrial center (n)

industrial district (n)

infant mortality rate (n)

infrastructure (n)

Inner Asia (pn)

interdependence (n)

internal structure (n)

Inuit (pn)

involuntary migration (n)

Iraq (pn)

Irish immigrant (n)

irrigation (n)

isthmus (n)

Italy (pn)

Khyber Pass (pn)

landlocked (adj)

land-use data (n)

land-use pattern (n)

language region (n)

leeward (adj)

levee (n)

life form (n)

linkage (n)

literacy rate (n)

local scale (n)

long-distance migration (n)

major parallel (n)

marine climate (n)

marine vegetation (n)

meridian (n)

Mesopotamia (pn)

midaltitude (n)

migrant population (n)

military campaign (n)

military installation (n)

mobility (n)

monsoon wind (n)

mortality rate (n)

multiculturalism (n)

Muslims/Moslems (pn)

natural resource (n)

natural vegetation (n)

natural wetlands (n)

Netherlands (pn)

New Delhi (pn)

Newfoundland (pn)

Niger River (pn)

Nile Valley (pn)

nonrenewable resource (n)

nuclear waste storage (n)

ocean circulation (n)

ocean pollution (n)

Ogallala Aquifer (pn)

old-growth forest (n)

origin (n)

overfish (v)

overpopulation (n)

Pakistan (pn)

pedestrian walkway (n)

pesticide (n)

petroleum (n)

Philippine archipelago (n)

Philippines (pn)

physical environment (n)

physical geography (n)

physical variation (n)

plant species (n)

Poland (pn)

political region (n)

political unit (n)

Polynesia (pn)

population concentration (n)

population density (n)

population distribution (n)

population growth rate (n)

population region (n)

population structure (n)

port city (n)

port of entry (n)

Portugal (n)

postal zone (n)

prevailing wind (n)

Prime Meridian [Greenwich meridian] (pn)

principal line (n)

principal meridian (n)

production site (n)

public housing (n)

public transit (n)

raw material (n)

reforestation (n)

regional boundary (n)

region of contact (n)

regrowth (n)

religious facility (n)

renewable resource (n)

residential pattern (n)

resource management (n)

ridge-and-valley pattern (n)

Riviera (pn)

runoff (n)

Rust Belt (pn)

satellite-based communications system (n)

Saudi Arabia (pn)

savanna (n)

school district (n)

seasonal pattern of life (n)

sea wall (n)

semiarid area (n)

settlement pattern (n)

shifting civilization (n)

Siberia (pn)

Sicily (pn)

Singapore (pn)

single-industry city (n)

soil erosion (n)

soil fertility (n)

solar power (n)

South Africa (pn)

South Asia (pn)

spatial (n)

spatial arrangement (n)

spatial perception (n)

spatial scale (n)

spread of bubonic plague (n)

spread of disease (n)

Sri Lanka (pn)

standard of living (n)

steel-tipped plow (n)

strait (n)

strip mine (v) (n)

suburbanization (n)

Sudan (pn)

sunbelt (n)

system (n)

technological hazard (n)

telephone area code (n)

temperature fluctuation (n)

terrace (n)

terraced rice fields (n)

thematic map (n)

topography (n)

trade advantage (n)

transportation hub (n)

tropical rain forest (n)

Tropic of Cancer (pn)

Tropic of Capricorn (pn)

truck-farming community (n)

tsunami (n)

tundra (n)

Twin Peaks [San Francisco] (pn)

urbanization (n)

Vietnamese (pn)

Virgin Islands (pn)

voluntary migration (n)

water rights (n)

watershed (n)

water spring (n)

water supply (n)

West Asia (pn)

White Sea (pn)

work animal (n)

Yucatan Peninsula (pn)

Zanzibar (pn)

High School

U.S. History

affirmative action (n)

Agricultural Adjustment Act (pn)

Algonquian (pn)

Alien and Sedition Acts (pn)

American Communist Party (pn)

American Federation of Labor [AFL] (pn)

Americanization (n) (v)

Asian civil rights movement (n)

baby boom generation (n)

Bank Recharter Bill of 1832 (pn)

Battle of Saratoga (pn)

Bay of Pigs (pn)

black legend (n)

Carolina regulators (n)

Carrie Chapman Catt (pn)

Chesapeake (pn)

Chief Joseph's "I Shall Fight No More Forever" (pn)

"City Upon a Hill" speech (pn)

Civilian Conservation Corps (pn)

Civil Rights Act of 1964 (pn)

Civil Works Administration (pn)

Cold War (pn)

Committee for Industrial Organizations [CIO] (pn)

Constitution of 1787 (pn)

covenant community (n)

crabgrass frontier (n)

crop lien system (n)

"Cross of Gold" speech (pn)

Dartmouth College v. Woodward [1819] (pn)

D day (pn)

de facto segregation (n)

de jure segregation (n)

Democratic nominee (pn)

Desert Storm (pn)

East Asian Co-Prosperity Sphere (pn)

economic depression of 1819 (n)

economic depression of 1837 (n)

economic depression of 1857 (n)

economic depression of 1873 (n)

economic depression of 1893 (n)

eighteenth-century republicanism (n)

election of 1960 (n)

emerging capitalist economy (n)

Emilio Aguinaldo (pn)

Ernest Hemingway (pn)

European land hanger (n)

farm labor movement (n)

federal judiciary (n)

fireside chat (n)

First New Deal (pn)

Five Civilized Tribes (pn)

"Four Freedoms" speech (pn)

full dinner pail (n)

gay liberation movement (n)

gay rights (n)

General Ulysses S. Grant (pn)

General William T. Sherman (pn)

generational conflict (n)

Gettysburg Address (pn)

GI Bill on higher education (pn)

Gibbons v. Ogden [1984] (pn)

Good Neighbor Policy (pn)

Grand Alliance (pn)

Great Migration (pn)

Greenback Labor Party (pn)

hammering campaign (n)

Hetch Hetchy controversy (pn)

Indian laborer (n)

Indian Reorganization Act of 1934 (pn)

International Ladies Garment Workers Union (pn)

Iran-Contra affair (n)

James K. Polk (pn)

Japanese American (pn)

Jay Gardoqui Treaty of 1786 (pn)

Jefferson Davis (pn)

John Collier (pn)

John F. Kennedy presidency (n)

John Locke (pn)

John White (pn)

Kansas-Nebraska Act (pn)

King's Mountain (pn)

La Raza Unida (pn)

labor conflicts of 1894 (n)

Lincoln's "House Divided" speech (pn)

Lone Star Republic (pn)

mainstream America (n)

Mark Hanna (pn)

McCulloch v. Maryland [1819] (pn)

Mississippi culture (n)

Mormon migration to the West (n)

mound center in Cahokia, Illinois (n)

mound center in the Mississippi valley (n)

National Industrial Recovery Act (pn)

National Recovery Administration (pn)

National Woman Suffrage Association (pn)

Native American origin story (n)

native population (n)

neocolonialism (n)

New England colony (n)

New Klan (pn)

New Woman (pn)

New World (pn)

New York City draft riots of July 1863 (n)

noble savage (n)

North American Free Trade Agreement [NAFTA] (pn)

Northwest Territory (pn)

November 10 proposal (n)

oil crisis of the 1970s (n)

Old Hickory (pn)

Omaha Platform of 1892 (pn)

OPEC (pn)

Panama Revolution of 1903 (pn)

parochial school (n)

Peace of Paris (pn)

Plessy v. Ferguson [1896] (pn)

pop art (n)

post–Cold War era (n)

Public Works Administration (pn)

Quaker (pn)

racial role (n)

Radical Republicans (pn)

relocation center (n)

resettlement (n)

Roe v. Wade [1973] (pn)

Roger Williams (pn)

Roosevelt Corollary (pn)

Rural Electrification Administration (pn)

Sacco and Vanzetti trial (pn)

Scots-Irish (pn)

Second New Deal (pn)

secondary education (n)

self-determination (n)

Shaysites (pn)

Sojourner Truth's "Ain't I a Woman?" (pn)

South Carolina (pn)

sphere of influence (n)

spirit of individualism (n)

Tennessee Valley Authority Act (pn)

Texas Revolution [1836–1845] (pn)

Theodore deBry (pn)

Title VII (pn)

traditional American family (n)

Upton Sinclair (pn)

U.S. Communist Party (pn)

U.S. Smoot-Hawley Tariff (pn)

Victorian values (n)

War on Poverty (pn)

War Powers Act of March 1942 (pn)

West Indian colony (n)

Western values (n)

William Jennings Bryan (pn)

William McKinley (pn)

Wilmot Proviso (pn)

Woodrow Wilson's Fourteen Points (pn)

Zuni (pn)

diffusion (n)

disease pandemic (n)

Dreyfus affair (pn)

duke (n)

Dutch merchant class (n)

Dutch West Indies (pn)

early modern society (n)

Emperor Aurangzeb (pn)

Ems telegram (n)

enclosure movement (n)

Encomienda system (pn)

enemies of the state (n)

energy crisis (n)

English Parliament (pn)

enlightened despot (n)

Enuma Elish (pn)

Erich Maria Remarque (pn)

Ethiopian art (n)

Ethiopian rock churches (n)

ethnicity (n)

Eurasian Empire (pn)

European country (n)

European Jew (pn)

European manorial system (n)

evangelical argument (n)

evangelical movement (n)

evil empire (n)

existentialism (n)

expansionism (n)

expansionist foreign policy (n)

expressionism (n)

expulsion of Jews and Muslims from Spain (n)

foot binding (n)

forced collectivization (n)

Franco-Prussian War (pn)

French colonization of Indochina (n)

French Declaration of the Rights of Man (pn)

French Estates-General (pn)

French West Indies (pn)

Freud's psychoanalytic method (n)

fundamentalism (n)

Geneva Accords (pn)

Genoa (pn)

genocide (n)

gentry elite (n)

German concept of Kultur (n)

German Empire (pn)

German Federal Republic (pn)

Germanic peoples (n)

Ghaznavid Empire (pn)

globalizing trend (n)

Golden Horde (pn)

Great Khan Mongke (pn)

Great Khan Ogodei (pn)

Great War (pn)

Great Western Schism (pn)

Greek comedy (n)

Greek Orthodox Christianity (pn)

Greek philosopher (n)

Greek tragedy (n)

guerrilla warfare (n)

guild (n)

hacienda (n)

Hadith (pn)

Hatt-I-Humayun (pn)

Heian period (pn)

Hernando Cortes (pn)

Herodotus (pn)

historical context (n)

historical continuity (n)

hominid community (n)

humanism (n)

Hun invasions (n)

Hung-wu [emperor] (pn)

Hutus (pn)

Iberian Empire (pn)

ideological conflict (n)

ideology (n)

Iliad (pn)

Imperial Mughal (pn)

imperial presidency (n)

impressionism (n)

Indian concept of ideal kingship (n)

Indian uprising of 1857 (n)

individualism (n)

Ismail (pn)

Islamic state (n)

Islamization (n)

Italian humanism (n)

integrate/integration (v) (n)

Jamal al-Din (pn)

Japanese invasion of China (n)

Jenne-Jeno (pn)

Jewish and Arab inhabitants of Palestine (n)

Jewish Diaspora (pn)

Jewish scapegoating (n)

Jiang Jieshi (pn)

jihad (n)

Joan of Arc (pn)

John of Plano Carpini (pn)

Joseph Francois Dupleix's theory of "divide and rule" (n)

Joseph II (pn)

Kashmir (pn)

Kerensky (pn)

Kievan Russian (pn)

King Joao II (pn)

Kumbi-Saleh (pn)

Latin (pn)

Latin American revolution (pn)

Latin Catholic Church (pn)

Lenin's ideology (n)

liberalism (n)

liberation theology (n)

Lingua Franca (pn)

Lord Dalhousie (pn)

Louis XIV (pn)

Machiavelli (pn)

Machiavelli's *The Prince* (pn)

Magna Carta (pn)

Magyar cavalry (pn)

Mahabharata (pn)

Mahdi Muhammad Ahmad I (pn)

Maratha (pn)

martyr (n)

Marx and Engel's *Communist Manifesto* (pn)

Marxism (pn)

May Fourth Movement (pn)

Mayan "Long Count" calendar (pn)

Mediterranean Empire (pn)

Mein Kampf (pn)

mercenary (n)

Mesolithic (pn)

mestizo (n)

Mexican Revolution (pn)

militarism (n)

military preparedness (n)

millennialism (n)

mobilize/mobilization (v) (n)

monotheism (n)

Mudejar Muslim (pn)

multiculturalism (n)

multilateral aid organization (n)

Munich Agreement [1938] (pn)

Muslim country (n)

national autonomy (n)

national identity (n)

nationalism (n)

national security (n)

National Socialism/Nazis (pn)

nation building (n)

natural history (n)

Nazi genocide (n)

Nazi ideology (n)

Nazi-Soviet Non-Aggression Pact, 1939 (pn)

Neo-Confucianism (pn)

Neolithic Revolution (pn)

New Granada (pn)

new scientific rationalism (n)

nineteenth-century literature (n)

Noh drama (pn)

Nok terra cotta figure (n)

nonhominid (n)

Northern Italian city-state (n)

October Manifesto (pn)

The *Odyssey* (pn)

Olympia de Gouge (pn)

one-child policy in China (n)

oppress/oppression (v) (n)

Orthodox Christianity (pn)

Otto von Bismarck (pn)

Pallavas (pn)

Pandyas (pn)

pan-Slavism (pn)

partition of Africa (n)

Pax Mongolica (pn)

Plato (pn)

Plato's *Republic* (pn)

poetry of Kabir (n)

poetry of Mirabai (n)

pogroms in the Holy Roman Empire (n)

Polish rebellion (n)

Popul Vuh (pn)

post-industrial society (n)

pre-industrial England (n)

principle of the "Invisible Hand" (n)

process of Russification (n)

Protestant clergy (n)

Protestant work ethic (n)

province (n)

Qianlong [emperor] (pn)

Qing position on opium (n)

Qizilbash nomadic tribesman (pn)

Rabbinic Judaism (pn)

radicalism (n)

Ramayana (pn)

Ram Mohan Roy (pn)

Rashid Rida (pn)

rationalism (n)

reactionary thinking (n)

realism (n)

realpolitik (n)

recurrent pandemic (n)

Red Russian (pn)

Red Scare (pn)

refugee population (n)

regulated family and community life (n)

religious evangelism (n)

reparation payment (n)

representative government (n)

retaliate/retaliation (v) (n)

reunify/reunification (v) (n)

rigid class (n)

Roman Empire (pn)

Romanization of Europe (pn)

Roundhead (pn)

royal patronage (n)

Rudyard Kipling's "White Man's Burden" (pn)

Russian chronicle (n)

Russian Revolution of 1905 (pn)

Sahara desert (pn)

sanctioned country (n)

sans-culottes (n)

Sargon (pn)

Schlieffen Plan (pn)

scientific racism (n)

sectionalism (n)

secular ideology (n)

Sei Shonagon's *The Pillow Book* (pn)

Seljuk Empire (pn)

Sikh (pn)

Sino-Japanese War (pn)

Slavic world (n)

social democratization (n)

socialist realism (n)

South African [Anglo-Boer] War (pn)

South India (pn)

sovereignty (n)

Soviet Non-Aggression Pact (pn)

Srivijaya (pn)

Stalinist totalitarianism (pn)

Stephen Spender (pn)

Strait of Malacca (pn)

Sufism (n)

Sui dynasty (pn)

Sumeria (pn)

Sunni and Shiite factions (pn)

Sun Yat-sen (pn)

surrealism (n)

Sykes-Picot Agreement (pn)

system of alliances (n)

Taiping Rebellion (pn)

Temple of Madurai (pn)

temporary dominance (n)

Teotihuacan (pn)

Tiahuanaco society (n)

Trans-Siberian Railway (pn)

Treaty of Nanking [1842] (pn)

Treaty of Shimonoseki [1895] (pn)

Treaty of Versailles (pn)

Tutsis (pn)

Umayyad Dynasty (pn)

"unified" India (n)

United States resolution (n)

universal language (n)

UN resolution (n)

urban bourgeoisie (n)

U.S.S.R. (pn)

Viking longboat (n)

Vladimir of Kiev (pn)

volunteerism (n)

wartime diplomacy (n)

Western hegemony (n)

Western political thought (n)

White Paper Reports on Palestine (pn)

White Russian (pn)

world influenza pandemic, 1918–1919 (n)

World War I (pn)

World War II (pn)

Young Turk movement (pn)

Yuan Dynasty (pn)

Zionist movement (pn)

Zoroastrianism (pn)

Civics

abortion (n)

absolutism (n)

adversary system (n)

advice and consent (n)

affirmative action (n)

"All men are created equal" (n)

allocation of power (n)

amendments to the U.S. Constitution (n)

American constitutional democracy (n)

Americans with Disabilities Act (pn)

amnesty (n)

Amnesty International (pn)

anarchy (n)

Antarctic Treaty (pn)

antifederalist (n)

arbitrary rule (n)

arbitrate/arbitration (v) (n)

arms embargo (n)

arms limitations (n)

Article I of the Constitution (pn)

Article I, Section 7 (pn)

Article I, Section 8 (pn)

Article II of the Constitution (pn)

Article III of the Constitution (pn)

Articles of Confederation (pn)

authoritarian system (n)

bilateral agreement (n)

bilingual education (n)

bipolar centers of power (n)

body politic (n)

boycott (v) (n)

bribe/bribery (v) (n)

British constitution (n)

Brown v. Board of Education [1954] (pn)

bureaucracy (n)

capricious rule (n)

charter local government (n)

chauvinism/chauvinistic (n) (adj)

checks and balances (n)

citizenry (n)

citizens and subjects (n)

civic center (n)

civil disobedience (n)

civilian review board (n)

civility/civil (n) (adj)

civil law (n)

civil liberties (n)

civil rights legislation (n)

Civil War amendments (n)

class boundaries (n)

class system (n)

clear and present danger rule (n)

collective decision (n)

common law (n)

communism (n)

Communist International (pn)

compulsory education (n)

concurrent power (n)

congressional district (n)

congressional election (n)

conservative (n) (adj)

constituency (n)

constitutional amendment (n)

constitutional democracy (n)

constitutional ideal (n)

constitutionalism (n)

constitutionality of laws (n)

consumer product safety (n)

copyright (n)

cruel and unusual punishment (n)

defense policy (n)

defense spending (n)

democracy (n)

democratic legislature (n)

Democratic Party (pn)

democratization (n)

direct popular rule (n)

distribution of power (n)

divine law (n)

divine right (n)

domestic tranquility (n)

double jeopardy (n)

due process (n)

electoral system (n)

eminent domain (n)

English Bill of Rights (pn)

enlightenment (n)

e pluribus unum (n)

equal protection clause (n)

equal rights amendment (n)

established religion (n)

establishment clause (n)

estate tax (n)

ethical dilemma (n)

ethnicity (n)

European Union (pn)

excise tax (n)

exclusionary rule (n)

executive branch (n)

Federal Communications Commission (pn)

Federal Reserve (pn)

federalism (n)

federalist (n) (adj)

federal supremacy clause (n)

Food and Drug Administration (pn)

franchise (n)

freedom of the press (n)

freedom to choose employment (n)

free exercise clause (n)

fundamental rights (n)

General Agreement on Tariffs and Trade [GATT] (pn)

general welfare (n)

general welfare clause (n)

Head Start (pn)

hearsay (n)

Helsinki Accord (pn)

higher court review (n)

House of Commons (pn)

House of Lords (pn)

humanitarian aid (n)

illegal search and seizure (n)

immigration policy (n)

impartial tribunal (n)

imperial power (n)

inalienable rights (n)

incorporation (n)

independent judiciary (n)

independent regulatory agency (n)

International Monetary Fund (pn)

jingoism (n)

judicial review (n)

junta (n)

jurisdiction (n)

legal code (n)

legislation (n)

legislative branch (n)

legislative districting (n)

legitimacy (n)

libel (n)

liberal (n) (adj)

liberalism (n)

litigate/litigation (v) (n)

lobby/lobbyist (v) (n)

Marshall Plan (pn)

moderate thinking (n)

monarchy (n)

Monroe Doctrine (pn)

moral obligation (n)

most favored nation status (n)

multilateral agreement (n)

National Democratic Party (pn)

National Education Association (pn)

national interest (n)

nationalism (n)

National Republican Party (pn)

natural law (n)

natural rights (n)

nonunion worker (n)

Northwest Ordinance (pn)

"one man, one vote" (n)

opposition group (n)

organized crime (n)

organized labor (n)

parliamentary government (n)

patent (n)

perjure/perjury (v) (n)

personal autonomy (n)

political cartoon (n)

political culture (n)

political efficacy (n)

political ideology (n)

political philosophy (n)

political rights (n)

popular will (n)

power of the purse (n)

power to declare war (n)

primary election (n)

private domain (n)

private sector (n)

property rights (n)

proportional system (n)

Protestant Reformation (pn)

public policy (n)

Puritan work ethic (n)

referendum (n)

republic (n)

republicanism (n)

Republican Party (n)

reserved power (n)

rights of the disabled (n)

right to due process of law (n)

right to life (n)

school voucher (n)

scope and limit (n)

search and seizure (n)

self-determination (n)

self-evident truths (n)

service group (n)

sexual harassment (n)

social contract (n)

social equity (n)

socialism (n)

social issue (n)

Social Security number (n)

social welfare (n)

socioeconomic welfare (n)

state bill of rights (n)

state constitution (n)

statute law (n)

supremacy clause (n)

Supreme Court justice (pn)

system of checks and balances (n)

term limitation (n)

third party (n)

time, place, manner restrictions (n)

two-party system (n)

Two Treatises on Government (pn)

unenumerated rights (n)

UNICEF (pn)

union movement (n)

unitary government (n)

urban decay (n)

urban riot (n)

U.S. domestic energy policy (n)

U.S. foreign policy (n)

vigilantism (n)

voting ward (n)

warrant (n)

"We the People..." (n)

winner-take-all system (n)

World Bank (pn)

world geopolitics (n)

writ of habeas corpus (n)

zoning (v)

Economics

absolute advantage (n)

affluence/affluent (n) (adj)

aggregate demand (n)

aggregate supply (n)

allocation method (n)

bait and switch (n)

balanced budget (n)

bank recharter (n)

black market (n)

budget constraints (n)

budget deficit (n)

budget surplus (n)

business deduction (n)

capitalism (n)

capitalist country (n)

capital stock (n)

circulation of money (n)

class conflict (n)

class relations (n)

collective bargaining (n)

collusion (n)

command economy (n)

commodity (n)

commodity flow (n)

commodity price (n)

common market (n)

communism (n)

comparative advantage (n)

complementary product (n)

consumer culture (n)

consumer fraud (n)

Consumer Price Index (pn)

consumer spending (n)

consumer's rights (n)

contemporary economic trade network (n)

cooperative (n)

corporate spending (n)

corporation (n)

cost-benefit ratio (n)

cost-push inflation (n)

creditor (n)

current interest rate (n)

cyclical unemployment (n)

default on a loan (v)

defer a loan (v)

deficit (n)

deflation (n)

demand curve (n)

demand-pull inflation (n)

depression (n)

deregulation (n)

developing/developed country (n)

discount rate (n)

disposable income (n)

Dow Jones (pn)

durable goods (n)

economic dependency (n)

economic disparity (n)

economic dominance (n)

economic incentive (n)

economic reform (n)

economic risk (n)

economics (n)

economic theory (n)

economy (n)

elasticity (n)

entrepreneur (n)

expected rate of inflation (n)

expenditure (n)

externalities (n)

Federal Reserve System (pn)

federal spending (n)

federal tax revenue (n)

financial institution (n)

fiscal policy (n)

fixed income (n)

fixed rate of interest (n)

fraud (n)

free enterprise (n)

free labor system (n)

free trade (n)

free-trade zone (n)

frictional employment (n)

frictional unemployment (n)

foreign capital (n)

foreign market (n)

functional distribution of income (n)

global economy (n)

global trade (n)

government directive (n)

government employee (n)

government security (n)

government spending (n)

government subsidy (n)

grant (v) (n)

home office (n)

income distribution (n)

income gap (n)

incorporation (n)

industrial parity (n)

inflation (n)

interest payment (n)

interest rate (n)

internal trade (n)

international company (n)

invest/investment (v) (n)

labor force immobility (n)

labor relations (n)

large-scale investment (n)

law of retail gravitation (n)

liability rules (n)

macroeconomics (n)

male-dominated job (n)

marginal benefit (n)

marginal cost (n)

market economy (n)

marketplace (n)

market revolution (n)

materialism (n)

maximum employment (n)

medical coverage (n)

medical expenditure (n)

mercantilism (n)

microeconomics (n)

military-industrial complex (n)

mining economy (n)

monetary policy (n)

money supply (n)

monopolize/monopoly (v) (n)

multinational corporation (n)

national debt (n)

national government spending (n)

national market (n)

natural monopoly (n)

negative externality (n)

net export (n)

nominal gross domestic product (n)

nominal interest rate (n)

nondurable goods (n)

nonexclusion (n)

nonprice competition (n)

oligopoly (n)

open market purchase (n)

payroll tax (n)

per capita (n)

personal distribution of income (n)

personal income (n)

physical capital (n)

positive externality (n)

prevailing price (n)

price ceiling (n)

price control (n)

price floor (n)

price stability (n)

primary economic activity (n)

private investment spending (n)

privatization (n)

production cost (n)

production method (n)

production output (n)

profitability (n)

profiteering (v)

profit motive (n)

propaganda/propagandize (n) (v)

propaganda campaign (n)

property tax (n)

proprietor's income (n)

public service commission (n)

public welfare (n)

public works (n)

real cost (n)

real gross domestic product (n)

real interest rate (n)

recession (n)

redistribution of income (n)

redistribution of wealth (n)

regulation (n)

rental income (n)

research and development (n)

reserve requirement (n)

return on investment (n)

seasonal unemployment (n)

service charge (n)

shareholder (n)

shift in demand curve (n)

shift in supply curve (n)

Social Security (pn)

Social Security withholding (pn)

socioeconomic group (n)

speculation (n)

stagnation of wages (n)

Standard & Poor's [S&P] (pn)

standard measure [of unemployment rate] (n)

standard measures (n)

standard weights (n)

state revenue (n)

status quo (n)

stock (n)

stockholder (n)

stock market (n)

structural unemployment (n)

subsidize/subsidy (v) (n)

suburbanization (n)

supply curve (n)

supply-side economics (n)

tariffs (n)

tax revenue (n)

telecommute/ telecommunication (v) (n)

tertiary economic activity (n)

theory of comparative advantage (n)

transaction cost (n)

transfer payment (n)

transnational corporation (n)

transportation cost (n)

underground economy (n)

virtual company (n)

Wall Street (pn)

war bond (n)

warranty (n)

wartime inflation (n)

welfare state (n)

workers' compensation (n)

work experience (n)

workforce (n)

Geography

absolute location (n)

acculturate/acculturation (v) (n)

adapt/adaptation (v) (n)

agribusiness (n)

agricultural soil (n)

AIDS (pn)

airborne emission (n)

air-mass circulation (n)

alluvial fan (n)

Americentric (adj)

Amsterdam (pn)

aquifer (n)

Arabia (pn)

Argentina (pn)

artesian wells (n)

Athens (pn)

atmospheric pressure cells (n)

atmospheric warming (n)

Austria (pn)

Basque minority (n)

Bible Belt (pn)

biodiversity (n)

biological evidence (n)

biological magnification (n)

Bruges (pn)

bubonic plague (pn)

Burkina Faso (pn)

Cambodia (pn)

carbon cycle (n)

Caribbean Basin (pn)

carrying capacity (n)

cartography/cartographer (n)

Caspian Sea (pn)

census data (n)

census district (n)

center-pivot irrigation (n)

Central Europe (pn)

central place theory (n)

chemical cycle (n)

chemical fertilizer (n)

choropleth map (n)

circuit-court district (n)

city planning (n)

climate graph [climagraph] (n)

coastal ecosystem (n)

coastal flood zone (n)

complementarity (n)

concentrated settlement form (n)

concentration of services (n)

concentric zone model (n)

Congo, the (pn)

contaminate/contaminant (v) (n)

continental drift (n)

cost-distance (n)

crude birth rate (n)

crude death rate (n)

cultural diffusion (n)

cultural identity (n)

cultural landscape (n)

culture hearth (n)

culture region (n)

cycling of energy (n)

decolonize/decolonization (v) (n)

deforestation (n)

demographic transition (n)

demography/demographics (n)

depleted rain forests of Central Africa (n)

deposition (n)

desertification (n)

diffusion (n)

diffusion of tobacco smoking (n)

distance decay (n)

distribution of ecosystems (n)

doubling time (n)

downtown business area (n)

drought-plagued Sahel (n)

dust storm (n)

dynamic system (n)

Eastern Australia (pn)

Eastern United States (pn)

ecology (n)

edge city (n)

environmental degradation (n)

environmental determinism (n)

environmentalism (n)

equinox (n)

erosional agent (n)

ethnic elitism (n)

ethnic enclave (n)

ethnic minority (n)

ethnicity (n)

ethnocentric (adj)

Eurocentric (adj)

European Union (pn)

Eutrophication (pn)

exchange of fauna (n)

exchange of flora (n)

exurban area (n)

feedback loop (n)

fertility rate (n)

flowchart (n)

flow map (n)

flow of energy (n)

flow pattern (n)

flow resource (n)

formal region (n)

friction (n)

friction of distance (n)

functional region (n)

gentrify/gentrification (v) (n)

geographic technology (n)

geomorphology (n)

geopolitics (n)

GIS [Geographic Information Systems] (pn)

global migration pattern (n)

Great Barrier Reef (pn)

Great Plains Dust Bowl (pn)

greenhouse effect (n)

greenway (n)

gross domestic product (n)

gross national product (n)

groundwater quality (n)

groundwater reduction (n)

Guatemala (pn)

habitat destruction (n)

Han dynasty (pn)

hazardous waste handling (n)

health care facility (n)

high-latitude place (n)

High Plains (pn)

hinterland (n)

hub-and-spoke model (n)

human adaptation (n)

human control over nature (n)

human-induced change (n)

hybridization of crops (n)

Hydrilla (pn)

hydrologic cycle (n)

hydrosphere (n)

indigenous people (n)

industrialize/industrialization (v) (n)

industrial revolution (n)

inherit/heredity (v) (n)

intermediate directions (n)

international debt crisis (n)

interstate highway system (n)

intervening opportunity (n)

introduction of species (n)

Iran (pn)

Iraq (pn)

iron metallurgy (n)

Jerusalem (pn)

Kurds (pn)

Kuwait (pn)

lake desiccation (n)

lake ecosystem (n)

land degradation (n)

landform relief (n)

landmass (n)

land value (n)

land-survey system (n)

Latin America (pn)

life experience (n)

light-rail system (n)

location principle (n)

Malaysian rain forest (n)

megalopolis (n)

mental map (n)

metropolitan corridor (n)

microclimate (n)

midlatitude forest (n)

Midwest (pn)

migration counterstream (n)

migration stream (n)

monoculture (n)

moraine (n)

multinational organization (n)

municipality (n)

nation-state (n)

natural population increase (n)

Netherlands (pn)

network (n)

Nicaragua (pn)

North Korea (pn)

Nova Scotia (pn)

oblate spheroid (n)

ocean ecosystem (n)

Ontario (pn)

outward migration (n)

overcutting of pine forest (n)

oxygen cycle (n)

ozone depletion (n)

ozone layer (n)

Pacific Ring of Fire (pn)

Pampas in Argentina, the (pn)

perceptual region (n)

peripheral area (n)

petroleum consumption (n)

Philippines (pn)

phosphate reserves (n)

physical process (n)

physiological population density (n)

plant community (n)

plate tectonics (n)

population pyramid (n)

post-reunification Germany (n)

power bloc (n)

primary data (n)

primate city (n)

principal parallels (n)

pull factors (n)

push factors (n)

racial minority (n)

rain shadow (n)

rate of natural increase (n)

rate of resource consumption (n)

Red Sea (pn)

reduction of species diversity (n)

regionalize/regionalization (v) (n)

regional planning district (n)

relative humidity (n)

relative location (n)

religious ties (n)

relocation strategy (n)

remote sensing (n)

resource base (n)

rural-to-urban migration (n)

rutile sand (n)

Rwanda (pn)

salinization (n)

salt accumulation (n)

sand movement (n)

sector model (n)

sediment (n)

seismic activity (n)

sequent occupance (n)

silting (n)

sinocentric (n)

soil acidification (n)

soil creep (n)

soil salinization (n)

solar radiation (n)

South Africa (pn)

Southeast Asia (n)

Southern Europe (pn)

South Korea (pn)

Spanish settlement (n)

stage of life (n)

staple crop production (n)

statutory requirement (n)

subarctic environment (n)

Sub-Saharan Africa (pn)

subsistence agriculture (n)

subsistence farming (n)

subsistence method (n)

sustainable development (n)

sustainable environment (n)

synergy (n)

systemic (n)

tectonic plate (n)

tectonic process (n)

Thailand (pn)

thermal (n) (adj)

threshold (n)

threshold population (n)

tidal process (n)

topographical map (n)

toxic dumping (n)

toxic-waste handling (n)

transportation corridor (n)

transregional alliance (n)

tropical soil degradation (n)

tungsten (n)

Turkey (pn)

Ukraine (pn)

urban heat island (n)

urbanization (n)

urban morphology (n)

utopian community (n)

Venice (pn)

volcanism (n)

weathering (n)

wilderness area (n)

world atmospheric circulation (n)

world temperature increase (n)

zoning regulation (n)

REFERENCES AND RESOURCES

Haystead, M. J., & Marzano, R. J. (2009, August). *Meta-analytic synthesis of studies conducted at Marzano Research Laboratory on instructional strategies.* Englewood, CO: Marzano Research Laboratory.

Kasser, S. L. (1995). *Inclusive games: Movement fun for everyone!* Champagne, IL: Human Kinetics.

Marzano, R. J. (2004). *Building background knowledge for academic achievement: Research on what works in schools.* Alexandria, VA: Association for Supervision and Curriculum Development.

Marzano, R. J. (2009). *Teaching basic and advanced vocabulary: A framework for direct instruction.* Boston: Cengage Learning.

Marzano, R. J., & Pickering, D. J. (2005). *Building academic vocabulary: Teacher's manual.* Alexandria, VA: Association for Supervision and Curriculum Development.

Oklahoma State Department of Education. (n.d.). *Building academic vocabulary: Oklahoma academic vocabulary suggested words and terms.* Accessed at http://sde.state.ok.us/Curriculum/BAV.pdf on August 24, 2009.

Tennessee State Department of Education. (2006). *The Tennessee academic vocabulary project.* Accessed at www.rcs.k12.tn.us/rc/departments/ITS/Teacher_Resources/State_Department_WordList_Final.pdf on August 24, 2009.